The New York Knicks

The Official Fiftieth Anniversary Celebration

Photographs From the Lens of

George Kalinsky

Official Photographer of Madison Square Garden

Editorial Director, Dennis D'Agostino
Text by Phil Berger
Design by Vincent Gatti

Macmillan·USA

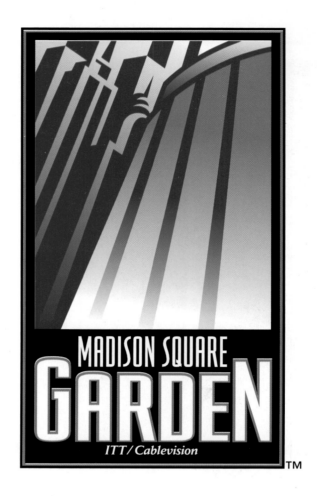

MADISON SQUARE
GARDEN
ITT/Cablevision
TM

MACMILLAN
A Simon & Schuster Macmillan Company
1633 Broadway
New York, NY 10019

Library of Congress Cataloging-in-Publication Data available

ISBN: 0-02-861444-5

Manufactured in the United States of America
10 9 8 7 6 5 4 3 2

Contents

To the loving memory of Ellen, my wife and best friend

introduction

You might not think that a young man growing up in Utah could ever be a New York Knicks fan. Well, think again.

The big team from the big city—the team of Reed and Frazier and DeBusschere and Bradley—cast a spell over a teenaged sports fan, one that could be felt even if New York was the most distant place in the world. I'd watch the NBA games on TV every weekend, and there they were. Pick up a magazine, there was Bradley or Reed on the cover. Open a newspaper, and there were the headline stories of another Knicks game, another Knicks victory, another Knicks championship.

And how they could play the game! They brought the "team" concept to a level never before reached. Spellbound, I watched on TV like any other rabid fan when the Knicks won a championship in 1970, and another in 1973. And I remember when my own team, the Utah Stars of Zelmo Beaty, Willie Wise and Ron Boone, won the ABA championship in 1971, and the people in Salt Lake started calling them "The Knicks of the ABA."

To be compared to the Knicks—what a compliment!

But it wasn't until I came to New York in 1990 that I realized exactly what the Knicks mean to the people of this city. Quite simply, the Knicks represent and symbolize New York City in a way that no other sports franchise does. From the schoolyards to the blacktops to the high school and college gyms, all the way to Madison Square Garden, basketball is The City Game.

And the Knicks are The City's Team. No one knows better than me how the Knicks are an emotional and spiritual rallying point for all of New York. The entire city has shared in the great success we have enjoyed in recent years, climaxed by our Eastern Conference championship in 1994. And our never-ending commitment to the city's young people through our expanded community service program serves to remind us of our obligations and responsibilities to New York's future.

And now the Knicks are fifty years old . . . the golden anniversary of one of the NBA's charter members. So many thrills, so many memories, so many great players and great teams.

Between the covers of this book, George Kalinsky's brilliant photography and Phil Berger's vivid prose tell the story of the first half-century of Knicks basketball. From Joe Lapchick to Jeff Van Gundy, from Carl Braun and Harry Gallatin to Patrick Ewing and Charles Oakley, and all the marvelous players and coaches in between, the history of the Knicks is one of the richest in all of sports.

Our team is blessed with an unmatched tradition of greatness. We hope that this book captures it all for you. Whether you're a Knicks fan from New York or some far-off place, enjoy!

David W. Checketts
President and Chief Executive Officer
Madison Square Garden

foreword

As a native New Yorker, I've always been a Knick at heart.

Remembering back to when I was a teenager, growing up in Forest Hills and learning the game, I can vividly recall watching and listening to their exploits as they won two NBA titles. How often I would dream about someday becoming a Knick, and be able to live out that dream right in my hometown.

That's why I know I'm extremely fortunate. My Knicks dreams came true in so many ways.

As a player, I was able to return to New York and be a part of the team that had the memorable run in the mid-eighties. As an announcer, I was at courtside and shared in the excitement that gripped the Garden with the arrival of Patrick Ewing, and with his maturation into one of the greatest Knicks of all time. As a front office staffer, I was able to learn how an NBA franchise worked from the inside, the intricacies and nuances that had to be mastered. As general manager, I worked with a talented, committed group of players, coaches and staff during one of the most exciting periods in the club's history. And now, as club president, I am tremendously excited about a bright new future for our ballclub, all geared toward the ultimate goal: an NBA championship.

Through all the years, I have always realized just how special the Knicks are, how rich their tradition is and how much they mean to the people of New York. They are a permanent, indelible part of the very fabric of the city. No matter where I go, people are always greeting me with "All the way this year, Ernie!" and "Hey, Ernie! How we gonna do against the Bulls?" On the surface, these people may be strangers. But, really, they're not. We are all linked together by our love and passion for the Knicks.

Leafing through the pages of this book brings back so many memories. Through the lens of George Kalinsky, we are able to share in all the drama and excitement of a half-century of Knicks basketball, and remember exactly where we were when The Cap'n walked onto the court for game seven, or when Bernard had his back-to-back 50s or when Patrick slam-dunked us into the finals. It's all here.

George likes to tell people that, in his longtime role as the official Knicks photographer, he is always the first person to see a player wear a Knicks uniform for the first time. That was the case with me back in 1982. And I know that, when I put on that Knicks uniform for the first time and posed for George on the first day of training camp, it was one of the biggest thrills of my life. That first day as a Knick, and all the years that have followed, remind me over and over that so many of the dreams I had as a youngster have come true.

Then again, the Knicks have been making dreams come true for a lot of us for fifty years. Hopefully, that will be the case for the next fifty . . . and far beyond!

Ernie Grunfeld

Ernie Grunfeld
President and General Manager
New York Knickerbockers

preface

The New York Knicks were created back in 1946 to feed the natural hunger that's always existed for The City Game of basketball. Great men have filled the Knicks rosters over the years, combining their talent with a little luck and some knowledge from their coaches to win two championship titles and many more NBA finals berths over the years. Added to that list of names are today's Knicks—including Patrick Ewing, Charles Oakley and John Starks—who usher in a new era under the management of Garden president David W. Checketts and the direction of former Knick and current president and general manager Ernie Grunfeld. They are the ones designated to carry the basketball tradition to another generation of those who live and die for The City Game.

For the fans, it's always been a source of pride to follow this team, through good times and bad. The experience of watching the Knicks is enhanced through George Kalinsky's expert photography. He is the quintessential professional, and he brings the history of the Knicks alive with his sensitive and excellent film artistry. What most people can put into words, Kalinsky has caught with his magic lenses. I trust you'll enjoy the views he has assembled in this book, as I have.

Congratulations for the New York Knicks on their fiftieth anniversary! I'm happy to be a part of this team's great history.

Red Holzman

Red Holzman
New York Knicks Consultant
Member, Basketball Hall of Fame

1

Nevele Country Club. Clockwise from left, Tommy Byrnes, Ossie Schechtman, Sonny Hertzberg, Hy Gotkin and their wives.

46-49 HUMBLE BEGINNINGS

The summer that the telegram came, Ralph Kaplowitz was living at his mother-in-law's place in Long Island City.

Mustered out of the Air Corps only months before, in February 1946, he was gearing up to return to New York University in the fall and secure a degree in accounting. With the diploma he would be able to get on with a life that had been put on hold for the five years he had served as a fighter pilot in the Japanese theater.

Fourteen missions he had flown, his P-47 single-engine plane often under heavy fire from Japanese soldiers entrenched on Pacific islands like Amamio Shima and Kyushu. But flight captain Kaplowitz had survived the war and now was ever-so-happy to know the normalcy of family life with his wife, Norma, and their three-year-old daughter, Barbara.

It was while waiting for the fall semester at NYU to begin that Kaplowitz signed on with the Philadelphia Sphas, a team that played in a weekend basketball league against clubs from places like Wilkes-Barre, Scranton, Trenton and New York. He received $150 a week from Sphas coach Eddie Gottlieb, who remembered Kaplowitz from the prewar years when Ralph was an All-American guard at NYU.

By July, though, the Sphas' American League season was over, and Kaplowitz assumed that basketball would be part of his past once he began hitting the books again. But on July 3, 1946, that telegram came, offering the intriguing prospect of basketball as a full-time job: INTERESTED IN

HAVING YOU PLAY WITH NEW YORK PROFESSIONAL BASKETBALL TEAM NEXT SEASON. PLEASE TELEPHONE ME. NED IRISH

In the 1930s, sportswriter Edward Simmons (Ned) Irish took note of how rabid college basketball fans were and came up with the idea of moving the game from undersized school gyms into New York's preeminent arena, Madison Square Garden. In those depression years, the Garden was dark often enough to prompt its president, General John Reed Kilpatrick, to try Irish's notion. On December 27, 1934, New York University defeated Notre Dame 25–18 at the Garden before 16,188 fans in the feature game of the first Ned Irish promotion.

In no time, college basketball doubleheaders became a mainstay on the MSG calendar, playing to sell-out crowds. Irish gave up sportswriting to take charge of the college basketball docket at the Garden, which was then located at Eighth Avenue between Forty-ninth and Fiftieth Streets. His success there helped the college game grow in popularity across the country.

The moguls who formed the Basketball Association of America (BAA), unlike Irish, were not sophisticated basketball men. They were mostly members of the Arena Managers Association of America, which controlled indoor arenas in many major American cities. Their past experience in professional sport was with hockey. For most of them, pro basketball was a marketing tool to keep their arenas filled during the winter months.

It was some two weeks after the June 16, 1946, meeting at which these arena owners formed the league that BAA teams in eleven cities in the U.S. and Canada began making offers to players like Kaplowitz. Each team paid the league a $10,000 franchise fee, the money going for operating expenses that included the salary paid to the BAA's president, Maurice Podoloff.

When Kaplowitz phoned to learn the details of the Knicks' offer, Fred Podesta, Irish's assistant, got on the line and told him the new franchise would pay him $4,000 for the season.

"The schedule called for sixty games and the playoffs, which meant I couldn't have an outside job," Kaplowitz recalled. "The BAA," Podesta said, "was a full-time occupation."

But when Sonny Hertzberg, who'd starred before the war at CCNY and, like Kaplowitz, had played the past year in the weekend American League for $50 a game—said he wanted to continue working for his father-in-law's Brooklyn-based optical company, the Knicks' front office told him no sweat, there would be time between games to grind those prescription lenses. Not true, it turned out, but the rush was on

to fill rosters and a little white lie here or there . . . well, what the hell.

Hertzberg was offered $4,500 to be a Knick, and he said yes without blinking. He, too, had spent the war years in the military—a tech sergeant stationed at the New York Port of Embarcation in the Bay Ridge section of Brooklyn. After the hardships and tumult of World War II, it was an enchanting prospect to be given a chance to make a living wage at a boy's game.

"I was excited," said Hertzberg. "It was a very glamorous prospect as far as I was concerned. Because it was the first time pro ball would be on that high a scale. Plus, we were to be pioneers of a major-league sport. And the money—well, it doesn't seem much by today's standards. But back then $4,500 was a great deal of money. I thought it was an excellent opportunity and I would get to continue in the optical business. Some of the players were shrewder than I and asked for more."

Fifty years later, the notes in the margin of the telegram sent to Kaplowitz attest to the negotiations he and the Knicks went through. "By comparison with what I'd made with the Sphas, I decided $4,000 was not enough," said Kaplowitz. "And see, as a kid I'd learned a thing or two about negotiating from my grandfather. Whenever we'd go to the Lower East Side to buy me a suit, Grandpa would ask the salesman the price and then tell me, 'Ralph, take off the suit.' The salesperson would say, 'Look, I'll do better.' And Grandpa: 'Ralph, put on the suit.' Six, seven times I'd have to take off and put on that suit until Grandpa got his price. With this in mind, I asked for $8,000. I later heard BAA teams had orders not to pay more than $5,000 a player. There was a sort of salary cap of around $50,000 per ten-man team. The idea was not to let the wealthy teams gobble up all the good players. Anyway, over the next four weeks Fred Podesta and I dickered over the phone. I ended up with a contract for $6,500, $1,500 of which I said I wanted, and got, up front."

Irish's objective was to form the nucleus of his Knicks from men who, like Kaplowitz and Hertzberg, had played on area college teams and still had marquee value in a city that doted on the undergraduate game. So when the Knicks went to training camp at the Nevele Hotel in Ellenville, New York, many among the score of players invited to try out were from New York metropolitan area schools. Ossie Schectman had played at LIU, Bob Mullens at Fordham, Nat Militzok at Cornell and Hofstra, Dick Murphy at Manhattan, Tommy Byrnes at Seton Hall.

The tryouts were held on the Nevele's outdoor concrete court—two workouts a day. The coach, like his players, was a New York guy, Neil Cohalan. Cohalan had been the head man for 13 seasons at Manhattan College and had coached a naval team during the war years. Cohalan accepted the Knicks' position with the understanding that it was just for the 1946–47 season and that he would be replaced the following year by Joe Lapchick, who was finishing his coaching stint at St. John's University.

"They were long and hard training sessions," said Hertzberg. "More than two hours in the morning, and then again in the afternoon. During and after practice we would do laps around the court and wind sprints. After two weeks, the team was narrowed to the ten men who would comprise it, and in the third week our wives were invited up."

The Knicks played their games in the 69th Regiment Armory, which seated 5,200, when dates were not available at the 18,000-seat Garden because of the busy schedule of college games for which the building was reserved.

In a city that was enamored of the college game, it was no easy feat to draw attention to the Knicks. While the team was covered in the press, Ned Irish, now president of Madison Square Garden, understood that he would need more than the printed word to overcome the market preference for the collegiate version of the sport. So badly did Irish want the Knicks games to be broadcast that when he met with Bert Lee, the general manager of radio station WHN, and Lee's crack young sports announcer, Marty Glickman, he was prepared to *pay the station* for the privilege of having the team's games go out over the air waves.

"He made that offer at the old Toots Shor's on Fifty-first Street," recalled Glickman. "Ned asked Bert Lee, 'How much will it cost me to have our games on WHN?' And Bert said, 'Not only will it cost you nothing but we'll pay you $250 a game.' Irish had vision. He could see what a selling tool radio could be."

The chief sponsor for Knicks broadcasts was Nedick's, a chain of orange-drink stands, including one that stood in the arcade outside the Garden, opposite the Adam Hats store. Glickman would punctuate Knicks baskets by saying, "Goooood . . . good like Nedick's." And pretty soon every schoolboy in city playgrounds was hollering out that expression whenever his shot dropped through the hoop.

The across-the-board coverage helped. For the Knicks' first home game, against the Chicago Stags at the Garden, 17,205 fans paid their way in—at ticket prices ranging from one dollar to five dollars. Among that large Garden throng was 11-year-old Stanley Asofsky, who'd grown up in Brooklyn as an enthusiastic fan of the college game. In those days Asofsky was too young to have his own G.O. (General Organization) card by which secondary-school students got cut-rate prices on their Knick tickets—"twenty-five cents, if I remember correctly," said Asofsky. So Stanley did what any basketball-crazy peewee would—he borrowed a friend's G.O. card, entitling him to sit in mezzanine heaven, to see Hertzberg, Kaplowitz, Schectman and company try out The City Game.

For Knicks players, it was a season filled with misadventures, some comical, some not, and yet the pleasure of being in the BAA was enough for them. "We had fun, took trains almost everywhere," recalled Butch van Breda Kolff, one of two Princeton men—the other was John (Bud) Palmer—to join the Knicks after the beginning of the season. "At times it took 24 hours to get to Toronto. We just sat and waited until the tracks were cleared of snow. My highest Knick salary in three years was $5,000 and we only had a $5 per diem. So we ate in the coach—35 cents for a cheese sandwich and 15 cents for a milk. A meal in the dining car cost $3.75, but that would wipe out our beer money. After games, beer was a dime a glass and we'd have a bunch of those."

The Knicks finished the 1946–47 season with a respectable 33–27 record, third in the six-team Eastern Division. Hertzberg would lead the team in scoring with an 8.7 points per game average, making New York the only franchise in the BAA without a scorer in double figures that year. But Irish would reward Hertzberg—by giving him a $1,500 bonus at the end of the season.

That the game would change, and change rapidly, can be seen in the turnover the Knicks experienced under Lapchick. As the 1940s drew to a close, most of the original squad was gone, having either retired or moved on to other teams. Of those 1946–47 Knicks, only van Breda Kolff remained on New York's roster as the 1949–50 campaign unfolded.

INTRODUCING NEW YORK'S NEWEST MAJOR LEAGUE SPORT

PRO BASKETBALL

RALPH KAPLOWITZ

Former NYU forward and All-American before going into the service. Ralph continues his brilliant offensive work for the Knicks.

MONDAY NIGHT, NOV. 11

N. Y. KNICKERBOCKERS vs. CHICAGO

MADISON SQ. GARDEN

This is the home-town debut of The Knickerbockers, "New York's Own," in the new Basketball Association of America league. Sponsored by Madison Square Garden, the Knickerbocker squad is made up of nationally-known basketball stars, coached by Neil Cohalan of Manhattan College. All-star squads from 10 other cities in the League play the Knickerbockers during the season. Four games are in the Garden; the remaining 26 games in the 69th Regt. Armory, 25th St. and Lex. Ave.

TICKETS NOW

Garden Box Office. For game Nov. 11 played at the Garden: Res. seats, $1, 2, 2.50, 3, 4.50, 5. For game Nov. 16 played at 69th Regt. Armory: Res. seats, $1.50, 2.75, 3.50. Tax incl.

MAIL ORDERS PROMPTLY FILLED

For 1946-47 schedule of home games and information on season subscriptions, write to Basketball Dept., Madison Sq. Garden.

In that first season, 1946–47, there were eleven franchises in two divisions—the Boston Celtics, the Philadelphia Warriors, the Providence Steamrollers, the Toronto Huskies, the Washington Capitols and the Knicks in the East; the Chicago Stags, the Cleveland Rebels, the Detroit Falcons, the Pittsburgh Ironmen and the St. Louis Bombers in the West.

Efforts to make the pro game succeed in the past had been plagued by the instability of the leagues, whose players might jump teams from month to month and whose teams did not always last the season.

For most BAA pros, their previous experience came in the college game, or in pro organiza-tions like the weekend American League or in the National Basketball League, a salaried setup with notable teams in Midwestern towns like Fort Wayne (Ind.), Oshkosh (Wisc.) and Sheboygan (Wisc.).

A few men were ostensibly amateurs, hired by industrial concerns such as Phillips Petroleum and given jobs that were often just a pretense. Their real duty was to represent the company by playing for its basketball team. The great film studio Twentieth Century Fox was among the companies that fielded such a squad. When the Fox team traveled to game sites, players wore the satin tuxedos and berets favored by film directors rather than coat and tie, and at home contests might play before crowds that included such movie stars as Henry Fonda, Victor Mature and Tyrone Power.

The first BAA game ever played saw the Knicks beat the Huskies 68–66 in Toronto on November 1, 1946, before 7,000 fans. A promising start to a season that would prove to be a year of constant improvisa-tion—not surprising, given the brief start-up time the league had. All those associat-ed with the BAA—players, coaches, refer-ees, writers, broadcasters and team execu-tives—would grope their way through the inevitable glitches that new enterprises occasion.

Take, for instance, the Knicks' return engagement in Toronto shortly before Christmas 1946. After losing to the Huskies 74–70, the team set out for Providence, where they were to play the Steamrollers the following night. "We had to travel by

PLAYERS CONTRACT

AS PRESCRIBED FOR THE

IMPORTA

Every play
all of the cond
therein, and if a
promises and a

BA

THIS AGR
(hereinafter cal
of the City, To

WITNES
In consid
and agree as
1. The
training seas
2. The

a salary of
for such sea

reserved to
pensation
All paym
In s
the club
be paid
the entir
ploymer
3.
other t
4.
"at ho
for vi
club
The c
to an
of th

keep
Clul
in r
mar
or

ga
pl
m
ci
P

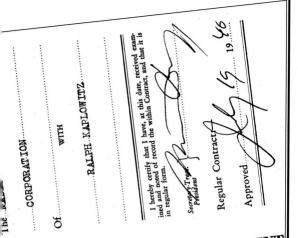

TO PLAYERS AND CLUB PRESIDENT

contract should carefully scrutinize the same to ascertain wheth
n between the Player and Club President have been incorpora
tted the player should insist upon having all the terms, conditic
in the contract before he signs the same.

ASSOCIATION OF AMERICA

—o—

NIFORM PLAYER CONTRACT

day of July '46 by and between Madison Square Garden
of the Basketball Association of America, and Ralph Kaplowitz
(hereinafter called the Player).

1946-47
NEW YORK
KNICKERBOCKERS
Madison Square Garden Entrant

IN THE BASKETBALL ASSN. OF AMERICA
307 WEST 49th STREET, NEW YORK 19, NEW YORK

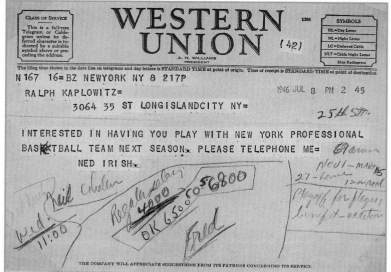

WESTERN UNION

The original telegram sent to Ralph Kaplowitz from Ned Irish. With this offer, Kaplowitz would become the very first Knickerbocker.

THE 1946–47 SEASON

Before joining the Knicks, Kaplowitz had played in the American League, a weekend operation, for a team coached by Eddie Gottlieb. Gottlieb had been promoting basketball tirelessly since the 1920s. His Sphas—the acronym of the South Philadelphia Hebrew Association—were an American League fixture, playing home games on Saturday nights in the grand ballroom of the Broadwood Hotel in Philadelphia. Admission price was 85 cents—35 cents for women, who stayed for the dance held after the game.

That was the old pro game, an image the BAA sought to put behind it. The new league hoped to make the kind of impact on the public that big-league baseball, football and hockey had. No more dances at halftime and after ball games. No more ramshackle gyms. Instead there would be a fast, savvy game in the best and biggest arenas this side of the Mississippi River.

Above, the Knicks took a score of candidates to their first tryout camp at the Nevele Hotel in Ellenville, New York. After two weeks, coach Neil Cohalan (far right, first row) cut the squad to ten men. Kaplowitz is fourth from left, second row. The team's leading scorer, Sonny Hertzberg, is second from left, back row. His best shot was the two-hand set, which he is seen releasing on the opposite page.

Below, in that first season, the players spent most of their off-hours with one another. During the team's training camp in Ellenville, New York, left to right, Jerry Kelly, Ralph Kaplowitz, Sonny Hertzberg, Ossie Schectman, Leo Gottlieb and Hy Gotkin over dinner. All but Gotkin and Kelly made the squad. Kelly played 46 games in 1946–47 for the Boston Celtics.

taxi to a point in Canada where there was a railroad crossing," recalled Kaplowitz. "There we would meet a sleeper that would take us on to Providence. We got into two cabs. I was in the cab with the starting team in it and, wouldn't you know, it broke down. What could we do? We got out and tried pushing it 'til finally we got it started. Well, when we got to that railroad crossing, we were out of luck. The train to Providence already had left. And there was no train until the next day, and that one wouldn't get us to Providence on time. So we made arrangements with a taxi cab company on the U.S. side of the border and drove ten hours in the snow to Providence. (We had) nothing to eat. We were all unshaven. By the time we got to the arena we were half an hour late. We told Cohalan that the cab broke down and we'd made arrangements, spending our own money. We changed quickly and settled onto the bench, where we stayed for the remainder of the game. None of us starters played a second. I have no idea what Cohalan was thinking. But he played the second team the whole game, and lost, 63–61."

In that first season, the Knicks relied on radio as well as the local newspapers to spread the gospel of pro basketball. To reach as wide an

1946–47 Bear Mountain training camp.

audience as he could, Ned Irish even tried pairing up Knicks announcer Marty Glickman with a female analyst in the radio booth.

"Ned thought that he could attract a female audience by teaming me up with a woman," said Glickman. "So he hired Sarah Palfrey Cooke, a former Wimbledon doubles champion, who was relatively well known at the time. I remember Bert Lee told me: 'She doesn't know much about basketball and your job, Marty, will be to teach her the game on the train ride from Penn Station to St. Louis, which was where the Knicks were playing the Bombers.

"Well, on the train I started with the very basics. To Sarah I said, 'A field goal counts as two points and a foul shot as one point.' She looked at me and said, 'What's a field goal?' Needless to say, it would be a long conversation that night."

The Knicks–Bomber game, which took place on November 7, 1946, started at 8 o'clock sharp rather than the customary 8:04 tipoff, leaving Glickman with no chance to introduce Ms. Cooke straightaway to their listening audience.

"So," said Glickman, "I couldn't properly introduce Sarah until we were six, seven minutes into the game . . . at which point I said, 'Here's Sarah Palfrey

N. Y. Pro Cagers Schedule 30 Home Games

The New York Knickerbockers of the Basketball Assn. of America will play four of its 30-game home schedule this season in Madison Square Garden and the remaining 26 at the 69th Regiment Armory. The Garden debut of Neil Cohalan's squad will be Nov. 11 against the Chicago Atomics.

The players include Ossie Shechtman and Hank Beenders of LIU, Hy Gotkin and George Pastushok of St. John's, Stanley Stutz (Modzelewski) of R. I. State, Forest Weber of Purdue, Sonny Hertzberg and Hank Rosenstein of CCNY, Nat Militzok of Hofstra and Cornell, Tommy Burns of Seton Hall, Ralph Kaplowitz of NYU, Bob Mullens of Fordham, Dick Murphy of Manhattan, Hank Lagerenberg of Villanova and Leo (Ace) Gottlieb.

The four games at Madison Square Garden will be on Nov. 11 against Chicago, Nov. 18 against Detroit, Dec. 8 against Boston and March 29, 1947, against Pittsburgh. The balance of the home games at the armory are as follows:

Nov. 14, Pittsburgh; 16, Chicago; 23, Cleveland; 27, St. Louis; 30, Philadelphia.

NEW YORK KNICKERBOCKERS
vs.
CHICAGO STAGS

MADISON SQUARE GARDEN   NOVEMBER 11, 1946   25c

24c, N. Y. C. SALES TAX 1c

Below, left to right, future Knicks Ralph Kaplowitz, Stan Stutz, Ossie Schectman and Sonny Hertzberg are seen from an aerial view during training camp in Ellenville, New York.

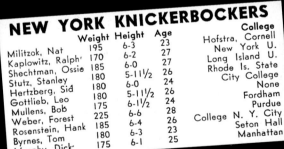

NEW YORK KNICKERBOCKERS				
	Weight	Height	Age	College
Militzok, Nat	195	6-3	23	Hofstra, Cornell
Kaplowitz, Ralph	170	6-2	27	New York U.
Shechtman, Ossie	185	6-0	27	Long Island U.
Stutz, Stanley	180	5-11½	26	Rhode Is. State
Hertzberg, Sid	180	6-0	24	City College
Gottlieb, Leo	180	5-11½	26	None
Mullens, Bob	175	6-1½	24	Fordham
Weber, Forest	225	6-6	28	Purdue
Rosenstein, Hank	185	6-4	26	College N. Y. City
Byrnes, Tom	180	6-3	23	Seton Hall
Murphy, Dick	175	6-1	25	Manhattan

Cooke, former tennis star and Wimbledon doubles champion. Sarah, what do you think of the game so far?' Well, she looked at me with a sort of blank expression and said, 'Marty, I'm speechless.' And she was."

The co-ed experiment lasted six games before it was scuttled. Stan Lomax was brought in as Glickman's broadcast partner. "And Sarah," said Glickman, "was as pleased as anybody else that she did not have to continue."

While the Knicks would have minimal television coverage for the first season on WCBS-TV, in those days the black-and-white TV was still a couple years away from being a common consumer item. WABD, the DuMont station in New York and WTTG in Washington, D.C., were, as future Knick announcer Bob Wolff remembered, the only stations doing daily TV in this country. Wolff, who announced the Washington Capitol games on WTTG that year, recalled, "In New York, games were mostly seen in Gimbel's department-store basement, where they were hard-pressed to sell this new-fangled contraption, television. In Washington, same thing—the games were seen mostly by appliance dealers who might stick a TV in the window to induce reluctant customers to buy a 12-inch television with a snowy picture. There were so few TV sets that my wife would take a bus to WTTG's studio to see what the heck I was doing. Face it: TV was in its infancy."

The across-the-board coverage helped the Knicks draw a nearly sell-out crowd for their first home game, which they lost in overtime to the Chicago Stags 78–68. *The New York Times* reported: "This being a play-for-pay circuit, it was most gratifying to those concerned that 17,205 spectators were on hand for the home debut of the Knickerbockers. Then there was a stirring regulation wind-up that saw Ossie Schectman, former LIU star, hit the target with a one-handed toss just thirty-five seconds before time ran out. This desperate shot brought about a 64–64 deadlock and, with the seconds ticking away, necessitated a five-minute overtime period, the first in the league.

"The crowd, which between halves had been treated to a fur fashion show and an abbreviated basketball exhibition, in which the Original Celtics—Nat Holman, Johnny Beckman, Dutch Dehnert, Joe Lapchick, Chris Leonard and Pete Barry—played a 1–1 tie with a team composed of New York Football Giants, was thrilled."

NEW YORK KNICKERBOCKERS
vs.
...AND REBELS
25¢

BIG GAME TONITE

NEW YORK KNICKERBOCKERS
vs.
PITTSBURGH IRONMEN
69TH REGIMENT ARMORY   NOVEMBER 16, 1946
25¢
24¢, N. Y. C. SALES TAX 1¢

✳ *As the forties wore on, BAA talent like Max Zaslofsky (below right), of the Chicago Stags, would be supplemented by players from the National Basketball League like Red Holzman of the Rochester Royals (below left). Both Zaslofsky and Holzman would later become part of Knicks history, Zaslofsky as a player and Holzman as a coach.*

In BAA arenas often so sparsely populated that players and fans alike could hear the echo of the bouncing basketball, the pro game took root. Not all of it was spectacular basketball. But across the league there were players who could excite the crowds such as Philadelphia's Joe Fulks, one of the few men back then who had a jump shot. Fulks, a self-described hillbilly from Kentucky, would lead the league in scoring in 1946–47, averaging 23.2 points per game.

Down in Washington, there was Bob Feerick, a 6' 3" whiz out of Santa Clara, the only BAA player to shoot better than 40 percent from the floor that first year and a man capable of the kind of spontaneous court wit that Bob Wolff still marvels over all these years later:

"The Knicks were playing the Caps at Uline Arena in D.C., and Feerick, an All-American type with a big shock of black hair, was racing the ball down the court, with a couple of Knicks in front of him. Well, from behind the top of the foul circle, he threw the ball intentionally against the backboard, cut by the players in front of him so he could catch it on the carom, and laid it in the basket. It was an ingenious move and players from both teams, I say *both teams*, applauded."

Fulks, Feerick, Stan Miasek (Detroit), Ed Sadowski (Cleveland), Max Zaslosfky (Chicago)—these were but a few of the better players the Knicks went up against that first season. Press Maravich, whose son Pete became an NBA legend, played with Pittsburgh. Matt Goukas Sr., whose son Matt Jr. would play and coach in the NBA, was with Philadelphia. Kevin (Chuck) Connors—a future star as TV's Rifleman—was at Boston.

✳ *The game in the forties was not the high-flying version seen now. Offenses were more earth-bound, with shooters often launching shots without leaving their feet. Two of the Knicks' better two-hand set-shot artists were Sonny Hertzberg (above) and Carl Braun (below).*

KNICKERBOCKERS
1946-47 HOME SCHEDULE

From 1940–60, the Knicks played a portion of their games at the Armory, which still stands today at Twenty-fourth Street and Lexington Avenue.

THE 69TH REGIMENT ARMORY

For Knicks fans paying anywhere from one dollar to five dollars at the Garden, even less at the 69th Regiment Armory, there remained suspicions about the quality of the pro game in 1946–47. The Knicks overcame the belief held by many New Yorkers that BAA ball was inferior to their beloved college games by scrimmaging local college fives and manhandling them. Word spread throughout the city.

BAA ball became attractive enough to Knicks patrons to ensure New York's being one of only two franchises that managed better than 100,000 paid admissions during 1946–47. Philadelphia was the other team to exceed the 100,000 mark. In all, net receipts for the first season would total $1,089,949—the salary of an NBA reserve these days or what the Knicks routinely grossed in two playoff games last year.

The game was more than a paycheck for those pioneer Knicks. It was fun. The camaraderie, the laughs and the competition made those years special. While money mattered, so did the game. With the war only recently ended and a peacetime optimism prevalent, the players, many of them ex-GIs, had a more innocent outlook than today's athletes. A recurring line from those first pros is: "I would have played for nothing." And while that may be exaggeration, remember: most athletes at that time were working stiffs, as these biographical blurbs from the Knicks' 25-cent game program reveal:

—During the off-season, Stan (Stutz) is a teacher-coach.
—Hank (Rosenstein) is single and in the off-season is a bookkeeper-manager.
—Nat (Militzok) is single and during the off-season is employed as an accountant.
—Richard (Murphy) is an apprentice pressman in the off-season.

Teams in those days traveled only occasionally by plane. That meant long hours going city to city by rail, which generated a closeness and rapport that was unique to those times. There were more than a few laughs during that first season.

Bud Palmer recalled the elaborate scheme that hyper-energetic Knicks guard 5' 11½" Stan Stutz (formerly Stanley J. Modzelewski) and 6' 7" teammate Lee Knorek, both of Polish extraction, pulled off toward the end of the season.

"It started innocently enough," said Palmer. "We were on the road on St. Patrick's Day and Knorek bought two black derbies—one for me, one for him—which we wore around on the trip. Anyway, we get to Cleveland and for some reason Stutz had on Lee's derby, which came down over his eyes almost. And he had on Lee's long blue navy coat, which came down to around his ankles.

"Lee wore my derby, which made him look like a pinhead, and my long blue coat, which fell way short on him. You get the picture? A rather odd-looking Mutt and Jeff pair. So we're at the hotel check-in desk in Cleveland, and Stutz marches up to the poor gal there and starts yelling in Polish for a room. And she, of course, couldn't understand. Up steps Knorek to act

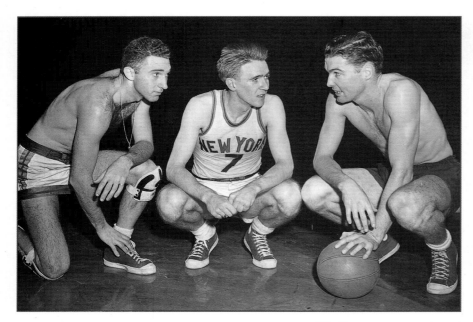

as an interpreter. He tells the poor girl that Stan is a commissar from the Soviet Union, an important man, and he was demanding a room immediately. Not only a room, but a limo. Meanwhile, Stutz and Knorek babbled back and forth in Polish, which the girl, I guess, couldn't distinguish from Russian.

"Anyway, Stutz and Knorek got a suite ... and a limo in which they later went to the airport while the rest of us rode by bus."

By then Cohalan's Knicks had undergone plenty of roster changes. Militzok and Dick Mullens were traded to Toronto, Murphy to Boston, Rosenstein and Forest Weber to Providence. Kaplowitz—unhappy with his playing time—had incited the deal that landed him in Philadephia.

Knicks such as Hertzberg remember the team's operation being top-drawer during a season where other teams often cut corners. "Ned Irish," said Hertzberg, "was a shy man and didn't mix well. People who didn't know him thought he was cold, aloof. But I had great admiration for Ned Irish. He quietly gave to charities, and he ran the Knicks first class. When Ossie Schectman suffered a ruptured spleen in Chicago from a collision with another player, Ned flew Ossie's wife out from New York to be with him. Which was typical of the way Ned Irish and the Knicks did things."

Above left to right, the 1948–49 Knicks squad, Sid Tanenbaum, Ray Lumpp and Bud Palmer.

Below, game action, 1948. Knicks in white jerseys, from left to right: van Breda Kolff, Tanenbaum, Palmer, Gallatin and Braun.

Facing page top, the Knicks, 1947–48. Front row, left to right: Paul Noel, Bill van Breda Kolff, Stan Stutz, Sid Tanenbaum, Tommy Byrnes, Ray Kuka. Back row, coach Joe Lapchick, Carl Braun, Lee Knorek, Dick Holub, Bud Palmer and trainer Jim Nevins.

Opposite page, bottom, Bud Palmer, #16.

Indeed, in the *New York Post* obituary for Irish that Leonard Lewin would write in 1982, he reinforced the point, noting: "In the early days of the pro basketball league, it was Irish who helped commissioner Maurice Podoloff keep it from folding. League salaries and expenses were paid by the Garden and from the pocket of Irish during the BAA's struggling years. Irish modestly never discussed his critical financial support that saved the league because he treated business secrets as though his life depended on it."

What was no secret about Irish's Knicks was

their lack of a big man. The Knicks' tallest player, 6' 10" Bob Cluggish, who'd played his college ball at Kentucky, lacked quickness and finesse and was derisively called "Sluggish" Cluggish by the newsmen following the team. That lack of a dominant center would turn out to be a problem for Knicks teams for many years—one that would turn into a quest on the order of the Arthurian pursuit of the Holy Grail. In a game that would grow increasingly airborne, as a new breed of springy-legged player appeared, the hole in the middle would haunt Knicks teams in the years to come.

During the 1951 finals, the Knicks enjoyed some special attention from a local car dealer. Shown here, standing next to the dealer, are (left to right): Dick McGuire, Vince Boryla, Sweetwater Clifton, Harry Gallatin, George Kaftan, Ray Lumpp and Connie Simmons. Seated are Tony Lavelli and Ernie Vandeweghe.

THE FIFTIES

When he turned up at the Knicks' Bear Mountain training camp in the autumn of 1947, Carl Braun viewed basketball as seasonal work. In his mind, he would play the 1947–48 season—and that year only—to keep in shape for what he regarded as his real future: baseball.

By 1947, Braun, a pitcher in the New York Yankee farm system, had moved up the Bronx Bombers' minor-league chain. But a shoulder injury to Braun's pitching arm would end his baseball career and give the Knicks the first of the nucleus of players who would build a franchise into a crowd-pleasing entity in the fifties.

In that 1947–48 season, Braun led the Knicks in scoring (14.3 points per game) and in assists (61 in 47 games), and was named Rookie of the Year. A wiry 6' 5" backcourtman, he was best known for a two-hand set shot that he released from over his head. Braun would be New York's first great pure shooter.

Some of the inside game the Knicks so desperately needed would be provided by the team's top draft choice in 1948, a broadshouldered, 6' 6" hayseed—or so his teammates would tease him—out of Northeast Missouri State Teachers College, Harry Gallatin. While he lacked the height associated with pivot play, nonetheless Gallatin would work around the basket using brute strength and an instinct for the basketball to make his living against bigger men for the better part of ten NBA seasons.

Gallatin's game would benefit from the Knicks' top draft choice in 1949, Richard J. (Tricky Dick) McGuire. For the 6' McGuire could find a moving target, like Gallatin, with passes threaded through the hoops equivalent of a needle's eye. And Gallatin, who had the knack of getting open, became the frequent, though not only, beneficiary of McGuire's clever playmaking.

McGuire's unselfishness was almost extreme. Frequently he would be so open for a shot that Knicks teammates and fans would shout for him to shoot. Sometimes McGuire would shrug his shoulders and reluctantly let fly. More often he would spy another opening for a pass that only a playmaking sophisticate like him could ever hope to find.

While Gallatin remained a bulwark around the basket, in this 1950–51 season he and the Knicks would get help beneath the boards from a 26-year-old rookie, Nat (Sweetwater) Clifton, the team's first black player. In a season that saw Chuck Cooper of Boston and Earl Lloyd of Syracuse break the NBA color barrier, the 6' 7", 225-pound Clifton followed soon after when the Knicks bought his contract from the Harlem Globetrotters.

Much to the delight of New York fans, Clifton still retained a bit of showmanship from his Globetrotter days. With his huge hands he liked to palm the ball and sometimes wave it around before making a move to the basket or deftly flipping a pass to a cutting teammate. But the role for which the Knicks had acquired him was that of a force under the boards. And while Clifton took some of the burden off Gallatin by defensing the big men that Harry the Horse often had to guard, by Lapchick's view he fell short for a man of his brute strength and athleticism as a rebounder. As Lapchick saw it, the trouble was that "Sweets," as he came to be known, was letting the opposition push him around rather than asserting his territorial prerogatives.

That all changed when, during an exhibition game against the Celtics before the 1951–52 season, Clifton took exception to the rough stuff of a Boston forward, Bob Harris. Words were exchanged, and then blows were struck, both of them by Clifton. With a left hook and right cross, he dropped Harris where he stood and then froze Celtic teammates, rushing to Harris' aid, when he brandished his fist and told them: "Come on. All of you."

"From then on the other teams kept their distance from Sweets," Lapchick would recall.

Clifton's rebound statistics improved markedly—from 491 in 1950–51 to 731 the following year.

There was one other Knick who would figure prominently in the success of those early-1950s New York teams, a man whose circumstances were unlike those of any other player in the NBA. Much as he loved basketball, Ernie Vandeweghe had career objectives that went beyond James Naismith's

game. Vandeweghe was studying to be a pediatrician, taking a full-time curriculum at Columbia College of Physicians and Surgeons on 168th Street and Broadway. The demands on a medical student like him would seem to have precluded the notion of playing NBA ball. But Vandeweghe's passion for the game overrode the common-sense notion of excluding it, and pretty soon he was shuttling between classroom and NBA arenas.

"Because of my situation, I was paid on a per-game basis," recalled Vandeweghe. "It was my discretion what games and what practices I would make. A day or so in advance, I would call the Garden and tell them whether I'd be making the game or not.

"People asked why I would try to play ball while going to med school. Well, see I was not much of a social butterfly. My social event was to turn up in Madison Square Garden in a Knicks uniform. It was what I preferred to drinking with the boys or going to the movies."

The 6' 3" Vandeweghe could run, shoot and defend. He was quick and aggressive—a strong competitor. For Vandeweghe the never-ending problem was to juggle his two demanding regimens and find time to do justice to them both. It wasn't easy. The dual roles invariably put him in a time crunch that, as Glickman recalled, "would find him stepping into the lavatory of a DC-3 in his street clothes to slip into his Knicks uniform." Like Clark Kent emerging from a phone booth, Vandeweghe now would stride down the aisle of the plane as Super-hoopster, in his Knicks warm-ups. Once the DC-3 had landed, he would race to find a cab to get him to the arena.

"We used to call the space behind the Knick bench 'Ernie Vandeweghe Avenue,'" said Asofsky, "reason being that Vandeweghe came late to ball games after making intern rounds, and used to warm up running up and down the floor in back of the Knick bench, even while the game was on—wind sprints and such. And on time-outs, he was the only ballplayer I've ever seen on time-outs shoot baskets to get set."

Even in the absence of Braun, who had been drafted into the armed services for two years, the core Knicks—Gallatin, McGuire, Clifton, Vandeweghe and a fine set shooter named Vince Boryla—got the Knicks to the seventh game of the NBA finals for two years running—the 1950–51 season and 1951–52. But both times New York seemed snakebitten.

In 1950–51, the Rochester Royals were the opposition. Rochester had big men like Arnie Risen and Jack Coleman, and capable guards like Bobby Davies, Bobby Wanzer and a man who in later years would be pivotal in the history of the Knicks, William

(Red) Holzman. As the seventh and final game of the playoffs counted down, New York had possession of the basketball and, as Knick reserve Ray Lumpp recalled, a one-point lead with half a minute left.

"Ned Irish thought he had his first championship—he had filled the plane with champagne for the celebration afterward," said Lumpp. "And he had good reason to expect the title. See, we had lost the first three games of the series to the Royals and come back to win the next three. If anybody had the momentum, it was us. And now all we had to do was keep possession of the ball and we were champions. But Bobby Davies hawked the ball, it bounced off (Knicks guard) Max Zaslofsky's foot and went out of bounds, giving the ball to Rochester. Well, the Royals took advantage. Arnie Risen threw in a hook. And that was it. Devastating. The champagne never got uncorked."

The following year, in the opening game of the championship series against the Lakers, the Knicks were victimized by an egregious oversight on the part of officials Sid Borgia and Stan Stutz—the same Stutz who had once played for New York. As Glickman recalled it: "The circus was in Minneapolis that night, so the opening game was played in St. Paul. A capacity crowd. Podoloff, the commissioner of the league, was there. Late in the second quarter, Al McGuire (brother of Dick McGuire) shoots from the top of the key and is fouled in the act of shooting. The ball goes in, meaning there's a chance for a three-point play. That's when Stutz, the outside official, says: 'Two shots.' Al says, 'No. One shot. The ball went in.' Maybe so, but Stutz didn't see it. And incredibly, neither did Borgia. Borgia was watching the bumping down low, and somehow hadn't caught the ball going through the net. "For 10 minutes, the officials are trying to sort it out. They even go over to Podoloff at one point and ask him did the ball go in. But Podoloff felt he should be an impartial observer, so he says, 'I can't say. It's not my business to.' So Stutz and Borgia had to ignore a basket that everybody in the building had seen go in—everybody but them. McGuire made one of two foul shots, the Knicks lost that night in overtime. And couldn't help but thinking about that play when they ended up losing the series to the Lakers four games to three."

The popularity of the pro game grew. In New York, when a college-basketball point-shaving scandal broke in 1951, many disillusioned followers of the undergraduate game shifted their allegiance to the Knicks. New York began to receive some of the perks associated with established sports teams. A local car dealer, for instance, gave the team access to free autos during playoffs for the promotional value he felt the Knicks afforded. The team's games were not only still broadcast by Glickman on WMGM, but also were shown to the expanding television market on WPIX, with Bob Wolff at the microphone starting in 1954.

When the team clinched the Eastern Division title in 1952–53, with Braun back in the lineup, Irish met the players on their return to Pennsylvania Station and transported them to Mama Leone's, an Italian restaurant, for a celebration that ran into the wee hours. Unfortunately, the good times ended in the playoffs when the Knicks were beaten in the championship finals four games to one by the powerful Lakers, led by big George Mikan, the league's first dominant big man.

But the Knicks were no longer a team groping for recognition. They were now a fixture on the New York sports scene. It was not long before a Brooklyn schoolboy, Marv Albert, formed a fan club for a Knick named Jim Baechtold, who joined the club in 1953. The enterprising Albert ended up merging the Baechtold club with fan clubs that sprang up for other Knicks and then consolidated them as the New York Knicks Fan Club, of which he was the first president. That exposure gave him an inside track to become a Knicks ball boy.

As the fifties ground on, the Knicks were having a tougher time of it. Starting in 1955–56, they would finish last three years in a row in the Eastern Division in spite of having virtually the same cast of players, and some very fine additions, like the hard-driving Richie Guerin, and Kenny Sears and Willie Naulls.

But that was simply not enough to cope with the power that other teams could muster under the boards. By the end of the decade Boston had Bill Russell, Philadelphia had Chamberlain—prototypes of the modern pivotman: sleek, athletic men, capable of soaring through the air with the greatest of ease and moving the game a giant step further from the earth-bound proposition it had been.

Through the fifties the Knicks had a hole at the center only slightly smaller than the Grand Canyon. The likes of Connie Simmons and Walter Dukes and Ray Felix and Charlie Tyra were not the antidote to the Chamberlain/Russell problem. Big men came and went for the Knicks, as did the coaches. By the end of the fifties, the Knicks coaching job was a revolving door: Lapchick, Boryla, Fuzzy Levane and Braun all were hired and fired through a period of dismal finishes by New York teams.

Ahead lay the sixties and that continuing search for the big man and the team chemistry that could revive a franchise badly in need of pepping up.

New York drafted wisely in the late forties, landing Harry Gallatin, below, seen rising up to the rim, and playmaker Dick McGuire, above seated at left, with team executive Ned Irish while coach Joe Lapchick looks on.

Opposite page, Nat (Sweetwater) Clifton, delighting Lapchick by palming a basketball in each hand. Clifton was the first African-American to play for the Knicks, joining the team in the 1950–51 season.

HARRY GALLATIN, New York Knicks

KNICKERBOCKERS vs. FORT WAYNE
SYRACUSE vs. ROCHESTER
MADISON SQUARE GARDEN   NOVEMBER 27, 1956   **25¢**
24c. N. Y. C. SALES TAX 1c

In the fifties the league would go through a shakeout period, as teams in the more obscure cities, like Sheboygan, Waterloo and Anderson, would disband for lack of financial resources. While it lasted, the inclusion of so many franchises in so many strange venues lent a certain raggedy charm to the game.

In Philadelphia, for instance, veteran Knicks made sure to bring their own soap because the Warriors management—read Gottlieb—was too budget-minded to include that in the visitors' dressing room. On the court, the home team often tried to take advantage too. These were times when uniformity in playing conditions was not the rule, as it is today. In Waterloo, a hot air blower located at one end of the court seemed to vent more vigorously when the Knicks were shooting at that particular basket; against that sudden stream of air the basketball might flutter like a knuckle ball.

At the Syracuse Fairgrounds, there were cables supporting the backboard that led from the four corners of the board to the edge of the balcony. At crucial times, when a Knick stepped to the foul line, the Syracuse faithful would yank on the cables, causing the basket to shake just as the shooter was about to release his free throw. Protests would follow, usually

KNICKERBOCKERS vs. ROCHESTER
BALTIMORE vs. SHEBOYGAN

MADISON SQUARE GARDEN   JANUARY 22, 1950 **25c**
24c, N. Y. C. SALES TAX 1c

Below, the fifties saw the advent of basket-ball's first dominant big man, George Mikan of the Minneapolis Lakers shooting a lefty hook over the Knicks' Clifton. Although only 6' 7" inches, Clifton often had to guard pivotmen who towered above him. Clifton, #8, is featured on a game program facing page, bottom.

Facing page, top, Mikan was so dominant and popular that when the Lakers were matched against the Knicks, the Garden marquee let his name appear in place of his Laker team, a tribute to his drawing power.

leading to the PA announcer saying, "Please don't shake the backboard." And until the next crucial juncture the shaking might cease.

At the Edgerton Arena in Rochester, the baseline at one end of the court was only three to four feet from an exit door that led out into an alley. One night, Knick Goebel Ritter was shoved from behind as he drove to the basket. Ritter's momentum sent him sprawling into the iron bar on the door. That caused the door to swing open and Ritter to go careening into the winter night. He went through the door and headfirst into a snowbank outside. Ritter shook off the snow and made his way back into the arena.

"In Baltimore," recalled Marty Glickman, "in the early fifties the Bullets played in a converted trolley-car barn. In fact, there were still trolley-car tracks leading into the building. It was a beat-up, decrepit facility with bleacher seats, about 4,000 capacity. I would broadcast from six rows up in those bleacher seats, sitting among the spectators. In front of my seat would be a two-by-six board for the radio equipment, (with) spectators in front and behind me.

"Well, in those days, Baltimore was a pretty wide-open town. Before the games, bookies would walk up and down the aisles taking bets. At halftime they would pay off for certain wagers—total points for the half and other propositions. I'd be broadcasting and, like nowadays you pass the peanuts along the row to the man who paid for them, in those days while giving the listening audience the halftime stats, I'd be passing dollar bills from the bookies to the bettors. And in the background you could hear the bookies hollering out their betting propositions for the second half. 'Five points second half Knicks.' 'Seven points second half Knicks.' At the close of the game I'd be giving the final stats to listeners while passing money."

Even more bizarre were the traveling arrangements the Knicks were obliged to make to reach certain NBA outposts—for example, when New York had to go from Rochester to Fort Wayne.

"There was no way to go straight from Rochester to Fort Wayne on a Saturday night," said Glickman. "No trains, no prop planes. So how do you get there? Well, the way it worked was you'd get a Twentieth Century Limited, going to Chicago. You'd climb aboard around midnight and wend your way through New York State, north to Buffalo, and from there due west to Chicago. We'd get aboard sleepers, with beds comfortable enough for a normal-sized guy like me but less comfortable for your fellows standing 6' 6" or better.

"Anyway, we had an arrangement with the railroad company. At five in the morning, the porter would wake us up. The train would make an unscheduled stop and leave us in the middle of a godforsaken

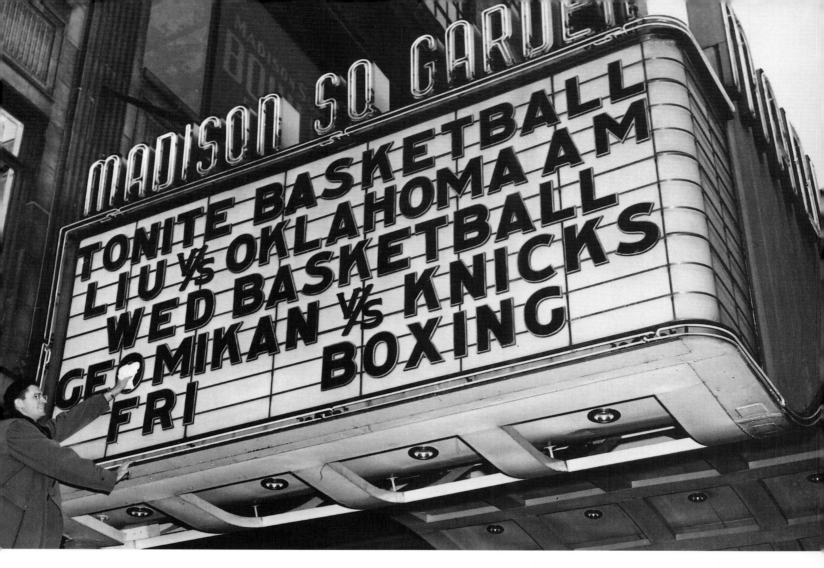

Indiana prairie. Dawn would just be breaking. Our instructions were to look for a yellow blinking light one mile away. Alongside the railroad tracks was a two-lane blacktop road, which led to this yellow blinking light. All of us—players, coach and broadcaster—would walk the mile, our bags in hand, the sun coming up. At a crossroads a good mile from where we'd been left, we would come upon eight or ten houses, the tallest house no more than two stories high, and at that crossroad would be the yellow blinking light. At this point we had instructions to look for the Green Parrot Cafe, which actually had a green parrot painted on its window.

"By now Carl Braun was mustered out of the Army and, given his pitching background, he was anointed to pick up a pebble and throw it up against the second-floor window. It might take two or three pebbles to wake up the drowsy-looking woman who lived there. She'd appear at the window in a nightdress and hair in curlers and say: 'Oh, the Knickerbockers. Be right down.'

"In the interim she would get dressed and would call three or four woman neighbors. They would materialize with cars. We'd get in and drive the forty miles to Fort Wayne. Get there at seven-thirty or eight in the morning and play that afternoon or night. That's how you went from Rochester to Fort Wayne in those days."

But getting there was only half the fun. The Pistons' home games were played in a high-school gym in which the spectators sat above the court and from up there heaped abuse and sometimes even spat on visiting players as they

NAT CLIFTON, N.Y. Knickerbockers

KNICKERBOCKERS vs. MINNEAPOLIS
BOSTON vs. ROCHESTER
MADISON SQUARE GARDEN   DECEMBER 7, 1954
24¢, N.Y.C. SALES TAX 1¢ **25¢**

entered and exited the court. Once, when a Syracuse National star, Dolph Schayes, got into a fight with a Piston, he was set upon by a fan who jumped out of the balcony and onto his back.

"You had the feeling when you walked out there . . . like you were a Roman gladiator," said Braun. "Forty-five hundred people, and there was no such thing as applauding a good play. These were home-town fans to the extreme."

That was typical of the provincial nature of fans back then. Many of the arenas in the league were compact, with courtside seats virtually arm's length from the floor. That made it easier for fans to be heard, and some of their remarks were personal enough to get the players' attention, particularly in Philadelphia's Convention Hall.

Above left to right, the nucleus of the successful Knicks teams of the early fifties were players Gallatin, #11, McGuire, #15, and Braun, #4, with Lapchick.

Below, the Knicks got added backcourt scoring punch when in 1950–51 they acquired Max Zaslofsky, having his ankle taped while McGuire watches.

Facing page, that's McGuire taking dead aim.

"There was a courtside group of guys in Philadelphia that bet on games," recalled Braun. "They all sat together, and they were very vocal—I mean, it was a concentrated twenty or thirty voices. And nasty. Referring to your wife and things like that. I mean, these guys would get pretty low.

"Well, if we had the game locked up, or if we had it lost, we'd send one of our guys cutting down the court right in front of these guys. As an ex–baseball pitcher I

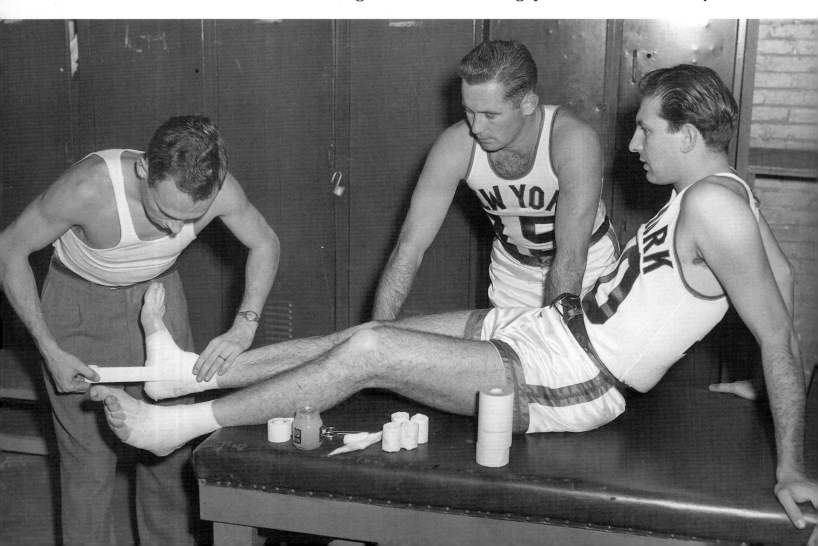

could throw that ball really hard. And I want to tell you, it could break your nose if it hit you square. I got one guy on the top of the head one night. If I hit him in the face, I would have hurt him, so it was probably just as well . . . But I want to tell you, it stunned him. The ball went up about forty rows. When I threw the ball, the fellow going to catch it would have his arms spread apart about a foot and a half, enough for the ball to go right through. He made as though he was going to catch it, but he let it go right through. And those guys in that section just couldn't be sure if it was done intentionally or not. I mean, it looked like my guy was trying to catch the ball."

Syracuse was known to the Knicks as "The Zoo."

"In the winter," said Braun, "for the people of Syracuse, basketball was their life. They were like the Green Bay of the NBA. And a Knicks game in Syracuse was *the* big event. Those folks were merciless. I can remember running down the court and having cigarette butts flipped at me as I went by. Live ash that got me in the legs and smarted."

So it went in Syracuse, where fans might smack players on the head with game programs as they made their way on or off the court, and where one woman came to the games equipped with a hat pin that she would jab at players, coaches and referees.

In the fifties, Syracuse was to NBA referees what Parris Island, South Carolina, is to Marines. In that city, officials discovered whether they could hack it or not. Those were the days when a gentleman known as The Strangler, a 300-pound local, would lurch out of the stands and apply full nelsons to refs who displeased him.

As Syracuse's Schayes recalled: "He left a few marks on one ref's throat. They had to talk the ref into coming back onto the court."

Richie Powers worked many of his early games as a pro referee in Syracuse. It was there, in fact, he heard for the first time what would become a familiar refrain: "Powers, you bum! You

Above, some NBA teams laid their floors over the ice that the local hockey team had used earlier in the day, resulting in the kind of slapstick spill that Ernie Vandeweghe takes.

Below, Al McGuire, left, is seen with his bar owner father, center, and his brother Dick, right. Al was the "other" McGuire on the Knicks roster during the early fifties. He was Dick's younger brother. Al liked to boast to newsmen that he could stop the Boston Celtics' great playmaker, Bob Cousy, seen driving to the hoop on the adjoining page, top.

Facing page, bottom, meanwhile, a more reserved Dick McGuire, #15, let his playmaking do his talking.

stink!" This was mild compared to what a fan shouted one night to Sid Borgia: "I know why you're bald, Borgia! They pulled out one hair for every bad call."

But through those rough and tumble days, the sheer fun of the game was the common denominator for the players. "We liked the game so much," recalled Braun, "that we'd have played almost for free . . . and many times we did. I used to play in charity games or somebody would ask me to go up to church and play, or synagogue. Where the ball was, that's where we wanted to be. It didn't make us good businessmen, but . . ."

In those days, Knicks players were often dispatched to playgrounds and recreation centers around the city to spread the NBA gospel to future ticket-buyers through the clinics they would stage.

"To Betsy Head Park in Brooklyn, or some place in the Bronx," Braun recalled. "We'd have team practice in the afternoon and do the clinics at night. A few of us would pile into a cab and off we'd go. They'd give us $12.50 in expenses and you'd get a free meal at one of the hotels afterward. And man, we used to kill 'em on that meal 'cause we wouldn't eat any lunch—we had a practice in the armory in the afternoon. And so when we sat down, I mean—two steaks, three shrimp cocktails. But we only got away with that for a couple of weeks and then they started to limit us . . . It was cheap at half the price. They got tremendous exposure and many of the years I played with the Knicks, after the game some boy who had seen me years before at a clinic would come up to me to shake hands."

It was an era long before multimillion-dollar player contracts and agents and a certain detachment from the public by the game's stars. Players still took pleasure in being part of a life that allowed them to extend their boyhood. Bill van Breda Kolff recalled the time when the Knicks bought water pistols that they carried on the road:

"Someone would drop a coin and when it hit the floor you drew and squirted. We were like little kids. When we flew to Chicago we'd shoot the stewardesses in the back of the neck. One night Joe Lapchick was going over the stat sheet on a bus. We squirted him and the ink ran down the page."

Lapchick, who had won recognition as the game's first legitimate pivot star as a member of the original Celtics, had played that barnstorming pro game from 1917 to 1936. He would coach the Knicks from 1947 to 1956. In keeping with the fraternal atmosphere the game had back then, he would hang out after home

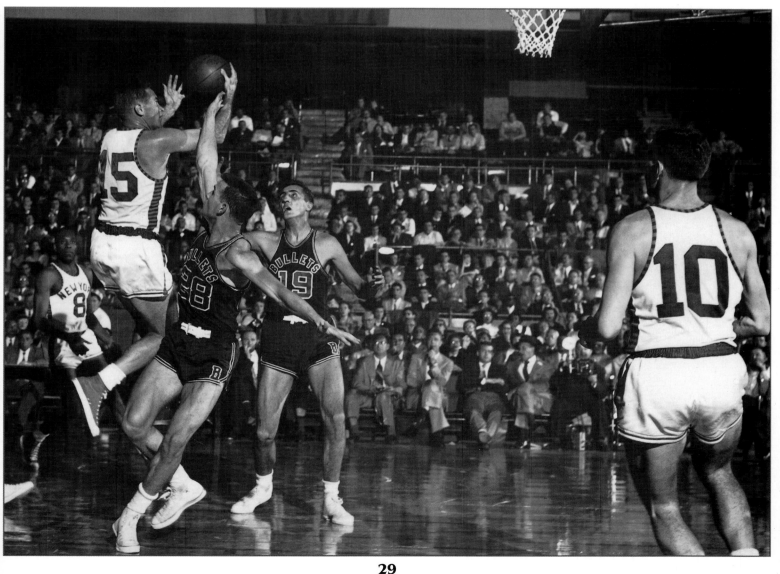

games at a West Side restaurant, talking basketball and chatting with sportswriters.

As Glickman recalled: "Everything was a laugh. Sure, they played hard and hated to lose, but we had fun. At that time, in contrast to the present, we were all in it together—writers, broadcasters and players, trainers, coaches and many of the owners. It was like one big happy family. We traveled by train almost exclusively. And Lapchick had a steady card game going with (*The New York Daily Mirror's* Leonard) Lewin and (*The New York Times'* Louis) Effrat—twenty-one and pinochle and poker. I was one-of-the-boys with them, even though I never played. There was a feeling of togetherness—we were truly friends. The players would have their card games going and Ernie Vandeweghe would be studying from a book. Every year for four, five years, I would have a party just for the players at my house in New Rochelle. And Dick McGuire, Al McGuire, Carl Braun, Harry Gallatin, Sweets Clifton and the others—they would all show. I remember I had a domed ceiling in the living room and we would hang a basket up there, and we'd spend the night eating and drinking, swapping stories and shooting at that basket. We'd have a ball. It was fun just being with each other. I can't emphasize strongly enough this feeling of camaraderie."

Boston's Bob Cousy dribbles between Kenny Sears and Richie Guerin.

Facing page at right, the 1957–58 team led the league in scoring with 112 ppg. From left to right: Ron Sobie, Carl Braun, Willie Naulls, Ray Felix, Kenny Sears, Guy Sparrow and Richie Guerin. Far left, Charlie Tyra.

KNICKERBOCKERS vs. PHILADELPHIA
3rd ANNUAL KNICK OLDTIMERS GAME
MADISON SQUARE GARDEN   OCTOBER 24, 1959 35¢

✳ *Above, Kenny Sears, featured on a Knicks game program, came to the club in 1955–56 and provided immediate scoring punch.*

While Al McGuire was, in his words, "a marginal player," he was one of the leading party guys on the Knicks, with a perspective skewed to laughter and the street-smart view of things.

"Those were different times, with different rules, and I don't mean just on the court," McGuire said. "There were no training tables and no hair blowers. The showers were about 5' 6" high and even the smallest basketball player could only get parts of their bodies under them. But it was a great time.

"Sweetwater Clifton was usually my roommate on the road with the Knicks. It was Sweets who taught me that 'aunts' didn't mean you're related. If he told me an aunt was coming to visit, I knew that meant I'd have to make

WILLIE
NAULLS   NEW YORK
Knicks

KENNY
SEARS   NEW YORK
Knicks

✳ *Far left, Willie Naulls arrived a year later, in 1956–57, and with Sears doubled the scoring potential of the Knicks front line. But neither Sears nor Naulls had the physicality or aggression that the Knicks needed in their front line in the late fifties.*

Merry Christmas
TO

The 1951–52 Knicks, with McGuire in center front row,
and Gallatin, back row, third from left.

* *While the Knicks sent Christmas greetings to their fans, above, Lapchick, holding the ball, yearned for Santa's help in securing a big man.*

ZASLOFSKY NITE

KNICKERBOCKERS vs. ROCHESTER
BALTIMORE vs. BOSTON

MADISON SQUARE GARDEN

MARCH 4, 1952 25¢

24c N.Y.C. SALES TAX 1c

MR. INSIDE & MR. OUTSIDE

In the early fifties, Harry Gallatin and Dick McGuire were Mr. Inside and Mr. Outside for the Knicks. Gallatin rebounded and scored near the basket. McGuire made the plays from the guard position away from the hoop.

When he first came to New York, Gallatin may have been somewhat in awe of his surroundings—Marty Glickman recalled Gallatin's hands "shaking" when he went up for the rebound in his first appearances. But Gallatin lost the jitters quickly enough and his aggressive style won over the Garden gallery. "Harry the Horse," the fans affectionately called him, an admiring allusion to the work ethic and the hustle Gallatin showed.

McGuire's selfless game owed to a mentality that was, as Michael Crosby would write in *Sports Illustrated*, "rooted partly in the Irish-Catholic ethos, in which self-effacement plays a large role, and partly in the reverse snobbery of old-fashioned New York cool. If you ask Dick McGuire . . . how he developed the passing game that made him famous, he says, 'We had to pass a lot because we weren't as good as the players today. They don't need to do what we did. They bring the ball up with one hand and shoot a 20-foot jumper right in your face. We had to look for the open man.'"

KNICKERBOCKERS vs. ROCHESTER
PHILADELPHIA vs. MINNEAPOLIS
MADISON SQUARE GARDEN   DECEMBER 6, 1955 **25¢**

Left to Right: Dick McGuire, Carl Braun, Harry Gallatin and Coach Joe Lapchick.

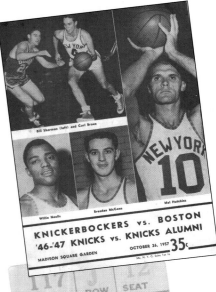

Bill Sharman (left) and Carl Braun

Willie Naulls   Brendan McCann   Mel Hutchins

KNICKERBOCKERS vs. BOSTON
'46-'47 KNICKS vs. KNICKS ALUMNI
MADISON SQUARE GARDEN   OCTOBER 26, 1957 **35¢**

✻ *Below, left to right, the big men the
Knicks had in the late fifties, Charlie
Tyra and Ray Felix, simply were no
match for Chamberlain and Russell.*

CHARLIE
TYRA   NEW YORK
Knicks

a trifecta and sleep in a room with two other guys.

"My regular running mate—off the court, I mean—was Connie Simmons (a 6' 8" center, who played five seasons with New York). Every now and then someone else would come out of the library and join Connie and me at our local watering hole, wherever we were, but usually it was just the two of us.

"We were arrested in Syracuse one time after some waiter wouldn't sing 'Happy Birthday' to Connie. It was barely a scuffle, no more than a push, but we were both charged with assault, along with my brother Dick, which was a joke because Dick wouldn't hurt a fly. After the season we had to go back to face the charges,

and we were fined. Ned Irish paid the fine, which I thought was very nice.

"Another incident I've never told publicly before was the time I had my jaw broken. It was three or four in the morning and Connie and I were in some after-hours place under the Third Avenue El. Connie or I said something someone didn't like and I was blindsided with a punch. I knew right away it was bad, the jaw was broken in two places, but I said to Connie, 'We gotta get out of this joint before reporters show up.'

"Connie got me to some hospital with a lot of foreign doctors, and I had one from, I think, the Yucatán Peninsula. It was five in the morning, he was probably thinking about some native relics or artifacts, and I'm thinking, 'How good can he be?' So my jaw was wired shut, and the story we gave out to the press was that I was hurt in a traffic accident on my way home at eleven the night before."

RAY
FELIX   NEW YORK
Knicks

NEW YORK
19

40
LOGE   C
ROW
SIDE LOGE   5
MADISON SQUARE GARDEN   SEAT
$1.50
SUN. AFT. 1:30 P.M.
JAN. 27, 1952   GAME
ARCUS-SIMON
TICKET CO.

K
SEC.
END PROME
69th REG
BASKETB
SAT. EVE.—7-13
JAN. 18, 1

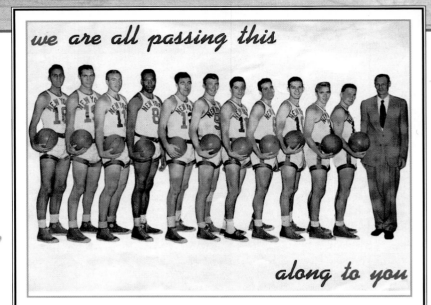

An early 1950s Christmas card.

THE EARLY NBA

In the early 1950s, the Knicks organization was regarded as one of the stronger ones in the league—a solid entity that could be relied on to maintain a big-league image for the NBA.

But in other cities, the teams were often run by individual proprietors whose bankrolls were not as fat as the Garden's. And in these places, team owners often did what made short-term economic sense for them, though in the long run it might not gild the NBA's image.

Marty Glickman recalled the day in the early fifties when the league had just acquired national TV exposure and wanted to create the best impression on the viewing public:

"The TV game on this particular day was up in Rochester, and (NBA commissioner) Podoloff warned the Royals' owner, Lester Harrison, not to display local advertising because it would diminish the league's image. Well, wouldn't you know Harrison had a huge papier-mâché drawing for a local sponsor, directly in camera view. Podoloff got nuts, shouting, 'You know you can't do this.' And when Harrison didn't respond, the NBA commissioner climbed a ladder and by himself tore the drawing down."

CARL BRAUN — NEW YORK Knicks

NEW YORK Knicks — RON SOBIE

As much fun as playing NBA ball was for the hired hands, it was also a treat for the young Marv Albert, who, in his role as a Knicks ball boy, had a backstage view of the game that he recalled years later:

"We'd play three-on-three until the players got there, then hang around with whoever might drop by: Wilt Chamberlain, Bob Pettit, Bill Russell, whoever. Some days they'd have doubleheaders at the Garden, maybe Boston against the Lakers and then the Knicks versus the St. Louis Hawks. Sometimes between game days there would be a major concert, so they'd have a lot of the orchestra equipment backstage. Between games once, Cliff Hagan, a star of the St. Louis Hawks, sat down at the piano and knocked out some wonderful stuff. I'll never forget that: standing around a piano backstage at the Garden while an NBA standout in full uniform sat tickling the ivories. It was wonderful.

"I knew them all. Bob Cousy, Frank Ramsey, Jim Loscutoff, Easy Ed Macauley . . . I spilled water on all the greats. Wilt (Chamberlain), Johnny Kerr, Larry Costello. I used to hear (Bill) Russell throwing up before the game. Red Auerbach would throw me out of his (Celtic) locker room when I'd try to hang around and hear his pregame talk. I knew Nat (Sweetwater) Clifton . . . they called him Sweetwater because he loved soft drinks . . . Sweetwater would give me a tip now and then. A good night's worth of tips was five dollars. That blew our friends' minds. Getting to sit on the bench of an NBA team *and* getting a tip? Get serious.

"I made my own contacts through that job. The best one might have been Marty Glickman, the most well respected sportscaster in New York when I was growing up. Did you know Jack Kerouac mentions Marty in *On the Road*? You can look it up. I must have pestered that poor man to within an inch of his life, because he finally started letting me do stats for him during games. From then on, everything I did or said, I did or said like Marty Glickman. If he

twitched, I twitched. If he had two lumps with his coffee, I had two lumps with my coffee. I wrote copy like he wrote copy. I was his alter ego.

"Sometimes I wonder what my style would have been like if it weren't for Marty. He hated cliches and hype and I learned to hate cliches and hype. He was the eyes of the listener, so I tried to be the eyes of the listener. He followed the ball. He developed a geography of the court. You bring it up along the right sideline. You cross the half-court line, you come across the lane. He brought forth the language of the game. For instance, he was the first basketball announcer to start using the word *swish*. People thought he invented it, but all he did was stand alongside Knicks starter Carl Braun one day and every time Braun shot it up Braun would say, 'Swish.' He just brought it to the booth. And the country."

The country that had stayed away from the pro game in the forties was warming up to it in the fifties, more so when the league adopted the

Above, while the Knicks gave it their best shot, sometimes in brawls against teams like Boston, the results in the standings were disappointing.

Below, Richie Guerin driving to the basket against the Chicago Packers and, opposite, shooting the left hook, was much admired as a hard-nosed competitor by New York fans.

24-second rule in 1954 to speed up the game. But by the late fifties the Knicks lagged behind the rest of the league, largely due to the lack of a powerful front line, like the best teams had.

The Minneapolis Lakers had been *the* team through the early fifties, with the 6' 10½" George Mikan teaming up with 6'7" Vern Mikkelsen and 6'3½" Jim Pollard, who jumped so well he was known as "The Kangaroo Kid." From 1948–49, the Lakers won the league championship five times in six years, overpowering teams on a home court that was narrower by several feet than any other NBA court and suited their power game. Mikan was so potent a force and

For one season, 1958-59, coach Fuzzy Levane, facing page with ball, managed to revive the Knicks. Under Levane, the Knicks were 40-32, finishing second in the East after three straight last-place finishes. But the Knicks fell back to last place the following season, unable to overcome the lack of a potent big man. From left to right: Richie Guerin, Willie Naulls, Ray Felix, Kenny Sears, Carl Braun.

Despite the efforts of center Ray Felix, laying the ball up, hard times returned.

such an attraction that when the Lakers came to New York the Garden marquee would read quite simply:

GEO MIKAN V/S KNICKS

As the Knicks became perpetual also-rans toward the end of the fifties, their players came to regard their work as an Excedrin headache. Take Richie Guerin, who'd sharpened his game in the mid-1950s with the Quantico (Va.) Marines and would bring a Marine's hell-for-leather aggression to the Knicks that quickly made him a crowd favorite.

But once he joined the Knicks, Guerin found that playing for the perpetually undermanned New York team took a toll on a player's psyche.

"We just couldn't compete against the Bostons, Philadelphias and Syracuses," said Guerin. "So we wouldn't make the playoffs. By mid-January, we'd be out of it. Under those circumstances it was difficult to bust your butt every night. Players came and went, coaches too. Each year you psyched yourself into believing that you had a chance. And then...and then reality set in again."

The reality? New York simply hadn't the capable large bodies to go up against Wilt Chamberlain or Bill Russell. Other teams had front lines that in combination could compete against Philadelphia and Boston—Bob Pettit, Cliff Hagan, Clyde Lovelette and Larry Foust at St. Louis; Schayes, Kerr and George Yardley at Syracuse. Connie Simmons and Walter Dukes and Ray Felix and Charlie Tyra were not the antidote to the Chamberlain/Russell problem.

Mel Hutchins played just one season for the Knicks, 1957–58, and won greater recognition as the brother-in-law of Ernie Vandeweghe.

Wilt Chamberlain, soaring above the rim, facing page, in the College All-Stars game against the Knicks in October 1959. The Knicks hadn't his equal in centers like Ray Felix, reaching for loose ball, below.

Left to right: Tom Gola, Len Chappell, Willis Reed, Art Heyman and Bob Boozer with coach Eddie Donovan in back.

3

THE SIXTIES

For Richie Guerin, the grim reality of being on one losing Knicks team after another turned surreal on March 2, 1962, in Hershey, Pennsylvania. That was the night Wilt Chamberlain couldn't miss. Shot after shot of his fell through the hoop.

"And at a certain point," recalled Guerin, "the Warriors decided to get Wilt the ball as often as they could so he could go for the record. Most points in a single game. Well, to do that they began fouling us in the backcourt to kill the clock and give Wilt more time to operate. To me it was embarrassing to play the game that way—a mockery of the sport. I just didn't want any part of it, so I began intentionally fouling, looking to get my six personal fouls and leave the court. I'd had enough. But talk of adding insult to injury. The referee, Willie Smith, wouldn't call the fouls on me. He was telling me: 'Eh, come on, Richie, play the game.' I was steaming. 'You're calling fouls on them when they hit us in the backcourt,' I told him. 'Why don't you call 'em on me?' Well, Willie looked at me and said, 'Cause I know why you're doin' it.'"

That night Chamberlain scored 100 points against the Knicks, a single-game NBA scoring mark that still stands.

From 1959–60 to 1965–66, the Knicks finished last in the Eastern Division. Meanwhile New York's quest for the talent that might upgrade its chances repeatedly backfired. Top draft choices like Darrall Imhoff (1960), Tom Stith (1961), Paul Hogue (1962) and Art Heyman (1963) were unsuccessful in New York. This left fans like Asofsky, now a season-ticket holder sitting first-row baseline with his croney, big Fred Klein, waiting for the proverbial light at the end of the tunnel.

So dismal were the Knicks that TV declined to cover New York's games from 1960–62, and there was a radio blackout during the 1960–61 and 1963–64 seasons.

But by the mid-1960s events that would reverse the Knicks' fortunes and bring unaccustomed joy to longtime Garden sufferers began to unfold. Six-foot-nine Willis Reed came to the Knicks in the 1964 college draft and had an immediate impact, averaging 19.5 point per game while totalling 1,175 rebounds, which broke the team record of 1,098 held by his own coach, Harry Gallatin. At the end of the season he was named Rookie of the Year.

By the next year, though, circumstances would conspire against Reed's progress. It started when the Knicks, starved for so long for a big man, opted for the luxury of having a second industrial-strength center. That's what the Knicks believed they were getting when they traded with Baltimore for Walter Bellamy, 6' 10½", on November 2, 1965. In Bellamy, New York had a man who was a proven scorer in his four seasons at Chicago and Baltimore—31.8 points per game as a rookie and no worse than 24 ppg since.

But in basketball, as in art, sometimes more is less. It would take a while for New York to discover that.

Another trade brought Dick Barnett to the Knicks that same season. A veteran guard who had played at Syracuse and Los Angeles, Barnett would be another important link in a chain of talent that would make New York a contender.

The 1965–66 season would also bring a pair of draft choices that at first would appear to be sadly wasted. After two seasons, the second-round selection, Dave Stallworth, of Wichita State, was diagnosed as having a heart condition that would rule out basketball as a career. One moment he was an NBA pro, the next he was a recreation supervisor in Wichita, Kansas, looking back in regret. The other draft choice, first-rounder Bill Bradley, well, he had opted not to play pro ball. Bradley, a banker's son who had been a major star at Princeton, had chosen instead the life of a Rhodes scholar at Oxford University. Like Stallworth, he did not figure to be in the Knicks' future.

But things happened that would alter first Bradley's and then Stallworth's plans. For Bradley, the apocalyptic moment came in the spring of 1967 when he wandered into Oxford's gym and straight into a vision. "I was alone," he told newsmen, "me and a basketball. I was both teams, the crowd, the officials. My imagination did the rest.

I came to New York and contacted the Knicks and told them, 'I'm in New York, let's talk.'"

By December 1967, Bradley was playing backcourt for the Knicks. For Bradley, that would turn out to be harder than any mental equation he'd been asked to solve at Oxford. The backcourt for him was a sort of Bermuda triangle which threatened to pull him under. Against NBA guards, he appeared too slow afoot, and too limited with his dribble.

It would take Bradley and the Knicks a while to find their groove. And the man who would preside over the crucial changes that would turn the Knicks into contenders would be a team scout who was elevated to head coach around Christmas 1967: Red Holzman.

Before Holzman took over, Knicks players were running the offense on the principle of boardinghouse reach, and teamwork be damned. As for defense, except for Walt Frazier, a rookie, they treated it with the aristocrat's contempt for sweat. Bellamy, who was now the center, bumping Reed to forward, was notorious for refusing to pick up an opponent who had slipped the Knicks defense. Bellamy simply watched the foe go by with the kind of respectful attention that English butlers affect.

In Holzman's defense-conscious operation, Bellamy's refusal to backstop his teammates was unacceptable. The solution came in one bold move: on December 19, 1968, the Knicks traded Bellamy and guard Howard Komives to Detroit for Dave DeBusschere.

The trade would be just the catalyst jolt the struggling Knicks needed. For the deal freed Reed to return from forward to his natural position, the pivot. And when Knicks forward Cazzie Russell broke his ankle in the middle of the 1968–69 season, Holzman shifted Bradley from guard to forward. The change allowed "Dollar Bill," as his teammates called him, to move unencumbered by the ball to spots on the floor where he could rapid-fire an accurate one-hander against larger but less nimble opponents. Not having to handle the ball against those slick, quick NBA guards, Bradley suddenly found that his entire game improved.

So did the Knicks once the 6' 6" DeBusschere, himself a force at both ends of the court, arrived. DeBusschere offered New York added muscle under the boards and was capable of shutting down the league's best large-sized forwards—the Gus Johnsons and Connie Hawkins of this world. Where both of those men played with crowdpleasing flourishes, DeBusschere's was a lunch-bucket style. Nothing fancy. Just results.

Before the trade, New York had had a record of 18 wins and 17 losses. With DeBusschere in the lineup, the Knicks won 36 of 47 games, the most successful record in the NBA over that period. Nor did they stop once the regular season had ended. In the opening round of the playoffs, New York swept four straight from Eastern Division top finisher Baltimore, igniting a basketball fever that hadn't existed in the city since the grand old days of the college game.

The 1969–70 season would be even better. From the 18-game winning streak early in the year to the most dramatic playoff finale as yet seen, the Knicks were a wonderful notion that year. They gave New Yorkers a brand of basketball—a game of finesse and smarts—that made the Garden a joyous place to be.

That season there was a particular crowd reaction not heard since—a swell of anticipated pleasure as the ball swung *zap zap* around the periphery, three, four, five passes so smartly executed, so selflessly conceived, that it was accorded a rippling murmur that built with each pass and ended in an explosive roar as the shot scored.

But the big noise was reserved for what the team did at the other end of the floor. The Knicks' aggregate hustle when they didn't have the ball would generate a new chant in the Garden: *"DEE-fense. DEE-fense."*

At the heart of that defense was Frazier, known as "Clyde" for the 1930s fashions he wore, similar to those Warren Beatty had donned in the film *Bonnie and Clyde.* But being Clyde meant more in those days. It was shorthand for glamour of a certain kind, an offhand indulgence for fancy cars, stylish clothes and alluring women.

He was Clyde on-court too: a sleek prowling basketball stud. On defense, he would sometimes feint at the ball before striking for keeps. He did that once to Boston's Jo Jo White, a rookie then—gave him a pronounced fake that sent Jo Jo stumbling backward in panic, as if a gust of wind had gotten into his shoes.

Through constant pressure, through double-teams, through Clyde's cat-quick strikes at the ball, the Knicks had other teams coming unglued all season. And when they took that defense—and their unselfish offense—into the playoffs, after compiling the best regular-season record, 60 wins and 22 losses, the city of New York fully expected them to win their first NBA title.

It was not quite so simple. What complicated things was the misfortune suffered by Reed in the fifth game of the championship series against the Los Angeles Lakers. With Los Angeles leading 25-15 at the Garden and the series tied at two games apiece, Reed fell as he drove against Chamberlain with 3:56 remaining of the first quarter. Marv Albert recalled: "To a man every Knick thought the season was over." But it wasn't. Holzman improvised, assigning DeBusschere to guard Chamberlain. The other Knicks helped on Chamberlain, and that defense pressure shut big Wilt down. Meanwhile, Knicks shots began to fall. At 5:19 left in the fourth quarter, Bradley hit a jumper from the left of the key that gave the Knicks the lead, 93–91. But the killing blow was the reverse layup that the medically cleared Stallworth scored on Chamberlain to up New York's lead to 103–96 with 1:32 left in the game. A smiling Stallworth, whom doctors had decided had not suffered a heart attack and had returned to the NBA at the start of the season, shook his fist against the night—and against the long road back to this place. For him...and for the Knicks. The final was 107–100, New York.

That there could be any more drama than this night seemed unlikely. Yet there was. Reed provided it in the crucial seventh game of the series at the Garden. As the teams warmed up, Reed, lips pursed and eyes fixed straight ahead, moved past the cordon of security with a deliberate step, like the baaadest marshall in Dodge City ready to take on those varmints from Los Angeles. Hoo-boy: the crowd went bonkers, and their relief at the sight of him was instantly audible in ear-splitting cheers.

That half-crazed Garden crowd did not have to wait long for The Cap'n, as Reed was known, to make his influence felt. Reed hit the first basket of the game from the top of the key and another jumper from 20 feet on the right side of the floor. The roars that followed were deafening.

For the rest, it was Frazier at his best. He was all over the floor, stealing the basketball, driving it to the basket, shooting it over Laker defenders, doing it all with the elegance of his Clyde alter ego. Sleek Walt: running the ball down the Lakers' throats. Tote it up afterward and it came to 36 points, 19 assists, 12 of 12 from the line, 12 of 17 from the floor. A game from hoops heaven.

And then, as the final seconds ticked down and Asofsky and the rest of the Garden gathering were on their feet, Marv Albert would call it like this: "DeBusschere holds the ball. Two seconds. DeBusschere holds the ball. That is it! The New York Knickerbockers have won the 1969–70 World Championship of Basketball!"

Carl Braun makes a noble effort to outshout officials Borgia and Toff, his efforts rewarded with a first-period ejection from a game against the Cincinnati Royals, who would go on to win this one, 124–118.

Below, Jim (Bad News) Barnes, #22, was the Knicks' first draft choice in 1964, ahead of Willis Reed, drafted in the second round. Barnes lasted one season in New York and then was traded. Reed became a Knicks legend.

The Knicks' return to respectability occurred through a chain of events by which the players who would mesh, eventually, as a team came together.

Emphasis on "eventually."

For in their quest to be a contender again, the Knicks would go through personnel the way a flu patient goes through Kleenex. Starting with the 1955–56 season, Lapchick was replaced by Vince Boryla, Knicks coaches were a disposable commodity. Lapchick, Boryla, Levane, Braun, Eddie Donovan, Harry Gallatin and Dick McGuire were the seven coaches who presided over a decade of mostly last-place finishes.

By the sixties, players came and players went too. Richie Guerin, for instance, found the agony of defeat too much to bear. By the 1963–64 season he was lobbying strenuously with Donovan for a change of climate.

"I figured I had three, four good years left and I wanted to be with a team that had a chance to win," Guerin said.

Two games into that 1963–64 season, Guerin got

The first major step toward upgrading the team came in 1964 when the Knicks made Willis Reed, with the ball below, their second-round draft choice, much to the pleasure of coach Eddie Donovan.

Donovan, like other Knicks coaches of that time, suffered through years of disappointing seasons that talented players like Willie Naulls, #6 above, or Tom Hoover, below, could not overcome.

his wish. He was traded to St. Louis, where over the next four seasons he would be in the thick of championship races.

"We never won the NBA title, but at least we were competitive," he said. "It brought back the joy of playing."

That joy was in short supply at the Garden. Knicks like Tom Gola, Len Chappell, Johnny Green, Johnny Egan, Tom Hoover, Bob Boozer, Gene Conley and Gene Shue simply were no match for their opposition.

The first step in reversing that cycle of gloom was Willis Reed, a second-round draft choice in 1964.

Life for Reed had been a succession of challenges he invariably met head-on. Even as a boy, Willis had struggled to help his family survive—and to satisfy his own basic needs. In recalling his childhood, he would say, "I picked cotton when I was nine in order to get me a pair of shoes."

That was in Bernice, Louisiana, a town ten miles from Hico, where Willis was born. "Moving to Bernice," Reed recalled, "was like moving to the big city. Bernice was two red lights long. Hico had no red lights, just a couple of stop signs."

As a ninth-grader in Bernice, Reed worked in a wheat storehouse, doing grownup labor. "I was a big kid then," he recalled. "Heck, I was in the ninth grade and I was six-five. But the money I made was hard money. I ended up with corns, calluses and blisters on my feet and hands. I looked at the men around me who had large families and I said to myself: 'I don't have enough money to do what I want to do. How can these people with ten kids take care of themselves and their families?'"

With a no-nonsense attitude, Reed used basketball to escape the hard life into which he was born. At Grambling, and later with the Knicks, Reed combined a shooting touch unusual for a man his size with a physicality around the backboard that gave New York legitimacy in the pivot for the first time. And though the trade that brought Walter Bellamy to New York bumped Reed, disadvantageously, to forward, he carried on, making the best of the change. That was how a professional went about his business, and Reed was ever that, giving his best effort wherever the team wanted him to operate.

Dick Barnett arrived in New York in 1965, the season in which Reed shifted to forward. Barnett

The ineptitude of Knicks defense allowed Wilt Chamberlain, above, to score 100 points in 1962, a record that still stands.

Below, in the mid-sixties, while Reed was establishing himself as a presence in the NBA, Dave DeBusschere, defending against Knicks guard Johnny Egan, was a player-coach at Detroit. But a trade during the 1968–69 season would bring both these men together for New York, and herald a new era in Knicks success.

Tom Gola, #6.

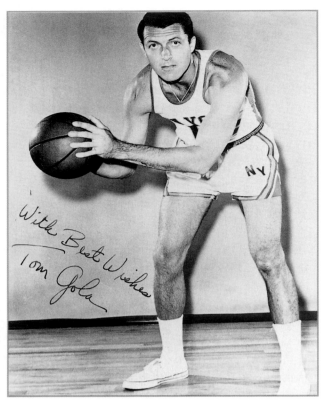

With Best Wishes
Tom Gola

was a man whose hooded lids and sleepwalker's gait belied the quick-enough moves and unorthodox shots he had. He had learned those moves practicing, usually by himself, in the back alleys of Gary, Indiana. As a boy he would shoot at a garbage lid with a Ping-Pong ball before graduating to a volley-ball and three chairs configured as a basket. It wasn't until he was 12 years old that he had the chance to play with a real basketball.

Barnett was deceptive. The sound-ness of his all-around game was obscured by the labored stroke of his jump shot and the herky-jerky way he moved on defense. But at both ends of the court, Barnett would prove to be a reliable talent. And never mind that he wasn't exactly textbook-smooth in get-ting the job done.

It took Bill Bradley a while to decide whether he wanted to keep his mind on textbooks or be part of the pro game. For as a Rhodes scholar, his objectives ran beyond the X's and O's of basketball to so-called serious matters. Bradley thought that through political office he could help create a better society, and was preparing for that with the curricu-lum he was taking at Oxford University.

Len Chappell, #24.

But on the way to that very adult life he was blind-sided by his love of a boy's game.

That passion for basketball landed him in a Knicks uniform in December 1967, but not before he did a bit of soul-searching. For as Bradley would put it: "The one thing I don't want to be is typed. I don't want to end up as just old satin-shorts Bradley."

Yet as a Princeton friend of his would tell a newsman: "The deepest thing he feels is playing basketball. Maybe he wanted to change, become a mainstream Princeton man, but he still has that small-town streak. He's like the guy from the small town who comes to Princeton and goes to the deb parties and says, 'Ah, this is me.' Then the little girl back home writes and he goes running back to her. Well, that's the way Bradley is with basketball."

The way he was with the Knicks was disappointing at first. Signed to a four-year contract worth $500,000—big money for that time—he struggled as a ball-handling guard. It was a major letdown for Knicks fans, who had anticipated him dominating NBA opposition the way he had conquered college foes while at Princeton. So keen were they for Bradley that when he made his pro debut on December 9, 1967, at the Garden, the 18,499 patrons even cheered his warm-up shots, and did so with such enthusiasm that the visiting Detroit Pistons turned to watch.

As the weekly *National Observer* would report: "In his first pro game, Bradley has made mistakes. He palmed the ball several times..., threw passes away, and missed three foul shots. As a Princeton freshman, he hit 57 free throws in a row.

★ *The Knicks reunion game in 1961 brought out, in front (left to right), Max Zaslofsky, Ray Lumpp, Stan Stutz, Ossie Schectman, Frido Frey, Frank Mangiapane; second row, Jerry Fleishman, Sonny Hertzberg, Dick Bunt, Dick Holub, Nat Militzok,; third row, Bob Mullens, Hank Rosenstein, Leo Gottlieb; back row, Bill van Breda Kolff, Connie Simmons and George Kaftan.*

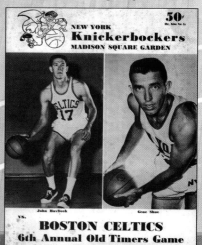

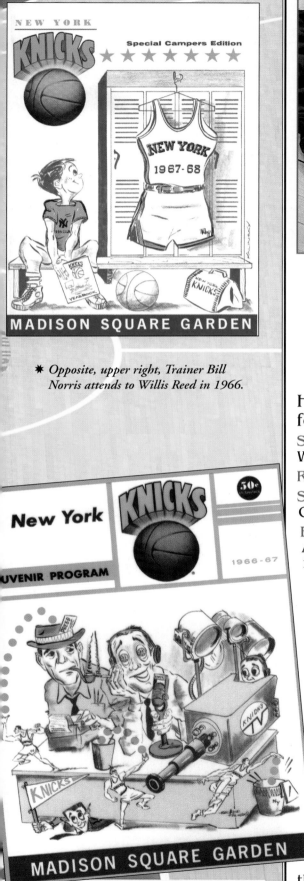

NEW YORK
KNICKS
Special Campers Edition
★ ★ ★ ★ ★ ★ ★ ★

NEW YORK
1967-68

MADISON SQUARE GARDEN

* *Opposite, upper right, Trainer Bill Norris attends to Willis Reed in 1966.*

New York
KNICKS
50¢
1966-67
SOUVENIR PROGRAM

KNICKS TV

KNICKS

MADISON SQUARE GARDEN

Ray Lumpp's practice jersey

LIFE AFTER BASKETBALL

Here's what happened to Knicks from the forties and fifties after their NBA careers:

Sonny Hertzberg became an executive with the Wall Street firm of Bear Stearns.

Ralph Kaplowitz went into the insurance business.

Stan Stutz became an NBA referee. He died on October 28, 1975.

Bud Palmer became a TV announcer, working for ABC-TV. Also worked as a good will ambassador for New York City mayor John Lindsay.

Ernie Vandeweghe became a pediatrician in southern California.

Sweetwater Clifton drove a taxi cab in Chicago. He died on August 31, 1990.

Bill Van Breda Kolff coached high school, college and pro basketball teams. While coaching at Princeton, one of his players was Bill Bradley.

Dick McGuire is presently Director of Scouting Services for the Knicks.

Al McGuire coached 1977 NCAA champion Marquette and later became a basketball commentator.

Carl Braun worked on Wall Street and is presently retired and living in Florida.

Harry Gallatin worked in the athletic department of Southern Illinois University.

Ray Felix worked for the Parks Department of the city of New York. He died on July 28, 1991.

Ray Lumpp is the athletic director at the New York Athletic Club.

Above, on a night the Garden PA system failed John F.X. Condon (also pictured below) used a bullhorn to keep the fans informed.

Photographers Bill Jacobellis and Larry Morris are kneeling; at the table (left to right) are timer Feets Broudy, Condon, Tommy Kenville, Jim Bukata, Jimmy Trecker, Cal Ramsey, Knicks PR director Frank Blauschild and sportswriter Leonard Koppett (standing).

"In Detroit's locker room afterward, the Pistons' Eddie Miles, who played both ways against Bradley, would say, 'His defense? I didn't see any basic weaknesses. He didn't turn his head when the ball was passed over him, which a lot of rookies do. Offensively, he looked for the open man and showed poise. Yeah, he had trouble with that dribble. He dribbles high, he's gonna lose the ball if he dribbles that high. Sure, the 18,000 might have had something to do with it. My strategy was to play him tight, get that 18,000 working for me.' Smiling now: 'Boy, what pressure. Ooo-eee. The unveiling of William B.'"

For Knicks fans, Bradley's unveiling came at a time when the team was floundering. The Knicks had won their opener, then lost six straight, then dropped eight of their first ten games after Bradley joined the team. In response, Dick McGuire was fired as coach and replaced by Red Holzman, who had been the team's chief scout.

It was not Holzman's first time as coach. That had occurred in the midst of the 1953–54 season, when he had succeeded his friend Fuzzy Levane as head man of the Milwaukee Hawks. The Hawks were not much of a team, and not even Holzman could figure how to make do with players lacking the talent and the focus he would eventually know in New York.

Marty Blake, general manager of the Hawks in those

days, recalled a halftime incident in the Milwaukee dressing room that typified what Holzman had to deal with:

"We had Frank Selvy then," Blake said. "And Frank was, like, a country boy. We're losing this game, but down there in the locker room Frank is slouched against the wall half asleep. 'Frank, Frank, wake up,' Red says. 'Frank, where are we losing this game?' Meaning, in what aspect of our game. Well, Selvy opens his eyes and says, 'Red, we're losing this game right here in Milwaukee.'"

During McGuire's reign, he urged his players to use the offense he'd installed, but they ignored the diagrammed plays for shots of their own. Shoot first and then ask questions. The defense had even less conviction.

All who knew McGuire regarded him as a very decent man, but that trait turned out to be a liability with his players, as the Knicks who

Richie Guerin is seen here posing with Garden executives, left to right, Muzz Patrick, Irving Mitchell Felt, Sam Slate of WCBS, Guerin, and Ralph Goshen of WCBS. Guerin was a stand-out Knick who eventually asked to be traded after years of playing on losing New York teams. Some of the slack caused by his departure was taken up by players like Dick Van Arsdale, below center, and Dave Stallworth, below right, shown with coach Harry Gallatin.

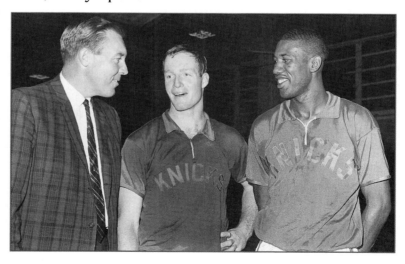

Willis Reed

played then recalled in the book *Miracle on 33rd Street*.

Phil Jackson: "Ballplayers would go out there and play one-on-one and Dickie would say, 'Come on, let's run some patterns.' And they'd go out and do the same thing, knowing, 'What else can he do, pull me in? What's gonna happen? They're gonna boo him and back I'll go.' So in effect you're paying ballplayers sixty, seventy, eighty thousand dollars, you're paying the coach twenty-five thousand. He was more expendable than the players were, which isn't right. Not that they're being overpaid, but the ballplayers can't be more valuable to the team than the coach. A coach has got to be the one that makes the ballplayer expendable or makes the ballplayers toe the line, and that was just what wasn't happening."

Walt Frazier: "If you made a mistake, McGuire

56

Walt Bellamy, #8, played pivot on the last Knicks team to play at the old Madison Square Garden on Eighth Avenue between Forty-ninth and Fiftieth Streets.

wouldn't tell you, but (would) take it out on himself. (McGuire confesses he had stomach trouble and was unable to sleep during the time he coached.) McGuire wouldn't like to hurt anybody's feelings."

Jackson: "(When McGuire was fired), there was an attitude of the ballplayers that we really hadn't done Dick McGuire justice, we really had much more talent than we'd shown. We were ashamed of ourselves the day they fired Dick. He said as a final speech, 'I just want to thank you guys for all you've done for us.' You know, that was enough to make us sit there and wanna cry or laugh or whatever, it was so black humory. You know, we hadn't listened to him, we hadn't done anything. So I think there was a basic attitude, 'Say what the hell, let's try to get together a little bit.'"

Holzman restored discipline on and off the court. He imposed fines on players who were late for team functions, and held them accountable for performance. When Bellamy continued playing as though the game were coming to him on delayed tape, Holzman cracked down. On road trips, Bellamy had been allowed a single room while other players took doubles, a privilege that Holzman revoked. "You don't get

Bellamy, #8, above, and Dick Van Arsdale, #5 below, endured the hard times of the sixties while Dick Barnett, #12, opposite page, would be an integral part of the Knick renaissance at the tail end of the decade.

Above, training-camp break during Dick McGuire's tenure as Knicks coach. From left to right, that's Neil Johnson, McGuire and Stallworth in chairs and Walt Frazier seated on ground. Cazzie Russell, #14 below, would break his ankle during the 1968–69 season, forcing Bill Bradley, opposite page, to be shifted from guard to the small-forward spot Russell had occupied.

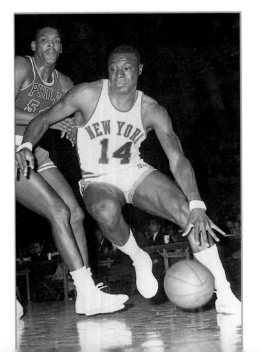

anything special," Holzman told Bellamy, "because you're not doing anything special."

"Holzman told the players he'd sacrifice ball games by not playing guys and they found out he meant it," said Knicks publicist Frankie Blauschild. "It didn't matter who it was. Red didn't play favorites. Take Willis Reed. He's probably the most popular player on the team. But Willis had a tendency to get back on defense slowly. When that happened, Red bawled the hell out of him. Guys tried to do what they did in the past and found out it didn't go anymore."

But all that did not heal this ailing team. For one thing, guard Howard Komives and starting forward Cazzie Russell had a personal feud going that affected the other players. For another, Bellamy's continuing laissez faire attitude stymied Holzman's concept of team defense.

"I don't think anybody ever had any antagonisms against Walt Bellamy," said Phil Jackson. "Walt was the most honest guy on the club. He wasn't fooling anybody. He got paid his seventy, eighty, ninety thousand dollars—whatever he was getting paid—came, played basketball, went home and that was it.

The attitude of Bellamy and the enmity between Komives and Russell were serious problems for Holzman. In one bold move, Knicks general manager, Eddie Donovan, who had been building this team piece by piece, solved his team's problems. He executed the trade that brought DeBusschere to New York and sent Komives and Bellamy to Detroit early into the 1968–69 season. DeBusschere, 6'6", was a no-frills sort of player, who complimented Reed and operated with the same earnest, workmanlike air. Together, they would give the Knicks the physical presence beneath the basket that New York teams had lacked in the past.

But the arrival of DeBusschere helped in ways that the Knicks front office had not expected. With DeBusschere able to work the strong-forward position, Reed was now free to return to his more natural turf in the pivot. That was not all DeBusschere did for New York. He worked the facets of the game that do not necessarily show

up in a box score. He defended. He made the smart pass. He set picks. He dove for loose balls. He scored crucial baskets. He walked, talked and played the team game.

This was not exactly a shock. For DeBusschere's maturity on the court, his grasp of the team concept, was so apparent that in the midst of the 1964–65 season, when Piston coach Charley Wolf was fired, DeBusschere was named to replace him as player-coach. He was 24 years old at the time and in only his third season as a player.

Team chemistry is an elusive reality. At Detroit, DeBusschere was widely recognized as a superior player. But recast in the Holzman system, and surrounded by new teammates, DeBusschere seemed to galvanize a change in the outlook and attitude of the Knicks team. The sum of the parts turned better with DeBusschere in the lineup. Suddenly, the once-selfish team became savvy with the ball and tenacious on defense.

Just as suddenly, guys like Frazier and Bradley turned extra potent. Frazier's ability to hawk the ball

Bradley, facing page, was a banker's son from Crystal City, Missouri. That was a long way from the famous arcade outside the old Garden, where Knicks fans would have a hot dog and orange drink at the famed Nedick's stand. But the distance between Crystal City and Eighth Avenue was bridged by the Garden faithful, who welcomed Bradley wholeheartedly during warm-ups on his debut night in December 1967 (far left).

Bill Bradley came to the Knicks during the tenure of Dick McGuire. McGuire, whose selfless play was so exemplary during the fifties, tried to instill that spirit in the Knicks teams he coached, like the 1966–67 club, facing page top. But his teams were outclassed during his regime by clubs like the Baltimore Bullets, whose star, Earl Monroe, facing page bottom, drives on Howard Komives.

on defense became more pronounced with Holzman's emphasis on defense. With his knack for stealing the basketball, Clyde became a kind of unofficial ringleader of the defense. A steal or two by Frazier would set off a defensive feeding frenzy by his teammates, who would go into overdrive, doubling and sometimes tripling the basketball and forcing myriad turnovers by the opposition.

In Holzman's set-up, Frazier's role expanded on the offense too. In 1968–69, his second season with the Knicks, Frazier began to take charge of the offense in a way he had not as a rookie under McGuire. The difference between the Walter Frazier Jr. of 1967–68 and the next season was startling. Frazier increased his scoring average from 9 ppg to 17.5 and his total assists from 305 to 635.

In the process, he went from a man who seemed to play on hold to one who played with a pleasure that was palpable.

The reaction of the crowd to these transformed Knicks was no surprise. For years the Garden crowd, teeming with aficionados who had learned the game in the schoolyards back when Chuck Taylor hightops were state-of-the-art basketball footwear, had been waiting for a team like this. A team whose players saw the court and applied a purist's selfless art, making that extra pass to free up a man for an open shot and strategically inciting mistakes when the other team had the ball.

It was the sort of fundamental approach to the game that brought roars of appreciation from fans who had endured all those years of Knicks inadequacy, fans like Asofsky. Once DeBusschere landed in New York, the Knicks found a chemistry that seemed almost mystical, with a lineup of Frazier, Barnett, DeBusschere, Reed and Cazzie Russell. Then Russell broke his ankle and the Knicks made their stretch run with Bradley shifting from guard to forward.

And just like that, Bradley was a new man. Freed from ball-handling responsibilities, he would run from corner to corner of the floor, moving smartly to get his open shot. That new-look Bradley would prove better able to exploit his particular skills—a quick-release out-

The 1966–67 team. Left to right, front row: Dave Deutsch, Emmette Bryant, Dick McGuire, Howard Komives, Dick Barnett; standing: Bill Norris, Cazzie Russell, Neil Johnson, Walt Bellamy, Henry Akin, Willis Reed, Wayne Molis, Dave Stallworth, Dick Van Arsdale and Red Holzman.

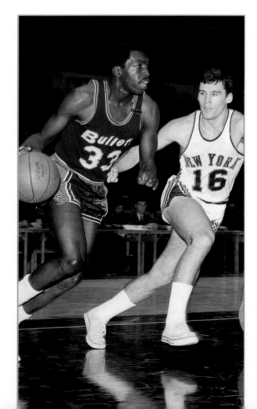

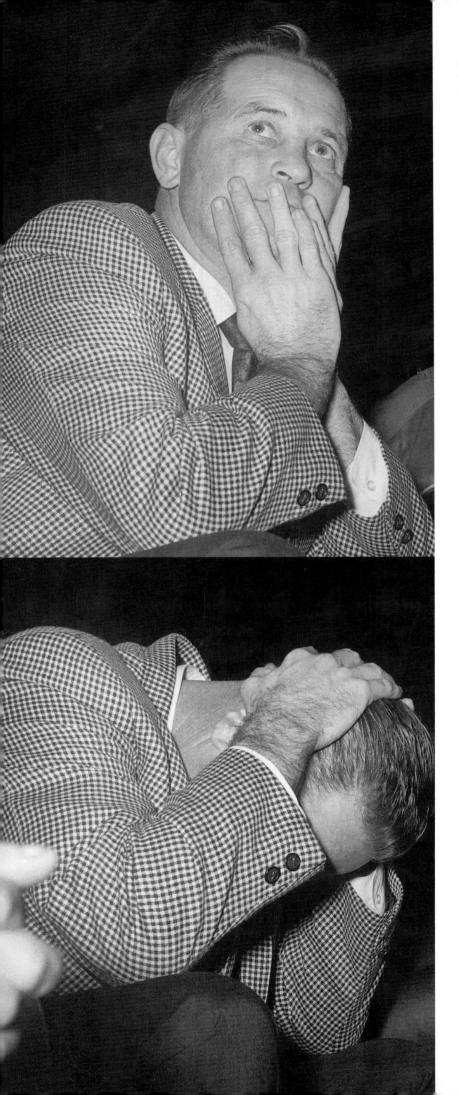

side shot and a passer's wide-screen view of the court. The continuity of the offense soared with Bradley at small forward. He became so integral to the success of the Knicks that when a healthy Russell returned for 1969–70, he found Bradley had usurped him as a starter.

Bradley and the rest of the Knicks found defense to be the key to the team's success. No surprise there. Defense was what Holzman preached nonstop. In practices, and during games, he was constantly shouting, "See the ball!"—a battle cry for defensive prepared-ness, for always being on the alert to the dam-age an offense could do. For the Knicks, defense started and ended with that prescrip-tive Holzman cry—*See the ball*. If a player had his eye on the ball, he could anticipate what-ever wrinkle the opposition might try.

But there was more to Holzman's defense than that, as explained in *Miracle on 33rd Street*:

"The targets of the Knick defense, the so-called pigeons, were those ball handlers who strayed into the strategically unsound pieces of the floor or, on safer expanses, got inoppor-tunely within pawswipe of a New Yorker. It was not by chance such bumbling occurred. There was to Knickerbocker defense a sinister logic that had for its foremost goal the creation of a moment come apart, an instant of court dislo-cation in which the unwitting dribbler found himself in the maw of a double-team maneu-ver, two Knicks thrusting and groping at him like slapstick buffoons, the purpose of their gymnastics to pry the ball from him or hasten a misguided pass. The way New York accom-plished this was by channeling the dribbler to locations on the wood where he was most vul-nerable to assaults on the ball. As the bullfight had a mathematics of terrain, so did basket-ball, and if a matador sought the more per-ilous stations of the grounds to enhance his show, a ball handler proceeded to these places for no such ennobling purposes, likely he was carried there by the drift of the game or the guile of Frazier and Barnett.

"The riskiest spots on the floor were along the sideline. The deeper into a corner the worse the peril. On the middle of the floor a ball handler whose dribble was terminated had outlets denied him on the sidelines. The Knicks deployed in such a way to ensure that a pass thrown in a territorial bind would end up a casualty. Two men applied pressure to the ball; the others edged toward the outlet men.

"If such a procedure left a man ostensibly uncovered, the vacated man was farthest from the ball. To make a pass to him under the presure of a double team was a feat akin to throwing accurately from the bottom of a well.

"Even if the short pass were completed, the opposition remained in trouble. The bustle engendered in keeping ball possession destroyed what theoreticians called *court balance*, a reference to spacious intervals between men. The result of doubling was to compress the action and force men less accustomed to handling the ball to work under pressure: it became an exercise in movable pigeons.

"The instigator of New York's doubling was usually Frazier. To give him more range for troublemaking, he was matched against teams' weaker guards."

Facing page, the likable McGuire became frustrated as the Knick teams lost despite the best efforts of men like Emmette Bryant, dribbling the ball, above.

Dave DeBusschere, #22, hits his first shot in his first home game as a Knick.

At right. Feets Broudy, Garden timekeeper.

In 1968–69, as the Knicks flexed their newly discovered muscle on defense *and* offense, Bradley's switch to forward would be the final piece in the chain of events that had begun back in 1964 when the Knicks had drafted Reed.

The drafting of Reed, the trade that brought Barnett, the hiring of Holzman, the trade that put DeBusschere in a Knicks jersey, the blossoming of Frazier as a result of the defensive orientation of Holzman and Bradley's change of position—here was a series of disparate moments that became linked, almost magically, in the making of a team. A team that would dramatically turn into a contender by winning thirty-six of its last forty-seven games in 1968–69 and give fair warning of what New Yorkers might expect in the future with a four-game sweep of the Bullets in the playoffs.

Never mind that New York lost in the next playoff round to the Boston Celtics. In the minds of rabid New York fans, the Knicks' elimination from the playoffs was because of bad breaks. For example, Frazier had played with a groin injury that limited him. Things figured to be better the next year with a healthy Frazier back, with Cazzie Russell coming off the bench as an instant offense sixth man, with the return of a medically cleared Stallworth and with the capable Mike Riordan in reserve.

New York at last had a team it could get crazy about.

Willis Reed

Above, the final score of the final game at the old Garden, on February 10, 1968, shown on the scoreboard fronting the lower mezzanine.

That night, members of the 1946-47 Knicks were on hand to mark the occasion. Below, left to right: Dick Murphy, Tommy Byrnes, Ossie Schectman, Ralph Kaplowitz, Nat Militzok, Stan Stutz, Hank Rosenstein, Leo Gottlieb, Sonny Hertzberg, Bud Palmer, Frido Frey, Butch van Breda Kolff and Lee Knorek.

And so it came to pass. The site of great college and NBA basketball memories was shuttered, as the new Garden on Seventh Avenue between Thirty-first and Thirty-third Streets opened on February 11, 1968. That evening, Bob Hope and Bing Crosby hosted the "Night of the Century," a salute to the USO. Three days later, February 14, 1968, the Knicks played their first game in the new building, a 114–102 victory over the San Diego Rockets.

But while the old Garden was gone, it was not forgotten. In writing about that last night at the hallowed Eighth Avenue building, Leonard Lewin would capture the look on Ned Irish's face as he walked off the floor. It was a moment caught in the photo at the right, a shot taken minutes after the final buzzer of the final NBA game to be played in the old Garden. Here is Lewin describing Irish as the Garden executive walked off the floor on his way out of the building:

"They were going to turn his building into a parking lot. He had his hat in his hand, his coat over one arm and he's biting his lips in a vain attempt to hide his emotions over the loss of a big piece of his life."

But by the end of the 1968–69 season, a Knicks ticket became a hot commodity and celebrities who didn't know a fish hook from a jump hook started showing up at courtside, Irish could feel a sense of redemption down there on West Thirty-third Street.

New York at last had the feel of a special

Ned Irish walks off the court for the last time.

Below, workmen disassemble a basket, marking the end of an era. Facing page: (inset) Boston's Bill Russell (with ball) versus Detroit in the first basketball game at the new Garden on Seventh Avenue and Thirty-third Street, February 14, 1968; (large) Walt Bellamy in the first Knicks tipoff, the second game of the double-header.

team—a team that moved the ball smartly until the open man was found for a shot. Their hustle when they didn't have the ball would generate a new chant in the Garden: *"DEE-fense. DEE-fense,"* and create a defensive hero in Frazier, about whom it was written: "Frazier had come to his defense the way the neighborhood shut-in arrives at his piano or palette, for lack of alternatives." At Southern Illinois, where Frazier played his college ball, he was declared academically ineligible in his sophomore year. Frazier's coach, Jack Hartman, allowed him to scrimmage during that season but only as a defensive scrub. Obliged to go up against the starting five, Frazier's focus, and pleasure, was in stymieing those first-stringers with his defense while rallying the other reserves to rise up collectively and do the same.

Whatever. After the abrupt turn-around in 1968–69, excitement built for

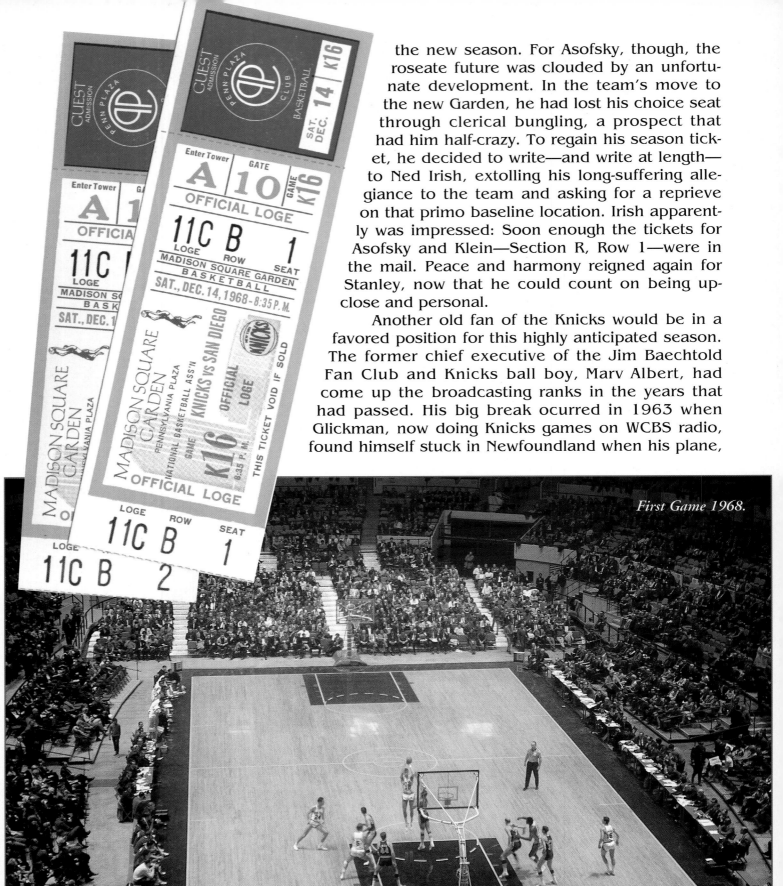

the new season. For Asofsky, though, the roseate future was clouded by an unfortunate development. In the team's move to the new Garden, he had lost his choice seat through clerical bungling, a prospect that had him half-crazy. To regain his season ticket, he decided to write—and write at length—to Ned Irish, extolling his long-suffering allegiance to the team and asking for a reprieve on that primo baseline location. Irish apparently was impressed: Soon enough the tickets for Asofsky and Klein—Section R, Row 1—were in the mail. Peace and harmony reigned again for Stanley, now that he could count on being up-close and personal.

Another old fan of the Knicks would be in a favored position for this highly anticipated season. The former chief executive of the Jim Baechtold Fan Club and Knicks ball boy, Marv Albert, had come up the broadcasting ranks in the years that had passed. His big break ocurred in 1963 when Glickman, now doing Knicks games on WCBS radio, found himself stuck in Newfoundland when his plane,

First Game 1968.

en route from Paris, had to make an unexpected landing there due to bad weather.

"I called ahead," recalled Glickman, "to say I wouldn't be able to get to the Boston Garden on time to do the Knicks–Celtics game the next day. I suggested Marv, who had worked with me on a weekend football review that I did on CBS radio—Marv gave the high-school results—and as an assistant producer on a high-school game of the week that I announced on WPIX channel 11 in New York."

Albert, 20 years old at the time, would later refer to this moment as "a wondrous, unbelievable, serendipitous thing." With his 14-year-old brother, Al, he rode an all-night train to Boston.

"Unfortunately," he recalled, "when we arrived at

The transition from the old Garden to the new Garden coincided with the rise of the rejuvenated Knicks, symbolized by players like Walt Frazier, above, looking back over his shoulder to watch the ball drop in on a driving lay-up, to score the first Knicks basket at the new arena. Knicks, 114; San Diego Rockets, 102.

the (Boston) Garden, the guard wouldn't let us in. I don't suppose either of us looked like Red Barber. *Right. You're calling the Knicks game. And I'm Jacqueline Kennedy.* The guy would not budge. We pleaded with him. Zippo. I even opened up my briefcase and showed him all my commercials and note sheets. He said anybody could have that. Yes, I'll bet half the fans in Boston were running around with WCBS commercials in their briefcases. There were only forty-five minutes until game time when we finally convinced him to call over Knicks general manager Eddie Donovan to vouch for us."

By 1967, when Glickman declined to do Knicks broadcasts on radio station WHN, he recommended Albert for the job.

As Glickman recalled: "They said, 'Who?' I said, 'Marv Albert. He's terrif-

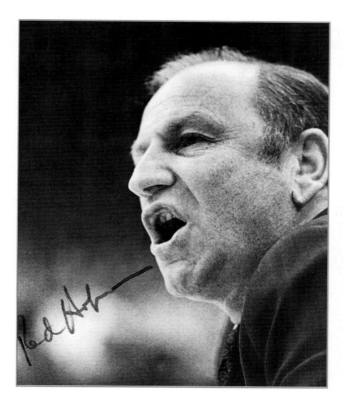

ic. He'll be great. Use him.' They set a date for Marv to go up to WHN. Afterward the guy from WHN calls and says, 'Sorry, Marty. He won't do. He's just a kid. Can you think of somebody else?' I said, 'No. He's the best.' Until finally they acquiesced."

Albert's opportunity to do the Knicks games in 1969–70 would prove to be a wondrous exposure for him. For, as he recalled: "In those days, maybe 30 games a year were on TV, and since nearly every game was a sellout, the only way someone could follow the team was on the radio. And so I became linked forever with that team too."

There were plenty other New Yorkers who wanted to be linked with the new-look Knicks in the months leading up to the 1969–70 season. Season ticket sales had doubled—8,000 seats sold for the 19,500-capacity arena. And the corporate world also wanted in, as Knicks began to sign on to do endorsements—Reed for Equitable insurance, Frazier for Supp-Hose socks, Russell for Ideal board games. Meanwhile, Frazier and DeBusschere contracted for books about the upcoming season.

All over New York, Knicks fans old and very new were eager for the new season to begin.

Facing page, top, Cazzie Russell, #33, being carried off the floor after breaking his ankle in 1968.

Facing page, bottom, Willis Reed, #19, diving for a loose ball.

The Knicks began to come together as a team under Red Holzman, left, shouting advice.

Frazier, #10, racing the ball upcourt.

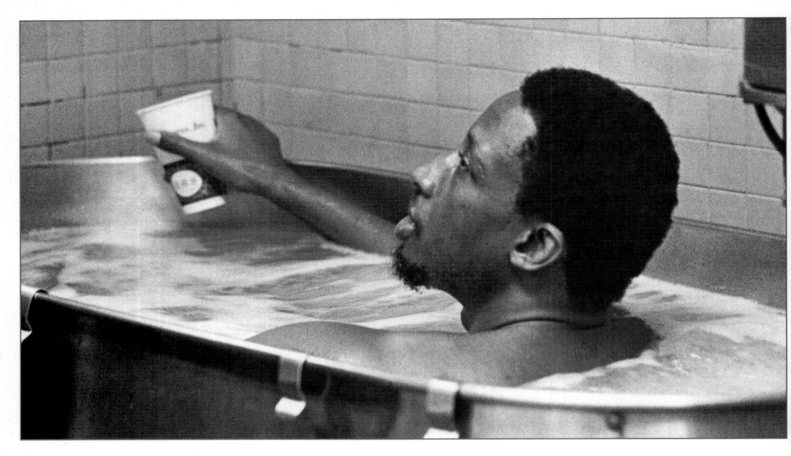

The city had grand expectations for these 1969-70 Knicks. As the Knicks dominated the league during the regular season with a league-best 60–22 record—that included their amazing last-minute come-from-behind victory against Cincinnati that gave them a record eighteen straight victories—so were Holzman's men counted on to blitz the opposition in the playoffs.

The sports public in New York figured this was it—the hour of conquest. Nothing short of an NBA title would satisfy those Knicks supporters who had waited more than two decades for the team's first championship.

In fact, no franchise had waited longer to win an NBA title than New York. Only two other teams, Boston and San Francisco (the Philadelphia Warriors until they moved after the 1962 season), had survived the original league that began in 1946–47. Each was a previous NBA champion.

Where once the Knicks had been shoehorned into the MSG schedule, now they were *the* event, their games bumping the circus to alternate dates. Indeed, on playoff nights circus rigging could be seen hanging above the court. Pro basketball was no longer a penny ante spectacle. When Holzman played on the 1950–51 champion Rochester Royals, total NBA playoff take was $50,000. Two decades later, the amount was $400,000—$118,000 for the winning team alone.

Players were more sophisticated about money matters by 1969–70. They now had attorneys to negotiate

The Knicks backcourt was comprised of the veteran Barnett, opposite in whirlpool, and the stylish Frazier, opposite below, and darting for the ball.

Dave DeBusschere playing with a broken nose early in the 1969–70 season.

their salaries, and representatives to contract for endorsements, public appearances and book deals.

Tickets for the playoff games were scaled down from a record $12.50—laughably inexpensive by today's standards but a heavy-duty price back then. But Knicks fans—so eager to be in on the coronation of their guys—did not begrudge management the price.

Many fans who were shut out at the box office phoned the Knicks at their Four Pennsylvania Plaza office and tried to lobby for tickets, angrily hanging up and, in some cases, cursing when secretaries there tried to explain that none were available.

When Asofsky's courtside pal, Fred Klein, went to pick up his clique's thirteen tickets, he was accosted by a man he described as a "seedy-looking Zero Mostel type" who grabbed his lapels and, with wild-eyed outrage, demanded to know what right he had to so many tickets. More softly, he said, "At least maybe give me one."

With an NBA title seeming to be this close, fans turned superstitious. On game nights, Asofsky took to parking his Volvo in the same place, in front of the Breslin Hotel on Broadway and West

Earl Monroe versus Walt Frazier, 1970 playoffs.

Twenty-ninth Street. Holzman's wife, Selma, wore the same orange- and mauve-striped dress to games and hung it by the same window at home. She did not dare send it to the cleaners for fear that the hocus-pocus in that garment would be gone on its return. Her husband was just as superstitious. When Reed's sneakers were falling apart during the 18-game victory streak early in the season, Holzman advised him to persevere with them until the string was broken.

In spite of these voodoo turns, the feeling that was afloat was that New York was a sure thing for the title. Who could stop the Knicks? For most New York fans, the playoffs were a confirmation of the obvious—their team was best.

Well, it would not be as easy as Knicks fans imagined. For New York's first playoff opponent, Baltimore, had a guard, Earl (The Pearl) Monroe, whose slithery moves were not only uncanny but also had a demoralizing effect on defenses, so improvisational and unorthodox were they. There were nights when Monroe could defeat the most tenancious of defenders, even double-teams, with those cunning slip-and-slide moves of his.

Baltimore had other men who could play, too. Gus Johnson fancied the showtime moves that his competition, DeBusschere, spurned. On drives to the basket he would swing the ball through the air in lovely twirls that made his drives picturesque.

Above, Baltimore's Jack Marin, #24, under pressure from Knicks defenders.

Facing page bottom, the Knicks defend against a young Lew Alcindor.

Below, Stallworth and fans exalt as the Knicks defeat the Bullets in the first round.

An intense Bradley drives to the basket against Baltimore's Jack Mann in the first round.

Jack Marin was the other forward. He was a quick-trigger jumpshooter, as was shooting guard Kevin Loughery, who would be playing with a lightweight protective vest for his damaged ribs. The team's hyperkinetic sixth man, Fred (Mad Dog) Carter, was not shy either about letting the ball fly.

That did not leave too many shot opportunities for the center, Wes Unseld, but that was no great problem for him. Unseld's area of expertise was rebounding and a rapid-release outlet pass that triggered the Bullets' fast break.

As for Milwaukee, the other Eastern team that New York figured to face, the Bucks had the next big-man legend, Lew Alcindor, who, at 7' 1" had the potential to carry an ordinary team by himself.

Milwaukee had acquired Alcindor through the draft only after a coin toss to decide whether the Bucks or the Phoenix Suns would draft first. Just prior to the draft, the management of the Suns staged a poll to let fans determine how to call the coin toss that would decide whether or Milwaukee was granted the rights to Alcindor. The Phoenix people chose heads, and shortly

Above, Reed and DeBusschere collapse on the Lakers' Elgin Baylor, as Baylor drives to the hoop. But for Reed it was against the legendary Wilt Chamberlain, facing page, that his biggest duels would be waged in the championship series.

Below, referee Mendy Rudolph orders Holzman back to the bench.

thereafter Alcindor purchased a Ural Mountains hat and the longest scarf in captivity and trundled off to Milwaukee.

Alcindor came in from the cold to a luxury apartment complex called Juneau Village, from where he made intermittent pronouncements on Milwaukee and its benighted culture. The feeling of Milwaukee, curiously enough, was not mutual. What Alcindor did for civic pride on the nights he worked for the local team privileged his remarks. In his first year, he led the Bucks from last place to second.

Meanwhile, in the west there were the Los Angeles Lakers, with Alcindor's high-rise predecessor, Wilt Chamberlain, as well as future Hall of Famers Jerry West and Elgin Baylor.

Not easy at all. The Knicks would find plenty of fight in the opposition and would have to raise their game to a level unimagined before the playoffs began. In the end, the drama would be provided by Reed—"The Cap'n" as his teammates called him. Through playoff series against Baltimore and Milwaukee, Reed was the man in the trenches, battling first the broad-beamed Wes Unseld, who stood 6' 7½" (more with his Afro) and was harder than a bread van to dislodge from around the basket and then confronting the rookie Alcindor, who later would take the Muslim name Kareem Abdul-Jabbar. Under both handles, Lew/Kareem was and would be as prolific a scorer as any big man since Chamberlain, starting with this 1969–70 season during which he had averaged 28.8 points per game.

But Reed did the job against both men.

In the overtime period of the opening game against Baltimore, he hit the clinching hook shot with 31 seconds remaining, breaking a 117–117 tie and securing the victory with the last of his 30 points that night. Final score: 120–117, New York.

So it went against Baltimore. With the series tied at two games apiece, and playing on aching knees that would require a pregame shot of cortisone, Reed went out and scored 36 points while grabbing 36 rebounds in leading New York to a 101–80 victory. It was a performance that inspired the ink-stained wretches covering the team to wisecrack about just what the good doctor had shot into The Cap'n that night.

Whatever it was, the Bullets were not prepared to concede the series to New York. With Monroe, Unseld, Marin, Johnson and Loughery, Baltimore would win the next game, taking the series to its climactic seventh game.

Before the game, as Knicks trainer Danny Whelan gave Reed a pregame rubdown, The Cap'n would exclaim, "Ow," when Whelan touched his right knee. But bad knee and all, Reed would fight the formidable Unseld in the

The Cap'n crumbles in game five against the Lakers.

determining seventh game of the series, and contribute mightily to the Knicks' 127–114 victory.

Then against Alcindor, Reed applied, let us say, dynamic tension—a euphemism for laying his body on the rookie and making it hard for him to get as close to the basket as Lew would have liked to be. The Knicks wrapped up the series in Milwaukee in five games through balanced scoring and the sort of defensive pressure that individually and as a team they had exhibited all year. But it would not have been so easy without Reed's work under the boards. Before the series, the Knicks appeared to outmatch the Bucks—Bobby Dandridge, Greg Smith, Flynn Robinson and Jon McGlocklin—except at center. Alcindor was the "X factor"—the one man who could undo the Knicks' position by position advantage. Reed didn't let him. The Cap'n clamped down.

But another super pivotman remained for Reed to contest. That was Chamberlain, who, with Bill Russell, had taken the game to the next dimension in the late fifties and early sixties, making it a sport played up at the rim. Chamberlain's Los Angeles Lakers had finished two games behind the Western Division champion Atlanta Hawks during regular-season play. But that was not necessarily a true indication of Laker strength. For Los Angeles had been without Chamberlain for all but twelve games of the regular season, the big man having spent most of the year rehabilitating an injured knee, some of the work being done by playing volleyball on the beaches of Santa Monica. Nonetheless, with Chamberlain in the lineup for the playoffs, the equation changed. The Lakers rallied to get past Phoenix in seven, blew out the Hawks in four straight games and came into the championship series a confident team.

The Lakers were not about to fall over for the touted New Yorkers. Although the Knicks won the opening game of the series at the Garden, 124–113, behind Reed's 37 points, L.A. gained a split on enemy turf when they beat New York 105–103 in game two.

The series shifted to Los Angeles, where game three turned out to be a beauty. A DeBusschere jump shot gave New York a 102–100 lead in the Forum with three seconds left. That's when West took the in-bounds pass and fired from 63 feet out—a desperation shot that went in as the buzzer sounded. The stunned Knicks pulled themselves together and won 111–108 in overtime. But the Lakers came back in game four and won 121–115 overtime victory behind West's 37 points and 18 assists.

MADISON SQUARE
GARDEN
PENNSYLVANIA PLAZA

PROFESSIONAL
BASKETBALL PLAY-OFF
Conducted by NAT'L BASKETBALL ASS'N
2nd PROMENADE
Est. Price $7.08
Sales Tax .42 $7.50
Maximum Broker Resale Prem. $1.50
Gen. Bus. Law of N.Y.S.

ENTER TOWER
GATE
A 19
SEC. ROW SEAT
308 G 1
0886
2nd PROMENADE $7.50
MADISON SQUARE GARDEN
PROFESSIONAL BASKETBALL PLAY-OFF
GAME
K10

The championship game, and here comes Reed, late but battle-ready, above, striding from the dressing room after being injected with painkillers. Reed would hit two early baskets to get the team rolling, and then Frazier, facing page, would dominate the game.

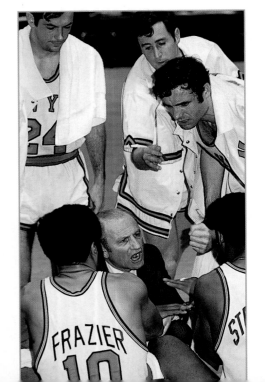

When Reed had gone down in game five against the Lakers, and the Knicks had shaken the Garden rafters with their comeback, they wrenched every last emotion from every single one of the more than 18,000 spectators. It was a game that would remain indelible in the minds of those who were there as well as those who caught the game on television. The night had the sheer drama of a Hollywood big-game finale.

The trouble was that game five was *not* the end of the series. When Los Angeles won game six on the West Coast, it meant the season would boil down to the seventh and final game in New York. One ball game for all the glory.

The city poised for battle. The question on the minds of Knicks fans was whether Reed would be in the lineup. And if he was, how much of his pit-bull tenacity would this damaged man be able to muster?

Reed's injury kept the lines of the MSG switchboard humming, as concerned fans called to inquire about his condition or to recommend "wonder" cures. And it was Topic One on the sports page, too, as game-day accounts tended toward the perfervid quality of this paragraph:

Like the cavalry thundering over the hilltop at the moment the beleaguered frontier fort is about to fall, or like Superman exploding from a telephone booth when Lois Lane is face to face with villainy of the worst order, Willis Reed (in the fantasies of thousands of fans of the New York Knickerbockers) will bound onto the court of Madison Square Garden tonight and save his team from worse than death.

Game day arrived—a warm and sunny day. At his office, Asofsky was analyzing inventory figures and trying to stay cool. But he was, as he put it, scared shitless. He divined foul things from his day. Leaving work early, he took the KK train to Brooklyn, and it was late. Though he had been anticipating a meat meal, his mother made dairy. Uptown, (Knicks secretary) Joanne Dinoia stepped outside Penn Plaza and a man with a walking cane offered her $100 for the ticket she had. She refused, and he told her she was crazy. All across the city people were making plans for the game. Ticketholders were taking early dinners and slipping into lucky wardrobes. Others headed straight from work to the bars on the East Side of Manhattan, where the game was to be shown on cable television.

The Cap'n met New York trainer Danny Whelan at the Knicks dressing room at two o'clock. He wore a red, white and blue shirt, a vest, a black and white bandana, blue and white trousers and a bush coat. His leg was treated with heat for ninety minutes in Whelan's room. Then he and the trainer dined at the Penn Plaza Club in the Garden. The place was empty. Reed ate a steak and salad.

At courtside, ABC was setting up for its national TV hookup that night. The network's Chet Forte, once a basketball star at Columbia University, and Ned Irish were discussing camera placements. Security chiefs were instructing their aides to have extra men stationed near Eddie Layton's organ in case fans wanted to disassemble it afterward. Maintenance men wet mopped the floor. The early arrivals among the press sat on a bench in the hallway outside the Knicks dressing room, where Reed was now resting. When Holzman passed by, newsman Leonard Koppett pointed to the writers on the bench and said, "Ellis Island." Holzman smiled. Minutes later, the first of the security forces trooped through the corridor. Many of them were in the social security bracket, others were

young and undernourished. "These guys," said a writer, "are going to keep 19,500 away?"

At 6:03 P.M., Reed stepped onto the court. He spun a lay-up on the rim and, when it dropped in, ushers applauded him. With Knicks reserve Don May feeding the ball, Reed slogged to spots on the wood for his arcing shots, favoring his left leg on liftoffs. In the aisleway to the locker rooms stood an interested observer. "Don't look, Wilt," a guy hollered. Wilt Chamberlain looked. Shortly after, Reed returned to the dressing room. On this final night of the season, it was closed to visitors and the press.

The Knicks took the floor without Reed.

As the players warmed up, the more than 18,000 patrons jammed into the Garden could see Frazier, DeBusschere, Bradley and Barnett out there hoisting up practice shots. But those worried spectators did not see Willis Reed. Throughout the afternoon, radio reports had assured Knicks partisans that The Cap'n would be game-ready. But having seen Reed crumble in game five, New York fans had no illusions about the injury. Nobody—Clark Kent notwithstanding—could suffer an injury like Reed's and come back two games later without being seriously impaired.

Suddenly a Knick was moving through the foyer leading to the court and stepping onto the Garden floor. The stirring of the crowd was abruptly terminated. False alarm. That player was Cazzie Russell, returning from New York's dressing room, where Reed was being injected with a shot of cortisone, an anti-inflammatory agent, and a shot of Carbocaine, a painkiller.

Well, as any serious student of Knicks basketball knows—and as those who were there will remember forever—Reed appeared, walking slowly, purposefully onto the court in the midst of warm-ups. Talk of drama. The sight of Reed thrilled the crowd. The cheers shook the building. And then, The Cap'n went out there and nail his first two shots, dragging his injured leg like Marshall Dillon's man Chester, as he put the Knicks on top, 5–2.

From the official play-by-play sheet, with the score 5–2, New York's favor:

	NY	LA
Chamberlain fouled by Reed—misses both tries. DeB rebds.		
Frazier fouled in act by Erickson—makes 2	7	
DeBusschere one-hander from top of the key	9	
(Time-out Los Angeles @ 9:42)		
Baylor uncontested one-hander from left of lane		4
Bradley quick spinning one-hander right of key	11	
(Erickson walks under pressure by Bradley)		
(Barnett loses it)		
West driving lay-in from the right		6
Frazier fouled by Garrett—makes 2	13	
DeBusschere off-balance one-hander from left baseline	15	
(Lakers lose to Reed)		
(Reed throws it to Garrett)		
Chamberlain flies thru to stuff rebound		8
Bradley with arm wide outstretched lays it in from left	17	

What Reed did and Los Angeles didn't do in the early minutes of the game gave New York an emotional edge that time and place and Walt Frazier sustained. Frazier was working the left side of the floor, using his suggestive gliding motion to con a step from the Lakers' Dick Garrett so that he could cuddle the ball at his shoulder and shoot it. Five straight

times in the first quarter Frazier swung room for his shot, and hit. It was not by shot alone that New York brought Los Angeles down. The defense accomplished incredible things. The Knicks stole the ball from Chamberlain and Keith Erickson and Baylor and even West. Frazier, lurking behind Riordan, came off him like a linebacker on a stunting move and cleanly took the ball from West at the middle of the floor. Eight seconds later, Riordan harassed West and made him step over the backcourt line for another violation. By the end of the first half, the Lakers had committed 15 turnovers to New York's 7. And the Knicks led, 69–42.

The Knicks did not suffer the letdowns they'd had earlier in the series. They were, in a phrase Frazier had used about the playoff state of mind, "psyched to kill." Asofsky had seen that even before the game: when the pop vocalist Steve Lawrence had gone to the Knicks bench to shake hands with DeBusschere, #22 had

given him a limp hand and a vacant stare.

In the third quarter Frazier went on another tear: he hit a jump shot, a free throw, got West to charge, stole the ball from Garrett and scored and stole the ball from Chamberlain and scored, all in a matter of minutes. By the end of that surge, the Knicks led, 79–54. Shortly thereafter, Reed left the game for the night. The rest was for savoring.

In one grand evening the ghosts of a sometimes chaotic Knick past were chased—Goebel Ritter executing a swan dive into a snowbank, the long walk to the Green Parrot Cafe, the dissension that Holzman had inherited. The scoreboard said it and the next day's headlines reflected it.

KNICKS WIN IT!—New York Post
WILLIS, CLYDE DO IT —*KNICKS WHIP LAKERS, 113–99, FOR TITLE*—New York Daily News.

At last.

More than 25 years later, those Knicks and that season are still regarded as quintessential by those who were there to see it.

It was not just that the 1969–70 team won an NBA title. Or that it was the first Knicks squad to do so. This was a group of strong, and distinct, personalities—the kind of diversity in characters a novelist might conjure up. Banker's son and Rhodes scholar (Bradley), enigmatic loner (Barnett), no-nonsense worker types (Reed, DeBusschere) and the fancy man (Frazier). New Yorkers were drawn to these vivid and contrasting personalities.

In combination, these Knicks were a smart team and given the futures they would make beyond the court— Bradley as a senator, Barnett as a Ph.D. in education, DeBusschere and Reed as NBA-team executives and Frazier as a polysyllabic color commentator—in retrospect it makes perfect sense that they were able to offer this city a game steeped in basketball nuances.

That year the Knicks had a play they called "X." Basketball mavens still speak of "X" in the sort of tones that theater buffs once reserved for Lunt and Fontanne. "X" was nothing but a variation of the backdoor play, unusual in that Bradley, a forward, brought the ball into frontcourt and ran the play for Frazier, a guard, an inversion of roles. Bradley would dribble to the middle of the floor,

with Frazier shuffling alongside him in that deceptive go-easy stride of his. Then Frazier would accelerate to the basket and Bradley would flick the bounce pass behind the defender. Frazier would look back and the ball would be in his hands for a lay-up.

Of all the players, it was Bradley who seemed to embody the Knicks sensibility, with its concern for team over personal gains. He had an artist's feel for basketball—a vision of the precise and heady works that the game could be. And when it was that, when the ball moved so smartly that it made Garden crowds rapturous, his pleasure was not merely professional. He used the word "sensuous" once in describing the feel of the game and seemed moved in a way other players weren't by the interrelations of a team.

But when the Knicks lagged, or momentarily lost the team concept, it was often Bradley who raised Cain. *"Move the damn ball!"* he'd scream on the court, or in huddles, his face reddening, his body stiffening. And because his team feeling was genuine, his harangues were not resented. Teammates appeared to regard those outbursts with secret delight, as proof of a wigged piece in the eminently rational individual. To see Dollar Bill turn angry at an official's call was

By the final minutes of the title game, Reed was on the bench, savoring the Knicks' mastery of the Lakers, along with Stallworth, Cazzie Russell and rookie John Warren, on opposite page. At the final buzzer, the bench emptied on to the court, below, while a downcast Chamberlain, #13, headed for the loser's dressing room.

NBA champions. Let the celebration begin. This page, Nate Bowman spills champagne on Howard Cosell. Facing page top, Ed Bradley (as a young reporter for WCBS Radio) catches the moment, with DeBusschere, Frazier and Riordan as they smile for the cameras.

Reed later accepts congratulations from New York mayor John Lindsay, facing page bottom.

amusing for its contrast to the other, more tranquil Bradley. Miffed, he would wander downcourt, as one writer described him, "like a sulky child in that peculiar, stiff-legged walk of his, muttering side-of-the-mouth words he would not have dared used in his scholarly dissertations."

In a year when these Knicks were a chic item, Bradley and the other starters were celebrated nonstop by the media, with Barnett proving most resistant to the process. He was the old guy of the team, 33 then, and the least impressed by the hoopla: *Newsweek* cover, network TV features and courtside celebs like Woody Allen, Robert Redford, Elliott Gould and Dustin Hoffman. It made no difference to him what people wrote or said, and there were all kinds of angles tried by the media. On a page labeled *food/fashion/family/furnishings, The New York Times* would note:

"There are five women who cheer a little louder, jump to their feet a little more often, and suffer a little more intensely whenever they watch the New York Knickerbockers play basketball in Madison Square Garden. They are young, slim and good looking. They have some of the best seats in the Garden. And it's no

wonder: They are the Knicks' wives." Barnett wouldn't buy into that hoopla. He would mutter cliches when reporters approached him and then act entirely different when they left, as this anecdote of Knicks reserve Bill Hosket will convey:

"Dick got 32 (points) one night and the news guy says, 'Dick, this 32 is the most you scored this year, how do you feel?' Dick says, 'It's sure great to win,' and looks down and starts tying his shoes. Like it doesn't impress him at all. Then the press left. Dick jumped up, yelled, 'GodDAMN! I was a monster out there tonight.' And he just starts talking about this move, that move and how he was dooooo-in' it tonight."

As elusive a character as Barnett was for the press, so, too, did his game resist ready labels. On the court, Barnett looked awkward. His jump shot seemed a battle with gravity, full of kinks and hitches, like a Rube Goldberg contraption. Barnett moved as if he belonged in the geriatric ward of Bellevue—the labored step matched his demeanor. He was uncanny, though. He could hit that junkyard shot of his with defenders soaring around him and his body reeling backward, as if he were experiencing technical difficulties. And on defense, it was Barnett who often drew the other team's hotshot.

Holzman also seemed to disdain the tumult of the media, giving pat answers whose objective was to quickly and efficiently deflect the spotlight from him.
Q: What have you done to help your team's success?

1969–70 World Champion New York Knicks, left to right: back row, coach Red Holzman, Phil Jackson, Dave Stallworth, Dave DeBusschere, Willis Reed, Bill Hosket, Nate Bowman, Bill Bradley, chief scout Dick McGuire, trainer Danny Whelan; front row, Johnny Warren, Don May, Walt Frazier, president Ned Irish, Irving Mitchell Felt, GM Eddie Donovan, Dick Barnett, Mike Riordan, Cazzie Russell.

A: Some stuff I have done has evidently apppealed to them.

Q: What do you mean, "stuff"?

A: Offensive and defensive stuff.

A Philadelphia writer listened to answers like that and said, "Holzman's as funny as cold oatmeal." Columnist Ira Berkow fantasized in print about the gradual disappearance of Holzman in clouds of his own ineffable modesty. Yet there was surely method to Holzman's muteness.

Holzman was like the poker player who kept confidences to himself, tabulated all the news on the table and only paused for chitchat on his way out the door with everybody's money in his pocket.

As with any season, there were moments that remain imprinted on the mind—snapshots, really, of one fleeting instant after another that in their cumulation still resonate a treasured time.

Holzman's New York–inflected voice was certainly part of that mélange of impressions.

Even now, all these years later, it is impossible to think of 1969–70 and not hear the echo of Holzman shouting, "See the ball, see the ball, dammit, see it, see it."

The coach willed the defense that his Knicks would play so expertly. He was crazy for his defense. He had been raised in a basketball era when the game was played closer to the ground and was full of ball handling and subtle motions—men feinted and moved their defenders and eyed for collaborators, the court was laid with foxy ruses. It was a

The NBA champions are photographed by LOOK photographer Arnold Neuman.

game that taxed a defender's wits.

The game changed with the advent of the jump shot, which allowed the player to spring into the air and shoot from an elevated vantage rather than with his feet planted on the ground. Suddenly, rather than delicate conspiratorial patterns and nurtured moments of freedom in which shooters lofted precise arcing set shots or, if trickery accomplished it, uncontested lay-ins at close range, there were all these free-form solos anywhere on the court.

All this made a defender's job more difficult. What happened was that defense became a virtue honored only in the abstract: scoring totals got higher and higher, and by 1955–56 teams averaged 99 points per game, or 31.3 more than in 1946–47.

The succcess that Boston had with its defensive pressure, backstopped by Bill Russell, showed that those free-form shooters could be stifled if a team was willing to invest in hard work.

Not all clubs reverted. But Holzman's did. Red sought to impose chaos on the foe, to panic every dribbler, and to do this without an ultimate nullifier like Russell but rather with five men working in concert.

Such a defense needed to be expertly tuned by a head coach. And so Holzman promoted collective attention at every juncture, in drills whose purpose was to get players to refocus the instant a score was made, or in the controlled circumstances that would follow such a drill, competitive two-on-two, three-on-three or red- and blue-shirted fives.

See the ball! See the ball!—jackhammer words to drive a player from his own petty defensive concern into a more communal frame of mind. A defender had to know where the ball was, had to see it, so that when Frazier made one of his darting thrusts for the ball and forced his foe to lurch like a man caught in wind, each of his teammates moved to the station on the floor that would make Clyde's move pay off. Barnett would come peeling in from behind the man to frisk the ball, and the rest of the defense rotated so that when the panicked dribbler sought to be

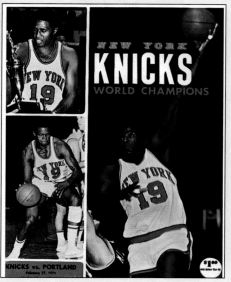

freed from the onus of incompetence and threw the ball to where his conditioned responses told him his people would be, Bradley or DeBusschere or Reed was there instead to steal the ball. And it would all happen because each man had seen the ball.

It was a long way from that night in Hershey, Pennsylvania, where Chamberlain had scored 100 points, to the postgame Garden locker room nearly a decade later where big Wilt sat looking stungunned by the defensive assault that the gimpy Reed and his Knicks teammates had mounted to win the 1969–70 NBA title.

Team ball had triumphed against a Laker club that was anchored in the middle by the man whose prolific scoring represented the double-edged virtues of the star system.

Not that Chamberlain was to blame for the Knicks championship game victory. No, New York had seized the game by the lapels, and shook it until the Lakers collectively rolled under. The Los Angeles team appeared immobilized by the fervor of the Knicks and their fans. The Garden crowd that night was unrelenting in the urgency it conveyed. Even Los Angeles coach Joe Mullaney seemed paralyzed with indecision. Mullaney stood pat, even when it was quickly apparent that Reed had to drag his right leg to defend and was vulnerable to motion. On his bench Mullaney had Mel Counts and Happy Hairston, either of whom would have given him a more nimble big man than 33-year-old Wilton Norman Chamberlain. Counts or Hairston, particularly Hairston, might have accomplished against Reed what the rovers, DeBusschere and Stallworth, did to Chamberlain in game five—they might have forced him to come away from the basket and expose his limited mobility.

But could-have and should-have belong to the vanquished. And credit to the Knicks, who, with heart, pressure and poise, hit Los Angeles that night like a wrecking ball and left the Laker season in pieces when it was all over.

And left us with the memory of 18,000-plus voices chanting *DEE-fense, DEE-fense* while history was being made.

THE SEVENTIES

70s

Three years later, New York was back in the thick of another NBA title battle.

The nucleus of the 1969–70 team was still there, but certain changes were apparent. Reed, who had played only 11 games the previous season because of injuries, was no longer capable of being the workhorse he'd been during the championship season. In 1969–70, he had led the team not only in scoring (21.7 average) but also in minutes played (3,089 in 81 games). Those stats were sharply reduced during 1972–73: Reed played 1,876 minutes in 69 games in what would be his penultimate year in the NBA. The wear and tear of nine seasons had taken their toll on The Cap'n.

Time had reduced Barnett, too, to a part-timer. Like Reed, he would play into the next season, and that would be it for him.

Other men would take up the slack.

One of them had been with the Knicks since 1967 but had missed the 1969–70 season because of an injury sustained the previous year. In fact, when the Knicks played that championship year, the injured Phil Jackson was often sitting baseline with a camera. Photography was a hobby he had taken up with some passion and for which he occasionally shot on assignment—$75 a game from *The New York Post*.

A few years down the road, Jackson would become more widely known as the coach of the Michael Jordan–led championship Chicago Bulls and a potent Knicks nemesis. That's the Jackson we see today, stepping onto the court in a smartly cut suit and with his gray-flecked hair and mustache trimmed neat as a pin. But back in the late sixties, and early seventies, Jackson, who had grown up in Williston, North Dakota, the son of a fundamentalist preacher, was as close to a counter-culture figure as you'd find on the Knicks roster then.

And Jackson at play, well, stylistically he was at the other extreme from most of those daring young Bulls who fly through the air these days with the greatest of ease. Jackson was no smoothie. Jackson back then was a lean and mustached forward, constructed, it sometimes seemed, from an Erector set. At 6' 8", with square shoulders and arms $40\frac{1}{2}$ inches to the sleeve, he was most effective going to the basket with the hook. But when he put the ball on the floor—another story. Then he tended to resemble Groucho at his crawl-walking best. This did not escape Holzman, who established a two-dribble limit for Jackson.

Jackson's entry into ball games would stir an uneasy murmur among the Garden's ticket-buying customers. What undid Jackson was the insult he gave form. His moves hadn't the silk most pros' do; with Jackson the hinges creaked. Yet the look was deceiving. In a career that would span twelve NBA seasons—ten with the Knicks, the final two with the New Jersey Nets—he was a legitimate force. On defense, he had the instinct for the ball and the windmilling arms to provoke turnovers. And though prone to personal fouls, he got them for the right reasons.

As unstylish as "Action Jackson" was, the imported Earl (the Pearl) Monroe was the essence of shake'n'bake improvisation with the basketball. Monroe had come to the Knicks in a trade for Mike Riordan, Dave Stallworth and cash in November 1971. But his game had come via the Philadelphia playgrounds, where a young Monroe had competed against established NBA stars like Wilt Chamberlain, Guy Rodgers, Wally Jones, Wayne Hightower and others. "I was only six-two, so I had to find a way to play with the big boys," he said. "I had to develop flukey-duke shots, hesitating in the air as long as possible."

On those Philadelphia playgrounds and in summer games for the Charles Baker League—the Philly equivalent of Harlem's Rucker Tournament—Monroe's reputation of being the closest thing to spontaneous combustion on a basketball court flourished.

At Winston-Salem (N.C.) College, Monroe liked to play to the crowd. Once, while cradling the ball in his left arm, he spotted a teammate heading for the basket, so he whipped his right hand behind his back and punched the ball to him. He was sometimes Earl, but more often that razzle-dazzle would inspire nicknames—Black Jesus, Magic, Doctor, Slick, The Savior and, in the pros, Pearl.

At Baltimore, Monroe had been the show, the focus of the Bullet attack. When he came to New York, the doubters figured that he and Frazier would have a hard time co-existing with one basketball. As Marv Albert would put it: "When the trade went down, the Knicks' players weren't so sure what they were getting. They were apprehensive about what kind of person Monroe was. Monroe had always been a mystery man, the sort of guy who keeps to himself, who just suddenly appears places and disappears just as quickly."

Well, the mystery about Monroe as a Knick was quickly solved. Monroe showed that beneath the flash was a mature basketball-playing man, one who would mute his game to accommodate the talent New York had in order to win ball games.

The other crucial element in the Knicks' quest to win another NBA title was Jerry Lucas, who was acquired in May 1971 in the trade that sent Cazzie Russell to San Francisco.

Lucas was 6' 8", 230 pounds, a strong rebounder and a man who had the ability to score inside as well as outside. His high-arcing one-handers from beyond the top of the key descended from the ozone. With Reed rehabilitating his left knee, Lucas did admirably in covering for him the 1972–73 season, averaging 16.7 ppg and nabbing a total of 1011 rebounds.

Even as he was establishing himself as an important cog on this reconstituted Knicks team, Lucas was also adding, in Marv Albert's words, "a bit of oddity to the team."

"He was obsessed," Albert recalled, "with his stats...At the end of quarters, he'd race to get a rebound nobody else cared about before time expired. He told me once if you could get two or three of those a night, you'd raise what would have been an ordinary five-rebound night to an eight-rebound night and it would pay off at negotiation time."

Lucas was always fascinated by odd facts and possibilities. He was widely known for magic tricks, and he had a photographic memory.

Although the 1972–73 Knicks would finish in second place in the Atlantic Division, eleven games behind Boston, their record was deceptive. For Holzman had been conservative about the playing time he had given to Reed. And with good reason. He wanted a hale and hearty Reed for the playoffs. So he spared those rehabilitated knees of Reed's during the regular season, hoping it would pay dividends come playoff time.

Well, the strategy seemed to work. The Knicks beat Baltimore four games to one and then took Boston in seven games. Once again, the championship finals would match New York against the defending NBA championship Los Angeles Lakers. Gone from the Lakers of 1969–70 was Elgin Baylor but not much else. Los Angeles' talent ran deep: Gail Goodrich, Jerry West, Jim McMillian, Happy Hairston, Wilt Chamberlain, Bill Bridges and Keith Erickson. In reserve was a veteran guard whose future would find him years later sitting on the Knicks bench as its head coach, Pat Riley. But in this series, the life of Riley would be as a player of secondary importance.

The Lakers won the opening game, 115–112. But it was to be their last hurrah. For Holzman and the Knicks responded to the defensive dominance of Chamberlain by sending either Reed or Lucas —whomever Chamberlain was guarding—downcourt on the run, looking to take advantage of Wilt's disinclination for the rapid-tempo game. By doing that Reed or Lucas would end up with open shots, forcing the 36-year-old Chamberlain to eventually race along with them, wearing him down.

The drama that had marked the 1969–70 series was not nearly so pronounced this time. The Knicks would win the next four games of the series, showing the smart ball movement and collaborative defense that were their trademarks. Reed would come up big for the Knicks on his rehabilitated and rested legs—21 points and 10 rebounds in game three, 21 points in game four.

The final game, in Los Angeles, saw the Knicks do what they had done all season—play their aggressive defense and unselfish offense and wrapping up the series 102–93. Monroe led New York in scoring with 23 points, Bradley had 20, Frazier and Reed ended up with 18 points apiece. For Reed, it was a fitting finale to a comeback year. In recognition, he was named MVP for the championship series by *Sport* Magazine.

Yes, the Knicks were champions. Again. But the good times did not last long on Thirty-third Street. The decade that had started with sheer glory, and drama, would end with a Knicks franchise gone awry again.

The difficulties that would plague the Knicks began in 1974–75, the first losing year since 1966–67, a season that highlighted the team's need for a big man under the backboards. The Knicks went the length and breadth of the U.S. to find that individual. They failed in attempts to secure George McGinnis or Kareem Abdul-Jabbar, or to lure Wilt Chamberlain out of retirement. In fact, when Knicks president Michael Burke and the team's general manager, Eddie Donovan, flew to the coast to meet with Wilt, Chamberlain stood them up.

The big men the Knicks finally landed were Spencer Haywood (traded by Seattle in October of 1975) and Bob McAdoo (traded by Buffalo in December of 1976)—name players with reputations as scorers.

McAdoo had led the league in scoring for three straight years, from 1973–1976. Haywood had two seasons in which he averaged 26.2 ppg (1971–72) and 29.2 ppg (1972–73). But as the Knicks front office discovered, the whole did not equal the sum of its parts, and all that firepower did not make for a winning team. Not only were McAdoo and Haywood incompatible playing together, they were flawed within the team setting.

McAdoo was, in the basketball parlance, a gunner, a shot-hungry player with a vision of the game that tended to be limited. He delighted in putting the ball in the hole, and would often declare a defiant "in-your-face" as he shot. So strong was his influence that the team-oriented game that Willis Reed, who succeeded Holzman as coach, tried to teach never took hold. The Mac-first orientation filtered down to other players, especially Haywood, who talked the team game in the locker room but played a different one on the court. Haywood's game turned out to be one-dimensional, too: It began and ended with his turnaround jump shot.

And the Knicks fell to the bottom of the standings.

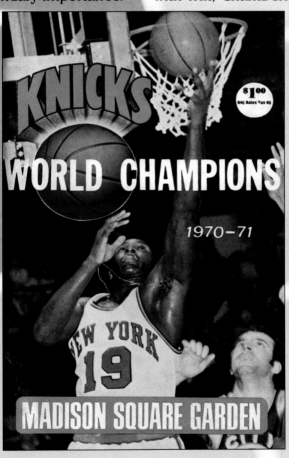

KNICKS WORLD CHAMPIONS 1970-71

NEW YORK 19

MADISON SQUARE GARDEN

$1.00

SHOOTING FOR A SECOND TITLE

In 1969–70, even before he fell in the dramatic fifth game of the championship series against Los Angeles, Willis Reed had been in pain.

Earlier in the series, on a charter flight to Los Angeles, he had risen from his seat and grimaced, showing the strain it was on his knees to perform even that simple maneuver.

Well, the pain that plagued Reed through that first championship run did not cease when the title banner went up in the Garden rafters.

"Funny thing," said Reed, "the doctors never really came out and said, 'Willis, you have to give up playing basketball. You can't do this or you can't do that.' They had told me during the 1970–71 season that I couldn't do any more harm to my knee by running and jumping. It was already so painful.

"If the medical men figured that way, then I decided I was going to play. That year I wound up with more minutes of game action than in any of the previous NBA seasons. Sure, I was in anguish most of the time. I realize that a good many other players wouldn't do the same thing, but I was of the opinion that I had to do it for the team.

"Between ball games, I'd try to grab a couple of days of rest and afterwards I'd feel really good. I'd play fairly well until the end of the game, by which time I'd seem to lose my ability to move. The only thing I could say about that was that I was

giving my best. And I know the guys on the club, like Bill Bradley and Dave DeBusschere and Clyde (Walt Frazier) and Dick Barnett, everyone, appreciated it. They never told me so but I knew."

A year later, he knew he could not continue playing with a left knee that rebelled against the pounding it took getting him up and down a basketball court. Reed would begin the new season, playing eleven games in 1971–72 before he decided it was "like a one-legged man trying to help an old lady across the street. Neither would make it."

After consulting with doctors, he went on the inactive list and began a rehabilitation program designed by Knicks team physician Dr. Andrew Patterson and by a man regarded as one of the foremost

The final buzzer sounds and the Garden erupts at the Knicks' 19–0 comeback rally that beats Milwaukee on November 18, 1972.

authorities on tendinitis in the country, Dr. Donald O'Donohue.

"What I thought was going to be whirlpool and ice baths, and rubdowns, turned out to be little more than a program involving weights on my legs," Reed recalled. "Dr. O'Donohue had charted four types of exercises for the area, all involving these weights. It was so simple that one might say it was sophisticated. He called these exercises a back lift, two side lifts and a front lift."

With or without Reed, the Knicks' reign as defending champions would not last. In 1971, Baltimore got its long awaited revenge, defeating the Knicks in the Eastern finals and capping the series with a two-point game seven victory that stunned a packed

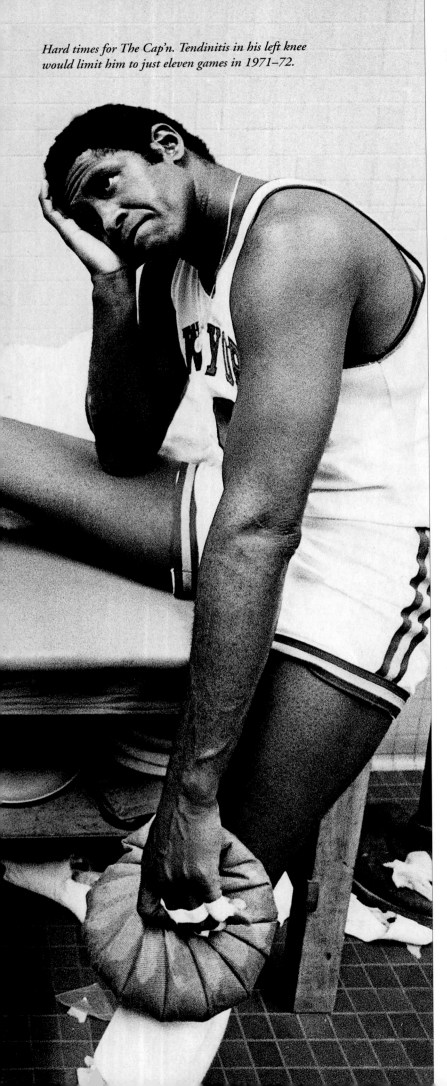

Hard times for The Cap'n. Tendinitis in his left knee would limit him to just eleven games in 1971–72.

Garden house. The following year, with Reed sidelined for all but eleven games, the Knicks won the East again, but were blasted out of the finals in five games by the Los Angeles Lakers team that finally hoisted its first championship banner.

As the 1972–73 season began, an optimistic Reed, with his knee strengthened from a year of strenuous rehabilitation, joined the team at its Monmouth College training camp in West Long Branch, New Jersey. He worked at his own pace to get in shape, eager to lend his brawn to the pivot that had been occupied in his absence by Jerry Lucas, acquired from the Warriors. Lucas also was plagued by knee problems and was forced to put ice packs on them after every game. Reed was hoping that between the two of them "we'd come up with a least one healthy center."

And those two were not the only Knicks coping with injuries. Monroe was bothered by bone spurs. For a while, New York more nearly resembled a trauma ward than a functioning basketball team. And what of their opposition? Well, in the Eastern Division, the Bullets were

a far different club from the one that had battled the Knicks in 1969–70. Gone were Loughery, Marin, Monroe and Mad Dog Carter. In their place the Bullets had acquired Elvin Hayes, Phil Chenier, Archie Clark, Flynn Robinson, Kevin Porter and Riordan and Stallworth in the deal that brought Monroe to the Knicks. They were none the worse for those changes, winning the Central Division with a record of 52 and 30.

Like the Bullets, the Celtics had lost some key players from their 1969–70 team—Larry Siegfried and Bailey Howell—but the men they added in the years since made the Celtics a stronger team. There was a redheaded pivotman, Dave Cowens, who ran without letup and could shoot from near the hoop or fire up a jumper from out a ways. Veterans Paul Silas, Don Nelson and John Havlicek provided a fine blend of muscle, hustle and scoring. Guard Don Chaney had long arms and loads of determination on defense, and the other guard, Jo Jo White, could score and defend.

Boston was the team to beat in the East. New York? Well, it was hard to tell how good they were, given the string of injuries that Monroe and Lucas had, and the cautious use of previously injured Knicks like Reed and Phil Jackson.

Jackson still unnerved many Knicks fans with his

Above, Jerry Lucas tips off against Houston's Elvin Hayes. Below, Don Nelson is restrained by referee and Bill Bradley by Willis Reed in the 1973 playoffs.

roughshod style. When he would dribble for a shot or hoist up a jumper the Garden throng would murmur uneasily. Certain players are like that. Their presence on the floor prompts negative reaction. Komives had often been booed when he played in New York. It used to be said that what he could use for pregame introductions was an armored truck. From in there, he might wave his arms to the Garden crowds when his name was announced and be spared the raucous reception that followed.

Though Komives was gone, the notion was not—not for Dick Barnett, who thought it up to begin with. He advised Phil Jackson that the armored truck would be rolling for him. Jackson was not unaware of his dubious standing with the local crowd, and could hear the insults some of his detractors would shout.

Pity was not a quality Jackson's critics had. They were like Nader's Raiders when it came to finding defects in his game. "And the thing is," Jackson said, ironically, "some of them know basketball."

Among his teammates, Jackson was better appreciated. From their point of view he was scoring better than ever and playing the kind of defense the team needed. "His timing was back and he was blocking as many shots as ever," Reed said. "That long arm span, combined with a new aggressiveness, made him one of the most valuable players on the club going down the stretch."

New York would have no men among the top ten scorers in 1972–73, but what they would show was a balanced attack, with five men in double figures during the regular season— Frazier (21.1 ppg), DeBusschere (16.3), Bradley (16.1), Monroe (15.5) and Reed (11.0).

More important was a team statistic for defense. New York led the NBA in that category, allowing the opposition only 98.2 points a game, making it the best defense in the league. By contrast, the Eastern Division champion Celtics (68–14 record) gave up 104.5 points a game.

Boston was the class of the division, but the Knicks had one shining moment in the regular season that has prevailed through the years. That was the November night when they scored 19

straight points down the stretch to defeat Kareem, the Big O and the rest of the Milwaukee Bucks, 87–86, on a chilly Saturday night.

"I was sitting on the bench and watching," said Milwaukee's Jon McGlocklin. 'This is ridiculous,' I was saying. 'There is no way they can catch us. The way we're playing, there is no way.' The next thing I knew, they won."

Holzman was a coach who put his trust in veterans. That second-year man Dean Meminger had significant playing time in 1972–73 owed to a simple fact: Dean the Dream could play defense. He was quick and aggressive. He got after the ball. Little had changed since 1969–70. Holzman still demanded that his men see the ball, and the game the Knicks put out there was still rooted in the team concept.

Of the Knicks who were starters in 1969-70 only Barnett would have a subordinate role three years later. At age 36, he was reduced to being a part-time player, but following his retirement after the

The Knicks of 1972–73 got outside scoring from Monroe, #15, above, and DeBusschere, #22, below. Facing page, from Holzman there were constant reminders to work together as a team—on and off the court.

1975–76 season Barnett would end up working as an assistant coach for Holzman. A clear sign of the respect Red had for his player.

As for the other starters, Reed was coming along nicely, Holzman using him sparingly to avoid putting undue strain on the rehabilitated knee. From training camp through the regular season, the idea had been to keep Willis healthy enough for the playoffs. And by playoff time he was ready.

So were the other holdovers from the 1969–70 starting team, Frazier, DeBusschere and Bradley. All of them were still performing up to standard, proven by their being named to the All-Star game earlier in the year.

That Bradley was still earning wages in the NBA was a surprise to William Warren Bradley. As he would observe in his book, *Life on the Run*: "I often ask myself why I continue to play. I was convinced that in 1967, when I first signed, I would play no more than four years, the length of my initial contract. After eight years, I'm still playing. One reason is the money. There is no question that it gives me a sense of security, and a greater feeling of freedom, mobility, and accomplishment.

"I heard a player say, 'Money alone makes you more of what you were before you had money.' Ultimately it is your work and the struggle that surrounds its daily practice that is important, much more so than money, because it is work, as Joseph Conrad has said, that provides the 'sustaining illusion of an independent existence.' Although I play basketball for money, and the amount of money is important, it is not the sole reason I play. The answer is not so easy to uncover. It lies much deeper in the workings of the game and in me."

Looking ahead to the playoffs, Reed would anticipate Boston as the big obstacle to New York's making it to the NBA finals.

"Boston," he said, "was relentless. They had a bunch of young guys there—Jo Jo White, Don Chaney, Dave Cowens—and we didn't really believe they would be able to keep up the pace from wire to wire. Yet with the help of a few seasoned veterans like John Havlicek and Don Nelson and Paul Silas, they were the scourge of the division.

"(Coach) Tom Heinsohn's boys had certainly proved themselves a team to be reckoned with. Milwaukee won its division, as did the Lakers. The Knicks, Golden State and Baltimore, Chicago and Atlanta completed the playoff bracket.

"The team defense concept paid off for us at the end of the regular season. We knew the Celtics had the division clinched and that we would definitely be in the playoffs, so Red rested us more liberally, and the defense was able to keep all the games within reach.

Ahead lay the playoffs.

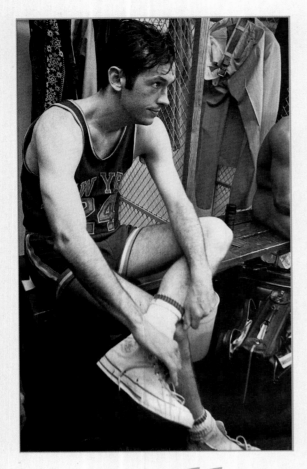

a will
to win

Below, Lucas mans the film projector in prevideo days.

From training camp through the regular season, the preservation of Willis Reed had been a key concern for Knicks coach Red Holzman.

Rehab or not, it didn't take a medical genius to realize that Reed was vulnerable.

So Holzman was not about to push The Cap'n beyond his limits. He took the conservative approach with an eye toward having the best Willis Reed possible available at playoff time.

"He was just great about it," said Reed of Holzman, "allowing me to set my own pace, work in with the team gradually. He told me to make my own timetable, just let him know when I was ready.

"Red tries to give one the impression that he's a hard, tough, impersonal coach. He's really just a pussycat with more knowledge of basketball than any man I've ever known. He's a warm, sensitive man. And every time I told him I was ready to participate a little more, Red would say, 'Make sure, Willis; if it bothers you just come right out.'"

Bradley recalled the gradual acclimation Reed needed: "It took him most of the year to get back a modicum of timing. His quickness was gone forever. With his knowledge of the game and his sheer physical bulk, Willis helped us sporadically during the 1972–73 regular season. Slowly, he began to try the old moves and rebound without fear of reinjury. "

In the meantime, the Celtics were running away with the regular-season competition. They would finish eleven games ahead of runner-up New York in the Atlantic Division. But Holzman, like the grinning trademark character of *Mad* magazine, adopted a "What? Me Worry?" attitude. He stuck with his game plan. Take it slow, take it easy, take The Cap'n to the playoffs.

It wasn't easy, to be sure, for the competitive Reed.

The pressure to help the team at the expense of a susceptible knee was ever-present. Reed was a team man, proud of being The Cap'n and demanding of himself. Add to that the pressure of a New York press clamoring for Knick management to ante up for a new center.

"The press," recalled Reed, "continued to demand that the Knicks trade for an established center. A few writers wrote me off after seeing my early-season performances. The guys on the team, however, remained as encouraging as ever.

"I was holding back a little, maybe. I had to work myself into condition. Although I trained as hard as ever, possibly it wasn't enough. These thoughts kept running through my mind. I kept wondering when I'd be able to answer my critics.

"Most important, the team had not jelled yet. Was it just a matter of time? I thought that to be the case.

"I may not have been the Willis Reed the fans at the Garden remembered before the 1969–70 season. But there were many good moments. The doctors were enthusiastic about my progress and I felt I was contributing more to the success of the team.

"There was still a long way to go. I knew it. I was having trouble with my jump shot, and I had to present some kind of a scoring threat. My maneuverability was not what it should have been, but with the help of DeBusschere and Clyde I was able to get the rebounding job done.

"Eventually, we became a steadier, more balanced club, and the defense began to mesh. It seemed as if each night someone else had the hot hand. There was no one scorer the opposition could double-up on. We could all score and now we were doing it."

Just in time. For the playoffs loomed.

Baltimore was the opponent in the opening round. The Bullets had their ever-reliable rebounder in Unseld, and four men who had scored abundantly during the regular season— Elvin Hayes (21.2 ppg), Phil Chenier (19.7), Archie Clark (18.3) and Mike Riordan (18.1).

Riordan, a member of the 1969–70 Knicks squad, had gone to Baltimore in the trade for Monroe and then developed his skills beyond the expectations of most observers. Indeed, Riordan's NBA career was a testament to that cockeyed mix of individual tenacity and just plain good luck. In 1967, when Bradley signed on with the Knicks, a workout was scheduled so the media could make an assessment. For lack of enough players—the season already had ended—Riordan, a Long Islander planning on studying for a master's degree in history that fall, was invited. He did well enough to be asked to training camp.

He did not make the team, but the Knicks monitored his progress in the Eastern League and eventually brought him up to the big team for the 1968–69 season. Holzman sent him

into games for the so-called *give-one foul*, the intent being to limit the opposition to a one-point free throw opportunity and create a mathematical advantage at the other end of the court where New York would have a chance to score two points on a regulation goal. The situation ended when a team collected six fouls in a quarter; at that juncture every foul automatically was worth two shots.

When Bradley's shift to forward created a need for a backup guard, Riordan got into the game more regularly and startled the public. "The people were surprised that I could make a jump shot or a decent pass," he said. "One fan said to me, 'Hey, I didn't know you could shoot.' Tell you the truth, I didn't care what people thought."

The rise of Riordan attested to the ever-changing fortunes of basketball talent. In New York, he had started out as a bit player. Now he was a star. Age, injuries and who-knew-what-else could alter, and radically, a player's status in the game. Age had diminished Barnett. Injuries had put Reed in a bind. But the careful nurturing of The Cap'n had brought him to the playoffs feeling rested and strong, secure in the conviction that for this second season, as the playoffs were sometimes called, he could muster up enough of the past magic to get the Knicks through.

"The postseason games are always like starting from scratch," said Reed. "What you did during the year doesn't count. You have to be ready to put out 100 percent, all the time, against the toughest opposition there is. We believed we were healthy and ready to go.

"The first game was played at home. It was a tough defensive struggle all the way. Neither team got 100 points, and we won, 95–83. It sounds a heckuva lot easier than it actually was. We were losing for the better part of

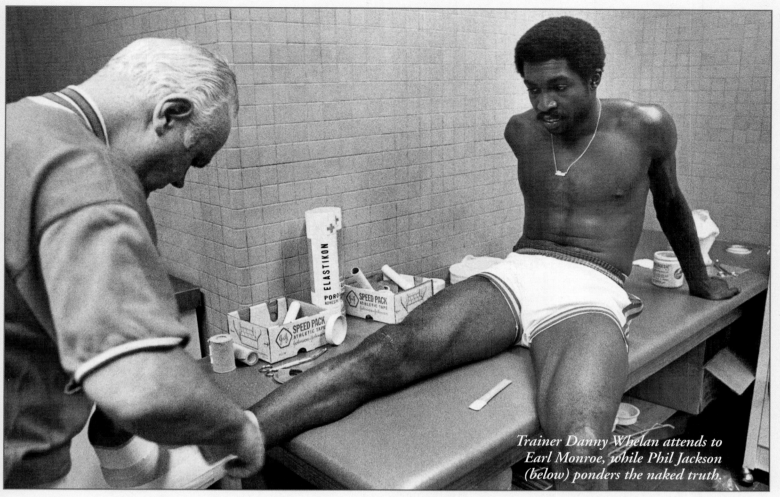

Trainer Danny Whelan attends to Earl Monroe, while Phil Jackson (below) ponders the naked truth.

three quarters and Baltimore unveiled a good running game with Elvin Hayes and Unseld getting their passes out quickly.

"Archie Clark was penetrating well and we were just trying to play our game, set up the good shot . . . work the ball . . . hit the open man . . . play tough defense.

"But the Bullets, not noted for their team play, were within reach . . . We were fortunate that Earl Monroe had the type of game that possibly only he is capable of playing. He looked far better than he had all season."

In game two, also at the Garden, DeBusschere and Reed hit early on jump shots, luring their defenders, Unseld and Hayes, away from the basket. That opened the lane for Frazier and Monroe. And they began flashing down it like there was a perpetual green light. Frazier, who had that gliding stride that made his moves seem effortless, and Monroe, who feinted and juked like a featherweight fighter and then let fly when he had the other man back on his heels—well, those two just blew by Chenier and Clark.

In the Baltimore press, Chenier and

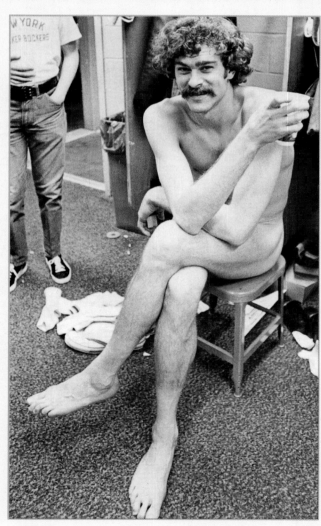

Barnett's unorthodox jumper.

Clark had been posited as the best pair of guards in the pro game. Well, Frazier and Monroe cast a dark shadow over that assertion with the ease by which they negotiated their way to the hoop. Monroe played 36 minutes and had 32 points. Frazier scored 29 points. New York won 123–103 to take a 2–0 lead in the series. Reed contributed 16 points and 10 rebounds in 36 minutes.

"The crowd," Reed recalled, "was yelling for us to pour it on and Red used every player. The fans at the Garden were amazing. Every one of the starting team received a standing ovation. I can't tell you how much that means to a player. It's like someone patting you on the back and saying, 'Job well done.'

"There's no other feeling like it in sports. After all those hours of hard work in the schoolyards and Boys Clubs, after hustling your way through college, and the learning stages of professional basketball, you get this recognition and sign of appreciation. It's unique and I don't think I'd trade it for anything."

The series shifted to Baltimore.

And still the Knicks mistreated the Bullets, beating them 103–96.

"If the Bullets hadn't gotten an exceptionally good performance from the Big E (as Hayes was known), 36 points, we would have run away with it," said Reed. "All of our starters finished in double figures, and we played a tough, never-let-up defense that shut off Baltimore every time it appeared to get close.

In earlier games, Riordan had outscored Bradley. In this game, Bradley had ended up with 23 points and 5 assists, Riordan had 14 points.

"Most of the experienced guys on the club hadn't even thought about a sweep," said Reed. "You just don't do such things against a tough club like Baltimore, but now DeBusschere and I saw it as a distinct possibility. After all, we hadn't thought we'd be three games up so fast."

"I remember (Baltimore coach) Gene Shue saying he thought his team had played well enough to beat the Knicks on most nights. That might have been true, but we had it that night and there

Below, Willis, #19, and Wilt tip it up; and Frazier, #10, launches over West, at right.

was no taking it away."

The Knicks were thinking sweep, but Shue made strategic adjustments to try to avoid that. Where Hayes had been guarding Reed, and Unseld had been guarding DeBusschere, Shue had them switch assignments on the chance that that might make a difference. He did the same thing with the backcourt match-ups, shifting Clark onto Frazier and Chenier onto Monroe.

Whether it was their coach's strategy or just the Bullets' pride, the result was dramatic. Baltimore's defensive pressure

Facing page, a valiant DeBusschere is helped off by Wingo and Bibby after spraining his ankle in waning moments of the championship clincher.

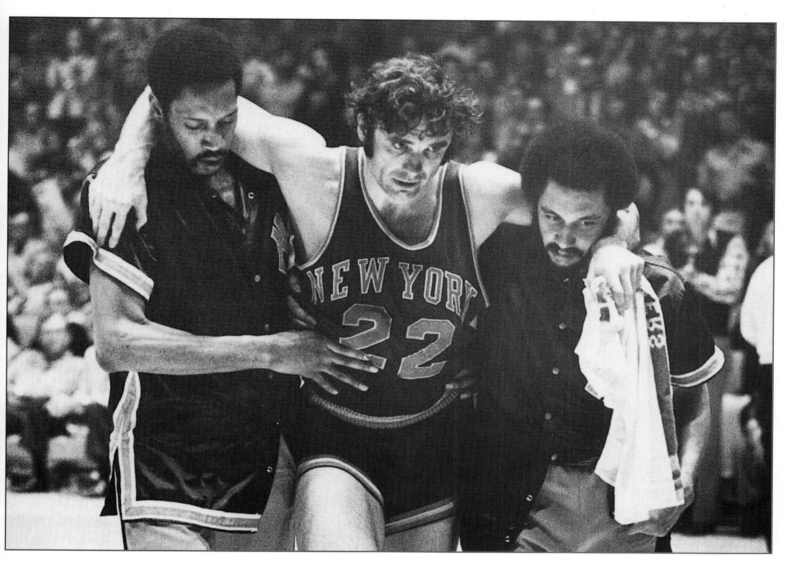

was fierce, forcing Monroe and Frazier into questionable shots and even impeding their progress over the half-court line. For the first time in four games, Baltimore won, 97–89.

Back to New York went the series.

"We received a fine welcome from the New York fans when we stepped out on the Garden floor for the start of the fifth game," recalled Reed. "It wasn't as easy a game as the score might indicate. We won by 10, 109–99, but at the end of three quarters we were up by only a field goal and the lead had changed hands almost more times than one could count.

"I think the major difference between the Bullets and our club was that we were much stronger on the bench and able to wear them down somewhat. This was never more apparent than in this fifth game when Phil Jackson replaced Bradley and scored 13 points while doing a whale of a job on the Big E defensively.

"Throughout the series we had depended on a lot of different players and it paid off. In each game a different guy took the starring role. All in all, I'd say our stingy defense and deep bench gave us the series against Baltimore. Our third- and fourth-quarter performances were encour-

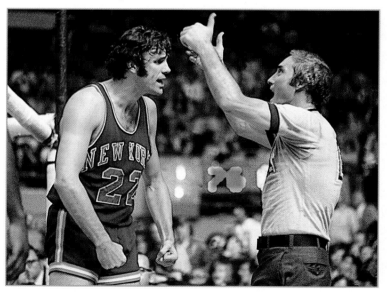

aging, another sign of bench strength.

"Earl again led the scorers. In the final contest, he had 26 points."

The Celtics were next. With the best record in the league, Boston would have the home-court edge for the first game and, if it came to that, the seventh game as well.

The Celtics' running man, the veteran John Havlicek, had 26 points and 11 assists. In 19 minutes, Don Nelson scored 21 points. Cowens had 18 points and 15 rebounds. Chaney had 18 points.

"The Celtics and Tom Heinsohn had a great day," said Reed. "And the Boston fans, some 16,000, were already beginning to compare this team with Red Auerbach's great teams of the past."

"But after game one—a 134–108 demolition job by the Celtics—it appeared

as though Boston's advantage was simply in having superior talent. In Jo Jo White, John Havlicek, Paul Silas, Don Chaney, Don Nelson and the big tough redhead in the pivot, Dave Cowens, the Celtics had a blend of seasoned players and Young Turks. The 6'9" Cowens in particular presented a challenge. He had, as Reed noted, "the moves and speed of a forward. He's got a good shot, can drive and is a bull under the boards."

But the Celtics were not infallible. The Knicks proved that back in Madison Square Garden by trouncing Boston 129–96, a remarkable turnabout that in no small part was aided and abetted by the support provided by Knicks fans. As Reed would recall: "From the moment we stepped on the floor, the whole place erupted in a frenzy of emotion. The

intense rivalry between the two teams is incredible. The fans began their applause with the pregame introductions and the pitch built so high that the crowd noise drowned out the national anthem. It may have been unpatriotic, but it sure was loyal to the team, and we really appreciated the backing after a 26-point loss two nights earlier."

DeBusschere jump-started the home team in game two. He had 2 steals and 7 straight points in the opening minutes.

Cowens was hit with three quick personal fouls by the middle of the second period, and when Heinsohn protected him by sitting him down, New York took advantage, going on a tear that put them 18 points up, 46–28. Say goodnight, Boston.

That evening the Knicks had eight men in double figures, and by the last quarter New York's reserves were getting liberal playing time. When Holzman saw the game was turning into a rout, he spared Reed. The Cap'n played just 17 minutes,

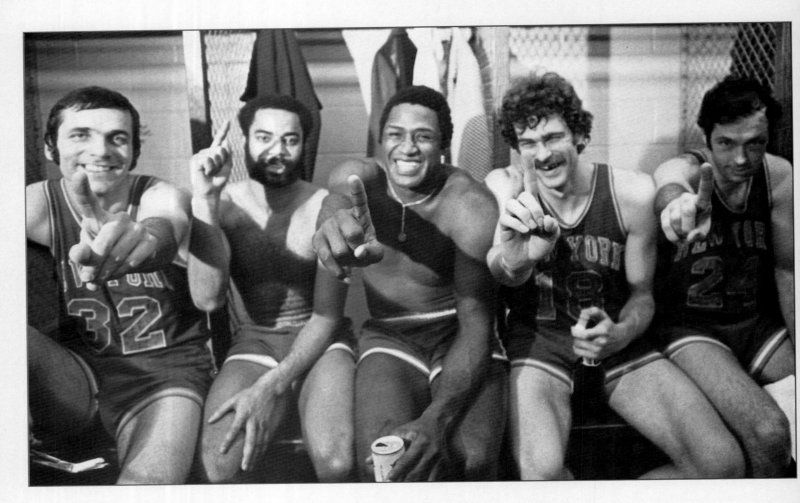

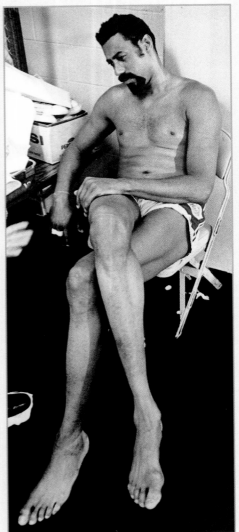

scoring 10 points.

New York beat the Celtics, 98–91, in Boston, in the third, nationally televised, game.

"Both teams came out using the fast break and it seemed like we were going to run ourselves into a state of exhaustion," said Reed. "The pace was tremendous and the lights from the TV cameras didn't help.

"Earl Monroe got a hip pointer in a collision with John Havlicek, and Dave DeBusschere complained of leg cramps and dehydration. But Meminger did a fine job in place of Earl, getting the step on Chaney and moving the ball club with the expertise of a ten-year veteran.

"We were more aggressive on defense, more physical than we had been in the first contest at Boston. We were going for the ball and getting it. The decisive action came in the second period when we outscored the Celts, 29–17. We left the court at halftime breathing fairly easily with a 58–46 lead. Boston came back with Cowens and Havlicek spearheading the attack, but a pair of field goals by Bradley and another by Clyde and we pulled away."

Reed was looking better every game, managing 18 points and 11 rebounds and moving fluidly about the court.

Back and forth the series went. Not unexpectedly it would go to a determining seventh game—in

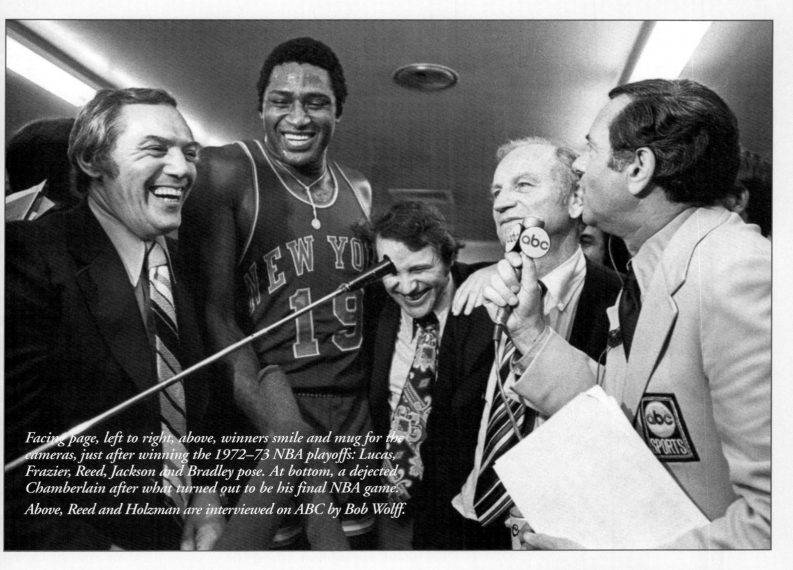

Facing page, left to right, above, winners smile and mug for the cameras, just after winning the 1972–73 NBA playoffs: Lucas, Frazier, Reed, Jackson and Bradley pose. At bottom, a dejected Chamberlain after what turned out to be his final NBA game.

Above, Reed and Holzman are interviewed on ABC by Bob Wolff.

Boston—no easy chore for any team.

In earlier contests, Cowens had proven difficult for either Reed or Lucas to contain. He had the advantage of youth on both men and the legs to run without fatiguing. Holzman's strategic adjustment was to add DeBusschere to the mix that would match up against Cowens: keep fresh bodies on him and work hard to keep the ball out of his hands.

DEE-fense was what got the job done against Boston. Not only did the gang defense on Cowens diminish his effectiveness, but Holzman brought Meminger in off the bench to harass White. The Celtic game withered from the white-heat pressure New York applied. Not even Havlicek, playing with torn shoulder muscles, could save the day. New York won easily, 94–78, clinching the series.

"Nobody can really say what would have been the result of the Boston series had Havlicek been able to go all out for seven games," said Reed. "I think our ball club would have won anyway.

"In the final contest, it was our tough, aggressive defense combined with good movement on offense which knocked the Celts out of the box. "

New York would now meet the best in the West, the Los Angeles Lakers, in the championship finals.

The strategy against the Lakers was to run the ball before Chamberlain could set himself on defense. At 36, Wilt hadn't the legs to play a fast-paced game, but let him get set up in the middle as a kind of one-man zone—his teammates would switch when necessary so he could stay in the hole—then the advantage was the Lakers'.

Reed committed to getting up and down the court as quickly as his legs could manage.

"With luck," he said, "they'd get the ball to me. If Wilt was there I'd give off to either Bradley or DeBusschere trailing and

121

1972 PLAYOFFS

KNICKS vs. LAKERS
$1.00

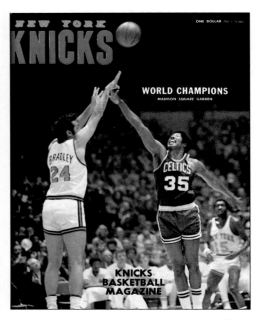

NEW YORK KNICKS
ONE DOLLAR

WORLD CHAMPIONS
MADISON SQUARE GARDEN

BRADLEY 24
CELTICS 35

KNICKS BASKETBALL MAGAZINE

KNICKS

NEW YORK 18

MADISON SQUARE GARDEN
$1.25

New York 1973-74 PRESS-TELEVISION & RADIO

KNICKS

MEDIA PASS

New York Knickerbockers

Madison Sq. Garden   NOT-TRANSFERABLE   163

they would have the open shot. If Wilt wasn't on me I'd just go right in toward the hoop. The big thing was to create a situation where there was going to be a free shot."

It was a fine notion, only it didn't work in the opening game.

Los Angeles won on its home court, 115–112.

But New York evened the series in the next game in Los Angeles as Bradley went on a scoring binge, leading the team with 26 points in a 99–95 victory. At one point in the game, when Laker coach Bill Sharman tried to create a mismatch for Bradley by bringing in 7' Mel Counts, Holzman shifted Bradley to, of all people, Chamberlain. Holzman's thinking was that at this point in his career, Chamberlain was not likely to take the ball to the hoop. He was right. Wilt would snare twenty rebounds, but he took only four shots and wound up with five points. Bradley survived on defense, and prospered at the other end of the floor.

Twice more the Knicks won in New York to lead the series three games to one as Reed was getting cranked up, reaching his peak, it seemed, at this opportune moment: 21 points in game three and 21 again in game four.

Reed would have 18 points in the fifth and final game of the series. DeBusschere would sprain his ankle late in the game and have to be helped off the floor. But by then the Knicks had the momentum, and minutes later they would race into each other's arms and savor congratulatory embraces as NBA champions. New York, 102; Los Angeles, 93.

For championship series MVP Reed, written off as old news earlier in the year, it was a sweet moment. Once again, he had come through in the money games. The Cap'n had redeemed his title. The Knicks were top of the heap. Again.

Bradley would later write of the 1972–73 season: "The euphoria lasted during a quiet postgame meal with friends in Los Angeles, through a marvelous night until

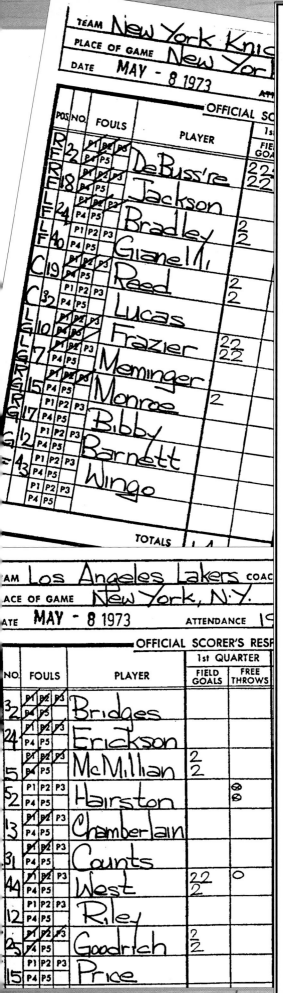

POS	NO.	FOULS				PLAYER	1st FIELD GOA
R	22	P1	P2	P3 P4 P5		DeBuss're	22 22
R	18	P1	P2 P3 P4 P5			Jackson	
L	24	P1	P2 P4 P5			Bradley	2 2
F	40	P1 P4	P2 P5			Gianelli	
C	19	P1 P4	P2 P5			Reed	2 2
C	32	P1 P4	P2 P5			Lucas	
L	10	P1 P4	P2 P5			Frazier	22 22
L	7	P1 P4	P2 P5			Meminger	
R	15	P1 P4	P2 P5			Monroe	2
G	17	P1	P2 P3 P4 P5			Bibby	
G	12	P1	P2 P3 P4 P5			Barnett	
F	43	P1	P2 P3 P4 P5			Wingo	
		P1	P2 P3 P4 P5				

TOTALS

NO.	FOULS			PLAYER	1st QUARTER FIELD GOALS	FREE THROWS
32	P1 P4	P2 P5	P3	Bridges		
24	P1 P4	P2 P5	P3	Erickson		
5	P1 P4	P2 P5	P3	McMillian	2 2	
52	P1 P4	P2 P5	P3	Hairston		⊗ ⊗
13	P1 P4	P2 P5	P3	Chamberlain		
31	P1 P4	P2 P5	P3	Counts		
44	P1 P4	P2 P5	P3	West	22 2	0
12	P1 P4	P2 P5	P3	Riley		
25	P1 P4	P2 P5	P3	Goodrich	2 2	
15	P1 P4	P2 P5	P3	Price		

Shutterbug Phil Jackson.

ACTION JACKSON

It is not exactly late-breaking news that most NBA pros come from impoverished backgrounds.

The 1972–73 Knicks were unusual in that two of their players did not. They had Bradley the banker's son and Phil (Action) Jackson, son of a fundamentalist preacher.

As NBA types go, Jackson was an improbable sort. In those days, he had interests that ran from mysticism to music to McGovern (he was co-chairman of Athletes For). And though he may be the only NBA player ever to have inquired if the league's major medical plan covered visits to the psychiatric couch (it did not), he appeared in no great need of it. But by his own admission, he came from a strange background.

Jackson grew up first in Montana and then in Williston, North Dakota, where his father, the Reverend Charles Jackson, served the Assembly of God, a Pentecostal faith.

"It was a fundamentalist type of belief," Jackson said. "There was no smoking, drinking, dancing or movies. TV was allowed but we didn't have one. The only records were religious and classical and Christmas music. The only sectarian magazine in the home was *Reader's Digest.*

"I can remember waking up one night when I was 11 and discovering no one was home. I panicked. Thought this was it. The Second Coming. And I'd missed out. I ran from room to room turning on lights, but nobody was there. I thought they'd all left, all gone to heaven."

morning, and through the plane ride back to New York. By the following day it too was over.

"I wonder if fans know that all the pressure, work and excitement makes for only 24 hours of joy. . . . If there is any broader social meaning to the championship, it is not that it diverts you from unpleasantness or inspires you to great achievements, but rather that it gives a glimpse of a better world—a world unattainable. A team championship exposes the limits of self-reliance, selfishness, and irresponsibility. One man alone can't make it happen: in fact, the contrary is true: a single man can prevent it from happening. The success of the group assures the success of the individual, but not the other way around. Yet the team is an inept model, for even as people marvel at the unselfishness and skill involved, they disagree on how it is achieved and who is the most instrumental. The human closeness of a basketball team cannot be reconstructed on a large scale. Groups in the real world cannot be like a championship team and ultimately the model of sport is dissatisfying for everyone but the participants.

"In the locker room after our second championship, as I looked around at my teammates I thought of how I liked something about each of them. They were good people, and from our sharing these unique moments they would be forever different from other people.

"I saw our reflection in the lives of nomadic Indian tribes on the Plains, making the group adjustments necessary to exist in a constantly changing environment, and also in the lives of Western gunslingers moving on from challenge to challenge with the knowledge that one day somebody would be faster and surer. Our friendship was based on deeds accomplished together. It even seemed at times like that night to seal the split between the black and white races. 'There warn't no home like a raft, after all,' says Huck Finn. 'You feel mighty free and easy and comfortable on a raft.' Being on a championship team is like being on that raft, floating down the Mississippi. Neither one can last forever."

✱ *Original program artwork (top) by George Kalinsky used all the names of Knicks players through the 1972–73 season.*

✱ *1972–73 World Champions. Left to right, standing: Bill Bradley, Phil Jackson, John Gianelli, Dave DeBusschere, Willis Reed, Jerry Lucas, Tom Riker, Dean Meminger, trainer Danny Whelan. Sitting: Henry Bibby, Walt Frazier, Ned Irish, Irving Mitchell Felt, Red Holzman, Earl Monroe, Dick Barnett.*

Willis Reed and Red Holzman accept 1973 championship trophy from NBA commissioner Walter Kennedy.

HOLZMAN THE PLAYER

By the seventies, Red Holzman had established his reputation as a championship coach.

Not as widely known was his background as a player.

Holzman, a 5' 10" guard, played six seasons in the NBA, five of them with the Rochester Royals and a final year with Milwaukee in 1953–54. He averaged 6.1 ppg and was known, not surprisingly, as a tenacious defender.

Holzman had come to the National Basketball League for the Royals back in 1945–46, after Rochester team owner Lester Harrison recruited Fuzzy Levane, a former star at St. John's. Harrison wanted Levane not only because he was a skilled player but also because Harrison thought Levane was Jewish. With a large and affluent Jewish community in Rochester, Harrison wanted a player with whom they could identify.

Trouble was Levane was not Jewish. "But," he said, "I was good friends with Red and with Dutch Garfinkel, who were Jewish, and I recommended both of them to Harrison, who brought them into Rochester."

FALL FROM GLORY

The thrill of victory soon turned to the regularity of defeat, as the Knicks franchise fell into decline.

Things had changed. The NBA was big business now. And since August 1977, Madison Square Garden Corporation had been a wholly owned subsidiary of Gulf + Western, a multinational conglomerate that also included Paramount Pictures Corporation, the Simon & Schuster publishing house and a Canadian theater chain.

"The arena," in the words of a Gulf + Western brochure, "is only one element of MSG's operation. The corporation also owns the New York Knicks professional basketball team, the New York Rangers hockey team, the Washington Diplomats soccer team and has interests in the International Holiday on Ice and thoroughbred and harness racing." Leisure Time Group revenues for fiscal 1978 were $302 million, of which $157 million were for "sports, racing and entertainment," the catch words for the Garden Corporation's share of the revenues.

At the time, the Garden Corporation's largest profitmakers were Roosevelt Raceway, a harness track in Westbury, N.Y.; Arlington Park, a Thoroughbred track just outside Chicago, and International Holiday on Ice. In addition, the Garden had taken to expanding its revenue base by broadening the operations of the building's theatrical productions department and by adding touring shows like "Bugs Bunny in Space" as well as by acquiring Market Concepts Inc., which developed programs and presentations for sales forces.

Managers at the Garden, like at other Gulf+Western holdings, were required to meet prior to each fiscal year with repre-

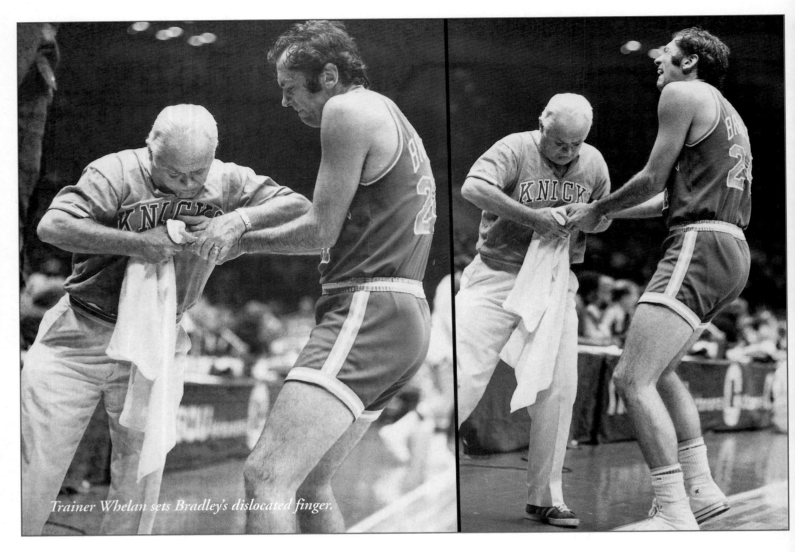

Trainer Whelan sets Bradley's dislocated finger.

sentatives of the parent company at a session where business plans were formulated. After that, prescribed financial forms—and sometimes subjective analyses—were forwarded to G+W's headquarters each month.

So the days of the $4,000 BAA contract offer were long past. The sports world was suddenly knee-deep in an era of coast-to-coast expansion and proliferating leagues, of players' agents and multimillion-dollar contracts, of lucrative connections to television and to conglomerates exactly like Gulf+Western. And in January 1978 the man behind the Knicks was David Abraham (Sonny) Werblin, the president of Madison Square Garden Corporation.

Werblin had been behind the scenes before. In the 1950s, he had been president of MCA-TV, a talent agency with clients like Jack Benny, George Burns, Martin and Lewis, Ed Sullivan, Jackie Gleason and Liberace. By the sixties he was legitimizing the New York Jets, by

signing quarterback Joe Namath to a three-year contract reportedly worth $411,000, unheard of money back then. The Jets that Werblin assembled, Namath included, won the Super Bowl in January 1969.

By June 1971, Werblin had become chairman of the New Jersey Sports and Exposition Authority, charged with converting 588 acres of swampland into a $342 million sports complex, and with bringing New Jersey its first established major-league sports team. When he left, in December 1977, the Meadowlands—as the sports complex is known—had a one-mile racetrack seating 40,000 fans and a 76,500-seat stadium, the permanent home for the New York Giants, which was also used by the Cosmos soccer team.

As a can-do kind of executive, Werblin was regarded as just the kind of man who could reverse the Knicks' skid toward the bottom of the Atlantic Division. He had his work cut out for him.

In 1973–74, the season following New York's second championship, the Knicks, finishing second in the Atlantic Division, were eliminated in five games in the Eastern Conference finals by Boston, which would go on to win the league title.

The Knicks were hurt by injuries to Reed, who played only nineteen games, and to Monroe, who played forty-one games. What injury didn't damage, the aging process did: Lucas and Barnett were shadows of their vintage selves, in what would be their final season in the NBA. DeBusschere, who had a strong season—18.1 points per game and 767 rebounds—also retired.

What's more, there was no new blood to reinvigorate the team. Meminger was a solid backcourt man but hardly the equivalent of Monroe. Henry Bibby, John Gianelli, Harthorne Wingo, Mel Davis and Tom Riker were young players with varying degrees of skill, none of whom a team would build its future around.

A year later, in 1974–75, New York slipped under .500 for the regular season, winning 40 games and losing 42, and was eliminated in the first round of the playoffs by Houston. Once again, the Knicks faced a future without a big man, as Reed had decided enough was enough and retired. To try to compensate for the loss of Reed, New York acquired 6' 10" Neal Walk from New Orleans late in the year. Walk had had big seasons at Phoenix, averaging 20.2 ppg in 1972–73, but he proved a disappointment in New York, scoring only 3.9 ppg in 30 games.

By the time Werblin came aboard, the Knicks were on a downward spiral that would require bold and dramatic moves to repair. The trouble was that neither Werblin nor the Knicks' team president, Michael Burke, was a career basketball man. Werblin's success through the years had been built on exploiting

big-name talent—be it Jack Benny or Joe Namath. That approach had worked at MCA and had worked with the Jets. It had even worked at the Garden with the Rangers.

For the Rangers, Werblin brought in a new coach–general manager, Fred Shero (at a price of $1 million for five years), and two Swedish stars from the rival World Hockey Association, Ulf Nilsson and Anders Hedberg (at $650,000 apiece each year for two years). The acquisitions made a difference as the Rangers charged into the finals of the Stanley Cup in 1979.

But the big-name tack was no guarantee in basketball. For a basketball team is built on the chemistry of the players involved, on their ability to co-exist and work for the good of the team. Corny as the saying is: there is no "I" in the word "team." Werblin had trouble, it turned out, with such nuances.

The big men New York ended up with, Bob McAdoo and Spencer Haywood, would turn out to be the sort of players that lacked the big picture. Each was used to being the focus of the offense on their previous teams.

McAdoo had done it at Buffalo, where he enjoyed three seasons during which he'd averaged 30 points or better while leading the league in scoring each year.

Similarly, Haywood had been a focal point of the offense in his one season in the ABA with Denver and in five seasons with Seattle. He had never averaged less than 20 points during those years.

Werblin's acquisition of Marvin Webster (at $3 million) was another case of more being less. At Seattle, the 7'1" Webster was a factor because he was surrounded by selfless players who blended Marvin's talents into their setup. But in the gimme–gimme Knicks game, Webster, known as "The Human Eraser" for his shot blocking, did not fit, underscoring the subtlety of putting together a *team* as

opposed to a gaggle of name players.

As the team descended in the standings, Knicks fans voiced their displeasure, booing the players and letting the executives in charge know they weren't happy.

Indeed, Asofsky had been so galled by the team's fall from grace that at halftime of one game he accosted the silver-haired, sartorially impeccable Burke as he strolled by after being interviewed on TV. Asofsky asked Burke: "What gives with the Knicks?"

To appease Asofsky, Burke handed over the gift he'd received for being the halftime TV guest—a pair of walkie-talkies. Asofsky gave the walkie-talkies to his twin nephews, who wrote their Uncle Stanley a note of thanks, ending by saying that, though the thought was appreciated, the walkie-talkies didn't work. For Asofsky, it was perfect—a neat correlative of the Knicks: a team that didn't work either.

"I'd love to give Werblin a basketball IQ test," Asofsky told one interviewer, who was plumbing the mood of Knicks fans. "If his life depended on passing it, he'd be a cadaver every day of the week."

For Asofsky, it was not just the losing that bothered him. It was the so-what attitude of the team.

It saddened Asofsky to see Reed—once the symbol of Knick greatness and by 1977–78 the coach of New York—become a victim of the unholy mess. And it galled him to see McAdoo and Haywood come out of the team dressing room at halftime and make a beeline for the statistic sheet that is generated for the media.

"At halftime," said Asofsky, "there was more concern about that statistics sheet than the game," he said. "Who looks at the stat sheet except the coach, who is supposed to? Me, I'd rather have a hungry $150,000 ballplayer than one who doesn't give a damn at $300,000."

FAREWELL, DOLLAR BILL.

T here was a certain irony that the very team concept that Bill Bradley held dear, with its emphasis on sacrifice and selflessness, was being torn asunder in his final years with the ball club.

What could he have thought watching the McAdoos and Haywoods gun it up for glory, with little apparent concern for what they might do to help the team?

It was a far cry from the harmonious workings that the earlier Holzman teams Bradley had been with had shown—those squads with Reed, DeBusschere, Barnett and Frazier. Those teams were now the standard against which Knicks fans measured excellence and repudiated the teams of the late seventies.

Not only did the Knicks of Bradley's twilight years fail to move the ball or look for the open man, but they treated defense with the sort of indifference not seen since Walter Bellamy's laissez faire approach. From the league's most tenacious defenders, the Knicks were by 1976–77, Bradley's last season, among

Bradley, above, played longer than he anticipated in the NBA, and most of his ten seasons were under coach Red Holzman. Below and on the adjoining page Dollar Bill is seen with teammates from his final years with the team. Note the "gag" photo of the 1974–75 team, below.

the worst, statistically, in the NBA. Neither McAdoo nor Haywood evinced as much interest in checking a man as they did in checking the box score for their stats. And as went the team's big guns, so went the Knicks.

In 1976–77, New York would yield 108.6 points a game to the opposition. In a league that now included twenty-two teams after the ABA merger, only Buffalo, Detroit, Milwaukee and San Antonio permitted foes more points per game.

While it was tempting to put such behavior to the times—players simply didn't care anymore, money talked and teamwork walked—the truth was that it came down to specific cases. By 1976–77 the Knicks were the antithesis of what Bradley had known during the glory years in New York. The atmosphere wasthe same as it had been before Holzman arrived in the late sixties, every man for himself.

In Bradley's final season, the team that would win the NBA title, the Portland Trail Blazers, seemed practically a clone of the 1969–70 Knicks in their smart ball movement and selfless attitude. Bill Walton, Lionel Hollins, Dave Twardzik, Maurice Lucas, Bob Gross—these men played the game with a purist's regard for the essential truth as Bradley knew it: Work together and the result will be better than you can imagine.

The 1975-76 Knicks, from left to right, front row: Butch Beard, Jim Barnett, Clyde Frazier, Red Holzman, Earl Monroe, Bill Bradley, Eugene Short; back row: Dick Barnett, Spencer Haywood, Phil Jackson, Neal Walk, John Gianelli, Harthorne Wingo, Mel Davis, trainer Danny Whelan.

Spencer Haywood

Toby Knight

The words Bradley had written a few years before in his book, *Life on the Run*, took on an eerie ring: "The success of the group assures the success of the individual, but not the other way around." Could he have imagined back then that he would see up close and personal the dark side of that precept? Likely not.

The 1976–77 season marked the end of an era. Reed, Barnett and DeBusschere had previously retired, Frazier would be traded to Cleveland for the 1977–78 season (and would receive a tumultuous ovation the first time he came to the Garden as a Cavalier) and now Bradley was moving on.

Among the Knicks Bradley had sometimes been enigmatic, sometimes accessible. But in his own way, he had been one of the boys. Teammates would kid him about his unstylish clothes and gave him as full a share of the verbal barbs they regularly traded as anybody else. One time, Nate Bowman had noticed Bradley wearing a pair of socks with a hole in them, and he let Dollar Bill know he was having a hosiery emergency, *wink wink*. Bradley asked that Bowman keep that bit of news to himself and thereby spare him from the merciless needling that was bound to follow, which Bowman, with the utmost sincerity, swore he would do. Of course, Nate, as instigator of much of the locker room hi-jinks, turned around and proceeded to issue a fashion update on Bradley's socks to his teammates.

The paradox of Bradley was that his own emotional restraint limited the intimacy that he could envision in an ideal sense. Introspection oppressed spontaneity

Jim Cleamons

135

for him, so that when he tried to authenticate himself for teammates in excursions that some Knicks affectionately referred to as "binges," he might come off wooden or vague.

Willis Reed: Bradley tells Hosket, says, "Be a man, pull my shirt pocket off." Hosket grabs his shirt and tries to pull his pocket off, and ripped the whole shirt, y'know, like the shirt came right across and made a big L.

Q: What did Bradley want him to rip the pocket off for?

Reed: I don't know. You know how Bradley is . . . he's so funny.

Q: What prompted him to do that?

Reed: I don't know, you know how Dollar . . . he's . . . he do those kind of things sometimes.

Jackson recalled another instance in Los Angeles: "He came in to get his tickets, signed his tickets out to somebody and was joking and, with kind of reckless abandon, throwing up quick shots and jumping in the locker room pretending like he was shooting baskets. Without a ball. He threw a hook shot and ran right into the wall and just knocked himself kind of silly. Once in a while he goes on these little crazy sprees. That's what the guys react to, like, this isn't the same guy once he's got his street clothes on."

While Bradley had worried back in 1967 whether playing ball for a living might be construed as taking the low road—that fear of being remembered as old satin shorts Bradley—he had lingered in satin shorts far longer than he had expected. "I realized," he said, recently, "that I loved the game far more than I thought and wanted to continue. I got tremendous satisfaction from playing. We played as a team. We were top of the league. They were a great group of people. And I was paid well those years. After my first four-year contract ran out, I'd play year by year, six one-year contracts. As it got toward the end, the team changed. There was not the same mesh of personalities. Which tipped it in favor of my leaving for politics."

And for that eventuality, he had

been, so to speak, in training even as he was running his perpetual patterns to get free for his shot during ten NBA seasons. In his first year with the Knicks, Bradley had been involved in street academies in Harlem that would focus young people there on objectives that could transform their lives, such as education and job train-ing. The summer before the 1969–70 season, Bradley had worked in Washington, D.C., as a volunteer for the Office of the Director of Poverty. So it went dur-ing a decade in which Bradley would average 12.4 ppg and offer bas-ketball wit that would fit nicely with the team on which he had landed. He would continue to find ways to broaden his experience, be it at the library in an NBA town or by working for Congressman Allard Lowenstein or on the Oglala Sioux Indian reservation in Pine Ridge, South Dakota, where, with Phil Jackson and Willis Reed, he would run a basketball clinic while absorbing, as always, the conditions of another part of his country.

"I'd use the off-seasons to travel around," he said. "All over the world. I remember I once went to Asia and later a guy on the board of Madison Square Garden, an admiral, spoke to me about being a secret agent there. I said, 'Gee, a six foot five Caucasian being a secret agent in Asia.' It gave me a real clue about our intelligence agencies."

He kept busy on the road with constructive programs that were a legacy for him, his moth-er once quoted as saying, "I wanted a Christian upright citizen, and I thought the best way to begin was by promoting things that would interest a little boy." In his youth Bradley had taken instruction in golf, tennis, swimming, piano, French, trumpet and danc-ing, and gained a feeling for the use of time that did not cease as a pro athlete.

"The problem," he would say during his

New York KNICKS

1978
PLAYOFFS
MADISON SQUARE GARDEN

playing days, "is the multiple fracture of an athlete's day. It gets a bit irritating, just because I think I play better when I do other things. On days I've had eleven hours' sleep, taken the proper number of limbering steps, eaten the right food, I don't think there's an *obvious* improvement. Some of the best games, I've had no sleep, five appoint-ments, worked in an office all day, walked around the city too much.

"What I'm trying to do is establish a certain discipline in other areas of my life, because that's always been there, provided by school. So I look at time as time to be used in that respect. Depending on where you are, there is always time to do something enjoyable and/or productive and, at times, that which is productive is enjoyable. Obviously you can't read economic theory on a plane or write poetry in first class. You become self-conscious, there are a lot of people looking. But you can read novels or reports, or when you're alone, you can do other stuff that requires more time and thought."

As the team traveled from city to city, invariably Bradley would be reading. His liter-ary tastes were diverse. In a trip he might go through *The Iceman Cometh* (O'Neill), *God Bless You, Mr. Rosewater* (Vonnegut), *Exile and Kingdom* (Camus), an anthology of poetry, periodicals and newspapers.

In retrospect, it was probably just as well that Bradley retired when he did. For it spared him the bad time that Reed, who succeeded Holzman as coach, endured. Reed surely deserved better from the players, and from the top brass at the Garden.

The failure of the Knicks did not fit with the Werblin image, so Sonny did what cagey moguls do. He set about to put as much dis-tance between an embarrassment and himself as he could. He did it with a scenario meant to

make Willis Reed the fall guy. To the press, Werblin repeatedly stated that Reed was his coach and that his only problem with Willis was his habit of putting blame on management when things went wrong on the court— the we-they syndrome.

In fact, though, there were indications that Werblin wanted a different coach: sly remarks about Reed to the press, and contact with potential replacements. But Reed was a mythic Knick, and in his first season as coach, 1977–78, Willis had taken the team

into the playoffs. So Werblin wanted his firing of Reed to *appear* proper.

On November 7, 1978, Werblin read a newspaper story in which Reed, as Sonny interpreted it, had given him an ultimatum for a vote of confidence. Harvey Araton, who wrote the story for *The New York Post*, phoned Werblin late that day and asked for his reaction. Werblin groused about Reed's demand for a vote of confidence.

"I said, 'Wait a minute,' Araton recalled. "'It wasn't a *demand* for a vote of confi-

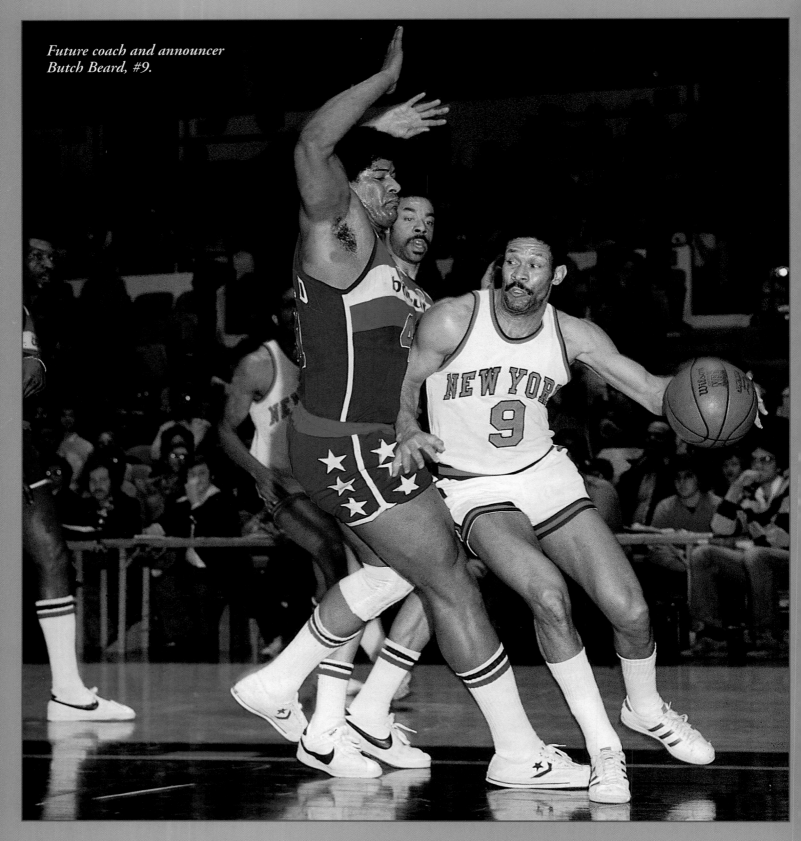

dence.' He said, 'What do you mean?' I said, 'Well, it wasn't like he said they'd better give me a vote of confidence.' What he was saying—and I explained this to Werblin—was: I need a vote of confidence because *they*—the players—think I'm going to be fired. He was saying that it's hard for any coach to have control of the team when the players think he's going to go. And with the rumors constantly swirling—it's hard to concentrate on basketball."

By the end of the week, Werblin had fired Reed, replacing him with Holzman. At the news conference announcing the change, Werblin said that Reed had given

him an "ultimatum" for a vote of confidence, and that he wouldn't be dictated to.

No matter. The Knicks continued their slide, finishing near the bottom of the Atlantic Division regularly toward the end of the decade. The grand experiment in Big-Name Talent was over: McAdoo was sent to Boston for three first-round draft picks in 1979. Haywood landed in New Orleans.

The way in which the McAdoo trade went down is the stuff of Knick legend.

On February 10, 1979, the Knicks played the Celtics at the Garden. Werblin was sitting in the stands with Celtic owner John Y. Brown and his wife, Miss America–turned–sportscaster Phyllis George. During the first half, Mrs. Brown waxed enthusiastic about how impressed she was with McAdoo's ballplaying ability, and how much her husband's team needed someone like him. John Y. was not one to disappoint his wife. At halftime up in Suite 200, or during a postgame stop at a midtown bistro, Werblin, Brown and George agreed on the trade. It was announced two days later. McAdoo was a Celtic.

1977–78 Knicks: Left to right, front: Jim Cleamons, Ray Williams, Bob Hopkins, Willis Reed, Dick McGuire, Earl Monroe, Butch Beard. Back: Jim McMillian, Lonnie Shelton, Phil Jackson, Bob McAdoo, Spencer Haywood, Glen Gondrezick, Toby Knight, trainer Danny Whelan.

The Knicks wound up with three first-rounders, who would turn out to be Bill Cartwright, Larry Demic and Sly Williams. Celtic president Red Auerbach, no fan of Brown, had been hoarding and stockpiling the picks over the years, expecting a talent bonanza in the 1979 draft. Now, in a single move that he wasn't even consulted on, they were gone. Just like that. Poof.

Auerbach was so incensed that he seriously considered Werblin's later offer to come down and run the Knicks. Red never did leave Boston, but one can only imagine the course of Knicks history had he said yes.

Another Knick, DeBusschere, would also be sullied when he was brought aboard the Knicks' sinking ship to set it right. Named the team's GM in 1982 he would quickly find himself the object of a tabloid press that derided him for lacking the hustle he had shown as a player. The attacks were personal and unrelenting. As the Knicks failed to revive, DeBusschere was fired in 1986, to the transparent glee of that part of the working press that had found his work less than satisfactory.

After the departure of McAdoo and Haywood, the Knicks were not without talent. But their best players hadn't the maturity that the championship-era Knicks possessed. Take Ray Williams. On physical skills, he was the equal of any backcourt man in the league. In 1978–79 the 6'3" Williams averaged 17.3 ppg and a year later 20.9 ppg. But over the years Williams would

142

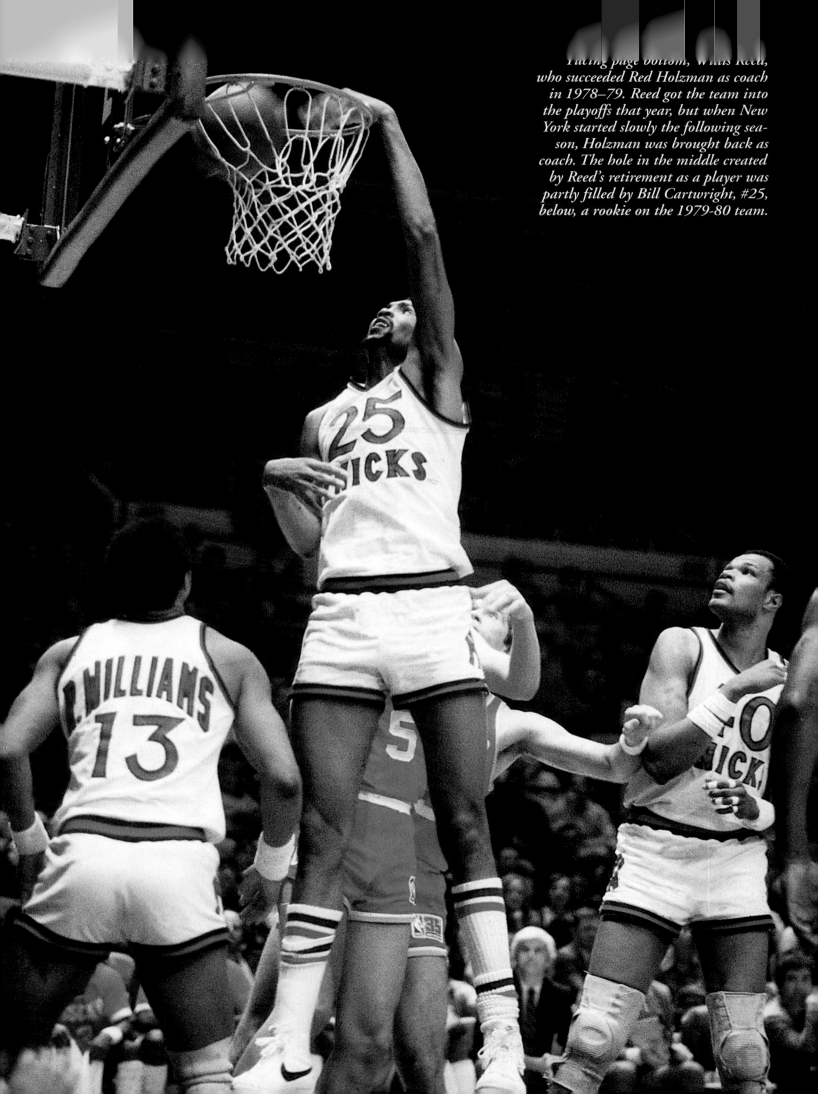

Ray Williams, #13.

play with a defective compass. For every crowd-pleasing, hang-glider drive shot, there were passes and shots that sometimes reflected bad judgment.

The other guard, 6'5" Micheal (Sugar) Ray Richardson, had superior natural talent, too—good outside shot, strong, often acrobatic drives to the basket. But he suffered, as Williams did, from an erratic streak that was most pronounced at crunch time, when the outcomes of games are decided.

Richardson's lack of discipline eventually extended to his personal life. He developed a drug habit that led to his supension from the NBA and his playing the final years of his career in Europe.

It was a decade that began with the Knicks racing off the court as NBA champions. When it ended, they weren't

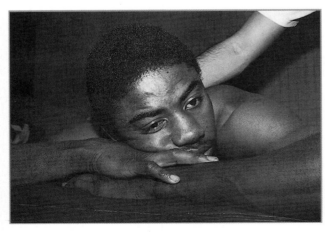

Micheal Ray Richardson, #20, below and opposite below.

Red's 500th NBA Win,
November 20, 1979

even a playoff team, with back-to-back seasons that resulted in thirty-one and thirty-nine wins.

New York's basketball fandom was not amused. From twenty-six sellouts in 1969–70 alone, the Garden produced just thirteen full houses over a three-year span from 1978–79 through 1980–81.

The Knicks didn't even look like the Knicks anymore. In 1979, Werblin and Burke saw fit to abandon the team's famous white, orange and royal blue uniforms in favor of a garish outfit of white, maroon and dark blue, which featured a block "KNICKS" on the front and represented about as big a break from

tradition as you could imagine.

In fact, everything around the Knicks, from the uniforms to the ball boys' suits, took on a maroon and dark blue hue. The official explanation was that the colors were changed in honor of the Garden's 100th Anniversary in 1979. The *un*official explanation was that maroon and dark blue just happened to be the colors of Burke's alma mater, the University of Pennsylvania.

By 1983, the club happily returned to orange and blue. And, just as happily, the switch coincided with another dramatic upturn in the club's fortunes, led by a scoring machine named Bernard and a fierce coach named Hubie.

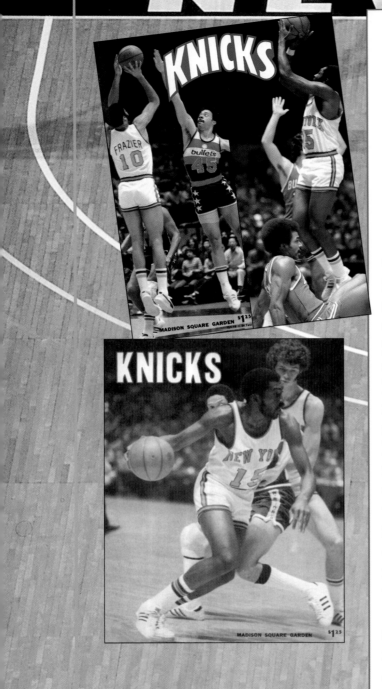

BRADLEY ON THE ATHLETE'S WORLD

"Athletes live in a very insulated sort of world. For one thing, you have to be very careful of the physical things you do. If you are a so-called conscientious athlete, you make sure of sleep and food, and do things that restrict your personal freedom. That limits your physical adventure, and your awareness. At Princeton, I would never take chances with myself. It was one of the things I was consciously glad about when I finished college basketball and went to Oxford. Now I didn't have to worry about sprained ankles. I could take a chance with drinking water. If I got a disease, who cares? The only person who cares is me. So I'd take a chance. At Oxford, I played soccer, wrestled and wasn't hesitant about climbing the Dolomites in Italy or trudging through the woods.

"On another level, you become very self-conscious, which leads to introversion, or narcissism–egotism, both of which militate against a kind of quiet experimentation or militate against something outside of yourself which you have to try to embrace or understand. Some of these people grow up in situations where everything focuses on them and how they perform. As a result they are not interested in other things, because they become so pleased with themselves."

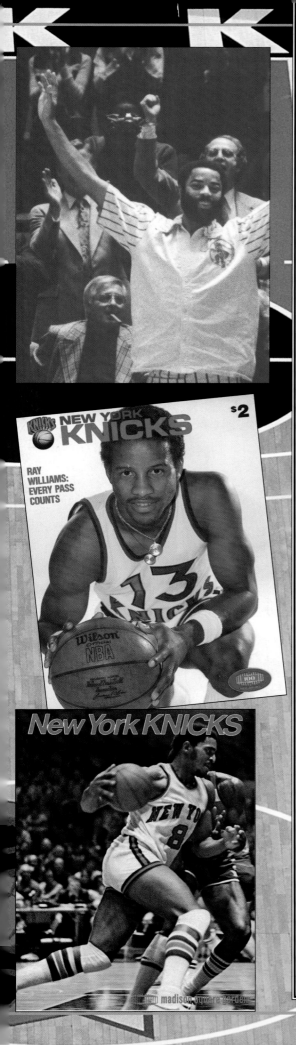

THE RETURN OF CLYDE

Marv Albert on the night Walt Frazier came to the Garden as a Cleveland Cavalier on October 25, 1977: "Clyde was nervous about how the crowd would react to him. After all, remember, New York fans are about as sentimental as traffic cops. These are the same fans who booed their legendary hero Willis Reed when he coached the Knicks to, apparently, not enough wins.

"When the night came and Frazier's name was announced, the sell-out crowd gave him a standing ovation. Frazier bowed his head. But then a funny thing happened. The ovation wouldn't die. It kept getting louder and more raucous. Suddenly, the wave of emotion seemed to hit Frazier flush in the face. He raised his head, then his hands, then raised them high and exultant. Then he went out and had a sensational game, hitting a jumper to win it in overtime, raising those same hands, soaking up the feeling."

The night ended as sweetly for Clyde, with his spearheading a Cavaliers overtime victory, 117–112.

THE EIGHTIES

As the Knicks were sinking to last place in the Atlantic Division in 1981–82, *The New York Sunday News Magazine* captured the frustration of Knicks fans through a profile on Asofsky.

"Never mind the ticket discounts and marketing gimmicks management was to try to fill the thousands of seats that would go empty every time the Knicks played. When a man like Asofsky gets to looking dyspeptic merely from being a spectator, you can mark down with a chisel on stone that there's trouble on Thirty-third Street. Or as Asofsky himself—slinking into his (baseline) seat—muttered: 'How much longer, Lord. How much longer can it be this rotten?'"

Relief, it turned out, was not long in coming. Under new coach Hubie Brown New York enjoyed its best back-to-back years (44–38 in 1982–83 and 47–35 in 1983–84) in a decade—not to mention playoff appearances that saw the Knicks reach the second round both years.

Brown came to New York with a reputation for ingenuity at the X's and O's of the game...and for driving his players to overachieve. He did it with a style that was unapologetically abrasive and unrelentingly demanding. Previously at Atlanta, Brown was forever barking at players, not worrying what effect his often profane language or insults had on them—be it scrub or top scorer John Drew, on whom he used various degrading names—"Cement Head," "Moron" and "Cinder Head."

In New York, Brown had nothing but superlatives for his star player, Bernard

King. The emergence of King as the Knicks' leading scorer (21.9 in 1982–83, 26.3 in 1983-84) was the payoff on a gamble New York had taken on a player widely regarded as a ticking time bomb. But New York rolled the dice on King's overcoming his admitted problem with alcohol. It was a problem that had entangled Bernard in an assortment of legal troubles and brought him to the brink of *persona non grata* in the NBA.

But in his first two years with the Knicks, King put his thorny past behind him, making believers of NBA players and coaches alike. What impressed coach Brown was King's ability to score so abundantly without throwing the offense out of whack. "He does not freelance or razzle-dazzle or break plays or call for the ball or yell at his teammates," said Brown. "He just takes good shots when they are there. He's got so much to give. Yet he remains in touch with the entire picture. All he wants to do is win."

It was no wonder that New York fans began anticipating a rapid return to the glory days. Bernard King had the kind of competitive will that conjured up the image of Reed or DeBusschere—a relentless player who knew how to win.

When he was healthy in 1984-85, King was as good as and often better than he had been before. There was a career-high 60-point game on Christmas night against the New Jersey Nets. A month earlier, he had scored 52 points against Indiana at the Garden. But a series of injuries would limit King's availability in 1984–85, though not his 32.9 scoring average, the best in the league. King became the first Knick in team history to lead the league in scoring.

But the injury bug that hampered Bernard would fell teammate Bill Cartwright, who could not play at all because of a damaged left foot that eventually required surgery that December. The supporting cast was diminished further when Truck Robinson and Marvin Webster had their seasons curtailed by injuries, too, and when Ray Williams was signed by Boston as a free agent.

Then on March 23, against Kansas City, a difficult season turned into a nightmare. That was when King, who'd suffered a sprained right knee in January, reinjured the knee so badly that his season was over. Worse, his future was in jeopardy because of the nature and extent of the injury—a torn anterior cruciate ligament and a partial tear of his lateral menscus cartilage.

Just when things couldn't have been darker, the Knicks finally caught a break. In the first-ever lottery draft, the luck of the draw gave New York first choice, which put the team in position to draft a potential franchise player, Patrick Ewing.

When director of basketball operations DeBusschere heard the news, he reacted like a quiz-show contestant who had hit the jackpot. He shook his fist, grinned and carried on. For DeBuschere, ordinarily a reserved individual, such a display of emotion could be excused. For by landing Ewing he had moved the team a giant step closer to being a very legitimate contender. And after a 1984–85 season in which the Knicks' medical reports had required him to have the forbearance of Job, a seven-foot lottery prize was a welcome change.

From the time he'd matriculated at Cambridge (Mass.) Rindge and Latin High, Ewing had been singled out as a special case. Why not? At the time he was 7' tall, 230 pounds, with arms and shoulders that had the sinewy muscle that comes from weight training on Nautilus machines. In motion, it got even better. Moving up and down the court, Patrick Ewing was your basic shot-blocking, slam-dunking unit and, according to the experts, the best schoolboy prospect in the country.

Ewing stood in that line of big men that stretched back to Wilt Chamberlain. Like Alcindor and Bill Walton in the sixties and Malone, Bowie and Sampson in the seventies, Ewing was already being called a dominating force in the game. HSBI Report, a scouting service used by colleges, referred to him as "the game's most dictatorial giant since Alcindor."

But not even Ewing, reportedly signed to a 10-year, $31.2 million contract (including $4.2 million in interest-free loans), could solve the manpower shortage that the absence of the injured King and Cartwright caused. The Knicks sank to dead last again in 1985–86.

Brown was fired early into the 1986–87 campaign, and the man who replaced him, Bob Hill, was not invited back for the following season. The short, happy era of Rick Pitino was upon us.

Pitino, the *wunderkind* of NBA coaches and a former assistant to Hubie Brown with the Knicks, was the perpetual gym rat who'd found a vocation in his obsessive need for basketball. At age 26, this New Yorker had taken over a moribund basketball program at Boston University and immediately turned it around. In five seasons, from 1978–83, his Terrier teams won 91 and lost 51 and for the first time in twenty-four years made it into the NCAA tournament. All of which made Pitino the most successful coach in the school's history.

Next Pitino performed a similar makeover at Providence College, whose 17–14 Friars would land a postseason bid to the NIT in Pitino's first season there, 1986, their first postseason berth since

1977–78. Then in 1986–87, Pitino led 25–8 Providence to the NCAA Final Four, a *tour de force* coaching job.

For Pitino, to be coach of the Knicks was a dream come true. He had grown up in New York as a rabid Knicks fan. The night Reed had limped onto the court in the final game of 1969–70, Pitino had seen it from the budget-minded blue seats.

Now he would be up-close and personal with a team in dire need of revitalizing. As the youngest coach in the NBA, the 36-year-old Pitino would be criticized at first for the rapid-tempo game he installed, a style that saw the Knicks using trapping defenses and full-court pressure while accelerating the offense. That emphasis on the up-tempo game—a style Pitino had won with at Boston and at Providence—was viewed by some as too taxing in the long run for an NBA team and more likely to crash at playoff time when defenses tighten.

But Pitino ignored the critics, and kept his Knicks playing on open throttle, in the process encouraging a shoot-first and ask-questions-later mentality on the three-point shot. To play this brand of basketball would require the new coach to use his bench liberally—as many as eight or nine players seeing serious playing time each night. Besides Ewing, there would be Gerald Wilkins, Trent Tucker, a healthy Cartwright and Pat Cummings, Kenny Walker, Johnny Newman, Sidney Green and the surprise of the 1987–88 season, rookie Mark Jackson.

Jackson, the Knicks' top draft choice, surpassed the expectations of even Pitino, who said: "No one in their right mind would have said Mark Jackson was going to be this good."

How good was that? Well, as a 23-year-old rookie, the former St. John's guard would average 13.6 ppg while leading the team in assists (868 in 82 games) and steals (205). Beyond the stats, though, there was an attitude that suffused his play. Jackson had adjusted to the pro game with an ease that was rare for a rookie guard. He exuded an air of self-assurance and repeatedly made the right decisions amidst the hurly-burly of large, quick-moving bodies with which a point guard must cope.

None of which surprised Jackson, who said: "Not being cocky or anything, I was born to play basketball. I don't feel like a rookie because I understand the game. I'm like Larry Bird. I may not have the God-given talent or quickness that other players do, but I'm smart and I understand what it takes."

There was a bit of the showman, too, in Jackson that the Garden crowds responded to initially—theatrical gestures when shots of his went in and the occasional fancy pass. With Jackson directing the team, and Ewing providing 20.2 ppg while leading New York in rebounding (676) and blocked shots (245), the perpetual-motion Knicks moved up in the standings, third place in the Atlantic Division with a 38–44 record. For the first time in in four years, New York made it to the playoffs, losing to the Boston Celtics in the first round.

But New York would do even better the next year, 1988–89. The Knicks jumped to the top of the Atlantic Division, with that foot-to-the-pedal game that once again brought the thrill back to the Garden. So often did Knicks players fire the three-pointers that its chief proponents—Jackson, Newman, Wilkens, Tucker and rookie Rod Strickland—became known as "The Bomb Squad." In their drive to the Atlantic Division title in 1988–89, the Knicks would make 386 of 1,147 three-point attempts, far and away more than any other team in the league. (Sacramento was the next most trigger-happy team with 824 three-point attempts.)

But New York's rise in the standings was owed to more than its long-distance shooting. Strickland's offense, the late-season acquisitions of Pete Myers and Kiki Vandeweghe (Ernie's son) and the preseason blockbuster trade that sent Cartwright to Chicago for Charles Oakley were all changes that helped bolster the nucleus of Pitino's previous squad and keyed New York's 52–30 record. The Knicks would make it to the second round of the playoffs before succumbing to the Michael Jordan led Chicago Bulls.

Of those new Knicks, only Oakley, 6' 9" of hard-nosed competitor, would endure in New York well into the nineties.

While the others moved onto other clubs or retired, "Oak," as his teammates called him, would remain here as that rare player who worked selflessly on defense and under the boards, providing grit and muscle in a thankless role year after year. The loose ball, the crucial rebound, the crunch-time stop on a big-name forward—these would be the province of Oakley.

Teaming with Ewing, he gave New York a power base that figured to make Pitino's Knicks even better. Trouble was, just when things were getting interesting, Pitino was gone.

Often at odds, philosophically, with New York general manager Al Bianchi, who preferred a more traditional half-court offense, Pitino decided to switch rather than fight. The boy-wonder mastermind left the Knicks to take the coaching job at the University of Kentucky, sending the Knicks into the nineties adrift.

Because of an alcohol problem, Bernard King, above, was on the verge of blowing his career when a trade brought him to New York. His brilliant career was marred by injuries which kept Dr. Norman Scott and trainer Mike Saunders, facing page top, busy. Other Knicks of the eighties: Hollis Copeland, #45, and Paul Westphal, #44.

It was hard to be happy as a Knicks fan in the eighties. Here is a glimpse of a suffering Stanley Asofsky from a profile on him that ran in *The New York Daily News Sunday Magazine* in 1982:

"Give him credit. It's early in the 1981–82 season. The New York Knicks are losing steadily and threatening to make 'Last Year at Marienbad' look like an action film. And still, Asofsky is not daunted.

"In his usual front-row baseline spot at Madison Square Garden—section R, row A, seat 1—he is working this game against Atlanta with a hard-core fan's passion, insulting the officials ('Hey, Jake (O'Donnell), you get paid by the bushel?'), riding the opposition 'Quit complaining, (John) Drew. When you cry, the mascara runs.'), encouraging the locals ('Good box-out, Bill (Cartwright). Big derriere, that's it. That's it.'). From the opening tap, he is in the game.

"But Asofsky's love of basketball goes only so far. By the fourth quarter in this game against Atlanta, his enthusiasm begins to wane as the truth rolls over him like heartburn: here is still another Knick team that can't hack it. The offense breaks down once a play's first option is diagnosed. Defense is by invitation only. Worse, there is no *esprit* among the players. And that, as much as any basketball flaw, is what has Asofsky bugged.

"Soon, he is mumbling about fat cats in the lineup, bad shots, the lack of conviction under the backboard. From his seat, he needles Knick coach William (Red) Holzman and shouts at Madison Square Garden Corp. boss David Abraham (Sonny) Werblin—discontent that underscores the hard times that have befallen the Knicks.

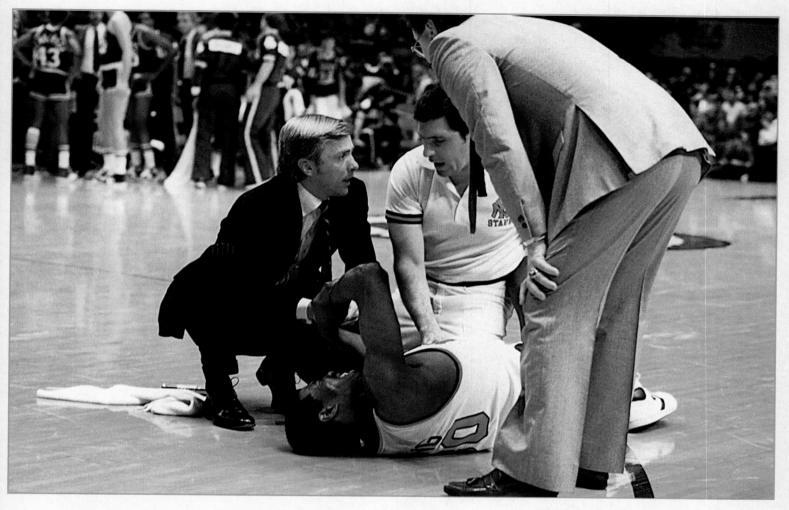

"Asofsky goes back to the days when the team played games in the Sixty-ninth Regiment Armory. In New York's glory years—it won NBA titles in 1969–70 and 1972–73—Asofsky was a happy man. The ball moved smartly from player to player. Defense was earnest. A graceful, informed game.

"In recent years, though, Asofsky has suffered a succession of bad Knick teams. He has not suffered in silence. Once, CBS-TV put Asofsky on camera for the six o'clock news and asked him what was wrong with the team. It was the last word CBS got in. Asofsky had plenty to talk about then—and still does."

Asofsky and fans like him looked at the inferior game the Knicks put out in the early eighties and reacted. It had taken but a few short years for the Knicks to bungle business badly enough to turn a rabid basketball city apathetic. They did it through a myopic approach that relied on the checkbook rather than court savvy, and sometimes got snagged in conglomerate politics.

Quickly, the supicion was abroad that the Knicks front office was not the same without Ned Irish running it. Irish, Michael Burke's predecessor, had a reputation for being cantankerous and hard-nosed about securing every possible advantage for the Knicks in the league's Board of Governors meetings.

When Hubie Brown took over the Knicks in 1982-83, he was able to turn them into winners. Brown often went beyond his starters, using many players, including Marvin Webster, #40.

But Burke was another story. The dapper executive hadn't the experience, or feeling, that goes with being around the game for years.

Case in point: In the summer of 1976, following Spencer Haywood's first season in New York, the NBA was preparing to take into the league four ABA franchises, including the New York Nets. At a league meeting, Nets president Roy Boe approached Burke. "In lieu of paying a territorial compensation to the Knicks," Burke said, "Boe offered us Julius (Dr. J.) Erving. But I felt the Nets were coming into the league on the basis of being a good healthy franchise. It was wrong to strip the team of its star."

Boe was not troubled by such high-minded considerations. He traded Erving to Philadelphia in a multimillion-dollar deal. Doctor J. became an integral part of the Philadelphia franchise and for a while the game's most popular player. Kids in the schoolyards and adults in the

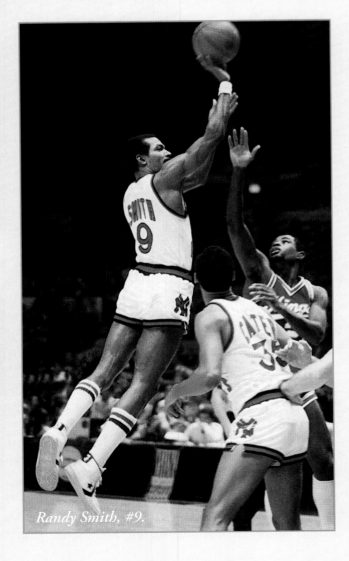

Randy Smith, #9.

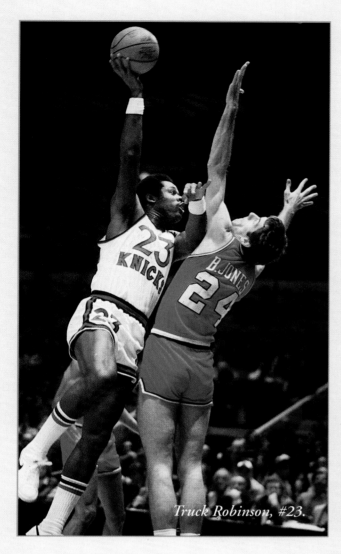

Truck Robinson, #23.

arena thrilled to Erving's midair moves—those gliding swoops to the basket that often ended with his casually stuffing the ball through the hoop.

Erving wasn't the only major star the team bypassed. As Marv Albert recalled: "Larry Bird was available for the 1978 draft after his junior year because he was a year behind his graduating class."

Albert remembers asking Sonny Werblin if he'd consider drafting him.

"Nah," Werblin said. "Our people don't think he's going to be any good."

As Albert would later recall: "Selecting two spots after the Knicks, the Boston Celtics that year took Bird as a junior and wound up winning three titles with him. The Knicks took Micheal Ray Richardson, and won zero titles with him. I believe Sonny's 'people' were the same ones who thought blue jeans were just a fad."

Knicks brass ignored the delicate chemistry that goes into building a team.

It opted to pile big name upon big name (Haywood/McAdoo) and discovered that star-stacking was not the answer. While in New York, Haywood and McAdoo would do exactly what they had in other NBA cities: they would score points in bunches. In four seasons here, Haywood would average between 13.7 and 19.9 points a game. In three seasons in New York, McAdoo would average 26.7, 26.5, 26.9, a model of point-producing consistency. But their scoring output did not compute to team excellence.

And the Knicks teams kept losing.

And in 1982–83, Hubie Brown would get his shot at straightening out the Knicks.

Success had marked Brown's coaching career at every level—from high school to pros. Brown's first stint as a coach was at St. Mary's High School in Little Falls, New York, in 1956. From there he moved on to coaching jobs at Cranford High School and Fair Lawn High School, both in New Jersey. His collegiate coaching began with a stop at William & Mary as an assistant in 1967, before heading to Duke University as the top assistant there one year later. The important first step into the professional ranks came in 1972 as an assistant to Larry Costello with the Milwaukee Bucks.

Brown had played his college basketball at Niagara University with Costello and Frank Layden, who also graduated to the NBA coaching ranks.

In an auspicious pro head-coaching debut with the ABA Kentucky Colonels in 1974–75, Brown led the team to a 58-win season en route to the American Basketball Association's championship. When the ABA merged with the

Bernard KING

NBA two years later and the Kentucky franchise folded, Brown took over the coaching duties for the Atlanta Hawks.

Brown was said to be the first NBA coach to call every play from the bench, which was a clear indication of his style as a coach. As Brown put it: "I want complete control."

But when he was at Atlanta, Brown's control had been a function of team economics. When the Hawks' owner, Ted Turner, bought the team in the middle of the 1976–77 season, he ordered the front office to unload all the high-priced talent. That led to the departure of stars like Lou Hudson, Truck Robinson and Thomas Henderson. The payroll for the 1977–78 Hawks would be a pared-down $800,000, and the symbol of the new-breed economy-model Hawk was a 5'8" guard, Charlie Criss, whom Brown brought up from the Eastern League and turned into a starter. The perpetual-motion, gutty Criss, rookie guard Eddie Johnson, John Drew and an assortment of NBA wanna-bes played Brown's pressing defense and orchestrated offense to the hilt. Brown goaded them into winning 41 ball games and making the 1977–78 playoffs for the first time since 1972–73.

Never mind that by 1980–81, when he was fired toward the end of the season, Hawk management would insist that his nonstop verbal assaults on the players had alienated them. The fact is that even in that final year the Hawks played better than .500 basketball and made the playoffs again. The Knicks, as they existed in the early eightiess, seemed in severe need of Brown's kind of authority.

Bernard King, driving to the basket below and wearing a crown on the opposite page, was the Knicks' leading scorer in the early eighties. In 1984–85 King led the NBA in scoring with a 32.9 ppg average.

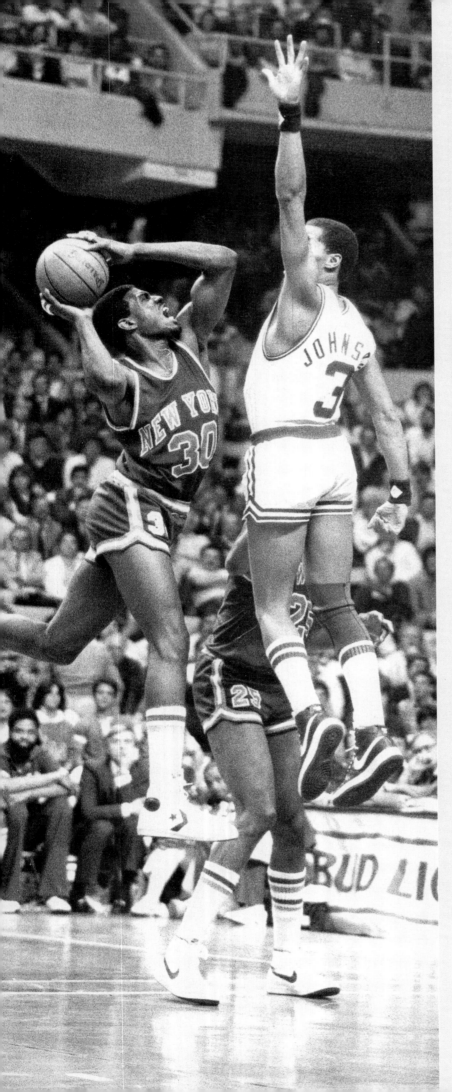

Brown's was an in-your-face style. He was a confident man—some would say cocky—and a coach of unshakeable convictions. At Atlanta he had often used ten players during a game and was the first coach to press the opposition night in, night out, eighty-two games a year. He would make substitutions in a clockwork fashion, rather than by the exigencies of the game. And when critics knocked him for these unconventional tactics, he would say: "We do a lot of radical things that pro basketball doesn't want to accept. But if you are an innovator, you will always be attacked. You can't ever allow that to stop you. The easiest thing is to just say you're going to let the players do their dance and let the talent win it or lose it."

In Brown's scheme of things, the coach was a factor. He was not simply a caretaker. He was an aggressor, pushing, prodding, demanding the best effort from his players while he was sorting out the X's and O's. And if sometimes he would scald a player's psyche with his blunt words, well, so be it.

As Bruce Newman would write in *Sports Illustrated:* "Someone once said that Hubie Brown burned his bridges *before* him. That speaks volumes about the effect Brown's personality has on people. Brown makes little effort to conceal his contempt for many of the other 22 head coaches in the National Basketballl Association, and yet he is plainly wounded by their disdain for him. He tells his players he doesn't want them to love him and doesn't care if they like him, but then expects them to play harder for him than they have played for any coach in their lives."

Indeed, Brown regarded himself as one of the few superior coaches in the NBA, and he did not hide behind anonymous quotes in voicing that.

By the time Brown showed up in New York, the team was in need of a major overhaul.

And Brown led that overhaul.

When he became coach of New York, he immediately reshaped the Knicks roster. Working with the new director of basketball operations, Dave DeBusschere,

he traded Micheal Ray Richardson to Golden State for Bernard King, and Maurice Lucas to Phoenix for Truck Robinson. Mike Newlin and Toby Knight were waived. Randy Smith became a free agent and signed with San Diego. In the 1982 draft, the Knicks took Trent Tucker, a sharpshooting guard from Minnesota, and Scott Hastings, a six foot ten center from Arkansas. Hastings was subsequently traded in February 1983 to Atlanta for guard Rory Sparrow. Ernie Grunfeld, who had played six seasons at Milwaukee and Kansas City, was signed as a free agent, he rejoined former college teammate King, with whom he had starred at the University of Tennessee in what sportswriters called The Bernie and Ernie Show. Another free agent signee was Louie Orr. Holdovers from the previous year were centers Bill Cartwright and Marvin Webster, guard Paul Westphal and forward Sly Williams.

Under Brown, the Knicks revived, becoming a better than .500 ball club and a playoff contender again. Bernard King, whose admitted alcohol problem had brought him to the brink of being *persona non grata* in the NBA, was key to the success of those Hubie Brown–coached Knicks.

While coach Hubie Brown (below) relied on King, #30 (opposite page), for the bulk of his scoring, he could look to others on the squad, like Louie Orr, #55 (above), to contribute.

161

In no time, King had players and coaches around the league remarking on his turnabout.

Julius Erving, Philadelphia 76er forward: "He has always had that intensity and will to succeed, and now you can see an acceptance of responsibilities that go with being a man, that go with being a club leader. He can be counted on night in and night out."

Dick Motta, Dallas Mavericks coach: "I'd hate to be guarding him. He's good. That's why he gets paid so much money. He earns his salary. That's why the Knicks pirated him away from Golden State."

Robert Reid, Houston Rocket forward: "Bernard King is the Moses Malone for forwards. He never stops working."

John Bach, Golden State coach: "Bernard is a Messiah. He flies where angels fear to tread."

M.L. Carr, Boston Celtic forward: "Bernard works as hard as a rookie, and he doesn't have to. He's just so talented."

Ernie Grunfeld, teammate: "Fans love Bernard because he gives that maximum effort every night."

The common thread, the consensus, among those in the league was that there was more to Bernard King than talent. King brought a big-league work ethic that maximized the talent. As King himself would say, "My motto has always been that if you work hard, success will find you."

That success was based on unique skills. King had an uncanny knack for getting off shots around the basket against taller opponents, even when double- and triple-teamed. Like certain great boxers—Willie Pep, Sugar Ray Robinson, Sugar Ray Leonard—who could work at close quarters and yet instinctively sense when punches were coming, King was able to anticipate the defense and beat them with a move just a lickety-split in advance of their effort. Through thousands of hours of practice, he had mastered an assortment of jump hooks, drives and one-hand pops, and he seemed blessed with the ability to get off his feet a little quicker than the

other man.

"He's like a bird," said Hubie Brown. "He's swooping toward the basket and you think he's descending. Then all of a sudden, at the last instant, he elevates and you'll see an incredible move."

All of which made King a prolific scorer. But King was able to get his points without throwing the offense out of whack, or making his teammates feel like an afterthought. King operated within the team concept, and it made a difference.

In 1982–83, King's first season in New York, the Knicks finished with a 44–38 record and went to the Eastern Conference semifinals in the playoffs, quite a turnaround from their last-place 33–49 season the year before. King led the team in scoring, averaging 21.9 points a game, with a high single-game mark of 43 points. The Knicks under Brown had balanced scoring, with Bill Cartwright (15.7 ppg), Sly Williams (11.9), Rory Sparrow (10 ppg average in 32 games after being traded to New York) and Paul Westphal (10). And Brown was not averse to using a deep bench as he had at Atlanta, with Truck Robinson, Trent Tucker, Louie Orr, Ed Sherod, Marvin Webster and Ernie Grunfeld getting significant minutes for New York.

King was even more potent the following year. In late January/early February 1984, on consecutive nights, he had 50-point games against the San Antonio Spurs and the Dallas Mavericks. In the playoffs, he had two 46-point games agianst the Pistons, in New York and at Detroit, and then came back with a 44–point scoring binge against the title-bound Celtics. In 12 postseason games, he would average 34.8 points.

The Knicks in 1983–84? Once again, they were a better-than-.500 ballclub—a record of 47 wins and 35 losses and a third-place finish in the Atlantic Division. In the playoffs, the Knicks eliminated Detroit three games to two in the opening round but were ousted by the Celtics four games to three in the Eastern Conference semifinals.

King again led the team in scoring with a 26.3 points per game average, with Cartwright (17), Ray Williams (14.8), Truck Robinson (10.8) and Sparrow (10.4) also in double figures. Williams had returned to New York after stints in New Jersey and Kansas City.

After two strong seasons under Brown, the Knicks and their fans looked forward to the 1984–85 season. But the upswing in the team's fortunes would be subverted by injuries. Serious injuries or illness struck down Bill Cartwright, Marvin Webster, Truck Robinson and eventually the indomitable King.

When King went down in Kansas City on March 23, 1985, with a knee injury, his future was clouded.

"I consulted with four or five world-renowned orthopedic doctors," King recalled. "I read as much material as possible. I think I received more medical and technical informa-

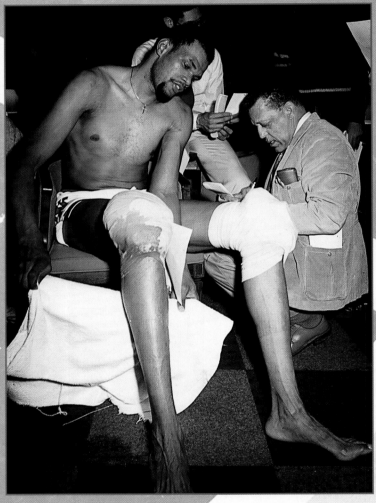

tion in one week than I ever received in biology or science classes. I actually did spend every waking hour gathering information on procedures, techniques and rehabilitation, you name it I tried to get it.

"After reviewing various surgical procedures I elected to have Dr. Norman Scott perform the operation. Dr. Scott and I felt his procedure of replacing the anterior cruciate ligament with the illiotibial band afforded me the best chance of achieving my goal, to return to the NBA as an All-Pro."

Well, in April 1985, when King had his surgery, there was no telling whether he ever would recover sufficiently to play at the All-Star level to which Knicks fans had become accustomed. (King, despite his injury, would still lead the NBA in scoring with 32.9 ppg in 1984–85.) As for the Knicks, their hard-luck season— King was one of several Knicks injured—had seen them drop to last place in the Atlantic Division with a 24–58 record.

Then came a happy addition to the Knicks franchise, lottery draft pick Patrick Ewing.

Ewing, a seven-footer, had not become acquainted with the game until he was 12 years old. That's when he had arrived in Cambridge, Massachusetts, from his native Jamaica.

In those days he was sensitive about his height—Ewing was 6'1" in seventh grade, 6'6" a year later. Classmates called him "Peking Man"—shortened to "Peking"—after an anthropological drawing found in textbooks, a figure that Ewing discovered was no charmer.

Ewing recalled his first varsity game for Cambridge Rindge and Latin High School: "People laughed at me that night too. All those people there, I was nervous. I scored one point and fouled out. They were saying I was clumsy. Yelling it out."

Well, Ewing would have the last laugh. While at Rindge and Latin, he quickly developed into a star and more: a landmark figure in the continuum of great big men of the game.

After dominant years under coach Mike Jarvis at Rindge and Latin, and after a hot pursuit by the biggest basketball colleges, on February 2, 1981, Ewing announced he would be enrolling at Georgetown.

There, under coach John Thompson, he became known as "The Hoya Destroya" for his dominance around the basket. He left Georgetown as the school's all-time leading rebounder (1,316) and shot blocker (493) while ranking second in all-time scoring (2,184) to Sleepy Floyd (2,304). With Ewing in the lineup, Georgetown became a collegiate power—three NCAA finals, including the national championship in 1984.

Ewing's NBA fate would be decided in the first-ever NBA Lottery, in which the league's seven non-playoff teams would have each of their logos placed in hermetically sealed envelopes and then revealed, one by one, to determine the top seven draft positions. The team with the number one pick, of course, had the clear path to Ewing.

The have-nots were the Knicks, Atlanta Hawks, Los Angeles Clippers, Indiana Pacers, Sacramento Kings, Golden State Warriors and Seattle SuperSonics. And as the lottery approached, each of them conspired to get the fates on their side.

In Indiana, Pacer owner Herb Simon held a gathering at his summer home and required each guest to

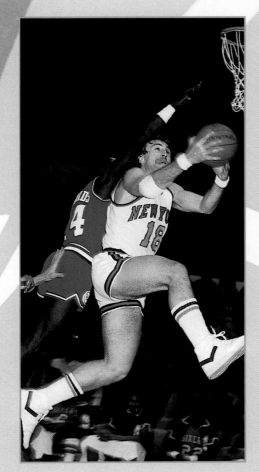

Ernie Grunfeld, driving to the hoop above, and speaking at a clinic for youth, below, played for the Knicks from 1982-86. He is presently the team's president and general manager. Marvin Webster, adjoining page, was a 7'1" defensive specialist.

bring a good luck charm. In Seattle, the Sonics proclaimed Lottery Day as St. Patrick Ewing Day. In Los Angeles, Clipper GM Carl Scheer joked about having Ewing's name changed in unison by thirty-three rabbis, matching Ewing's jersey, #33.

And in New York, Knicks public relations director John Cirillo carried in his pocket a horseshoe from a trotter named On The Road Again, given to him by veteran driver Buddy Gilmour, a friend from Cirillo's days at Yonkers Raceway.

It turned out to be the luckiest charm of all.

Lottery Day was also Mother's Day: May 12, 1985. The place was the Starlight Roof of the Waldorf-Astoria Hotel.

Before a packed ballroom and a national TV audience on CBS, NBA commissioner David Stern opened the envelopes, one by one. The number seven pick went to Golden State. Number six was Sacramento. Number five was Atlanta.

"I really didn't get into the lottery until after the early envelopes had been opened," said DeBusschere. "But when Stern was about to open the fourth envelope, I said to myself, 'God, get by this one, because now we're going to get one of those big guys we need so badly.'"

Number four was Seattle.

"But once we were one of three, I started to get a little cocky and told myself, 'Let's go all the way. Let's get the big one.'"

Number three was the Clippers.

"When it got down to the last two, I couldn't look. I couldn't listen."

And now, with DeBusschere staring straight ahead and his hands covering his face, Stern opened the next-to-last envelope and said: "The second pick in the 1985 NBA Draft goes to . . . the Indiana Pacers!"

Men whooped. Women shrieked. In a moment indelible in Knicks history, DeBusschere half-rose out of his chair and pounded the table in front of him, just once, before slinking, embarrassed, back into his seat.

Pat O'Brien of CBS said it all: "Basketball is back in New York City, my friends."

The Ewing Era had begun.

Immediately, he was dubbed a franchise savior. But he wanted none of that talk.

"I can only be Patrick Ewing," he said.

Fair enough, said New York.

"Bill Russell, with offense. A franchise center," said NBA draft guru Marty Blake.

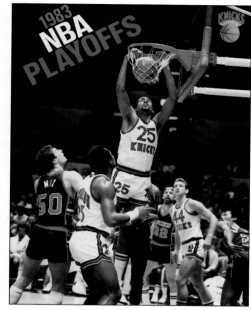

* *Knicks came and went during the eighties, as the team's fortunes rose and fell. Above, Bill Cartwright dunks; bottom, Bernard King slams it through. On the opposite page, from top to bottom, that's Maurice Lucas, #23; the threesome of Hollis Copeland, Cartwright and Micheal Ray Richardson; Ernie Grunfeld; and Darrell Walker, #4.*

WHAT BECAME OF...

Here's what happened to Knicks from the 1960s and 1970s after their NBA basketball careers:

Phil Jackson coached in the CBA and then became head coach of the Chicago Bulls.

Jim Cleamons became an assistant coach to Jackson with the Bulls and was named head coach of the Dallas Mavericks for the 1996–97 season.

Tom Hoover worked as a deputy commissioner for the New York Athletic Commission, which regulates boxing and wrestling. Presently gives basketball clinics for the Knicks and raises funds for student-athletes. His son, Jason, is a starting forward for Manhattan College.

Jerry Lucas is involved in memory training and lives in Templeton, California.

Earl Monroe owns an entertainment firm and makes numerous personal appearances.

Rory Sparrow and **Mel Davis** work for the NBA, helping former players get jobs and education.

Len Elmore became an attorney and player's agent.

Mike Glenn became a broadcaster with CNN.

Cal Ramsey is director of community relations with the Knicks.

Dick VanArsdale has been a longtime front office executive and broadcaster for the Phoenix Suns.

Neal Walk, paralyzed after spinal surgery, is the tireless community relations director for the Phoenix Suns.

Darrell Walker is head coach of the Toronto Raptors.

Bob McAdoo returned to the NBA in 1995–96 as an assistant coach for the Miami Heat.

Spencer Haywood tours the country, giving motivational speeches to groups and businesses. His autobiography, *The Rise, the Fall, the Recovery* was published a few years ago.

Artie Heyman is a restaurateur and entrepreneur involved in several business.

"This is a man who wins championships everywhere he plays. He is a fierce competitor, a real warrior," said Hubie Brown, who stressed the defensive end of the game as much as his new center did.

"Everybody likes to score. I like to score, but I like winning more than I like scoring," said Ewing. "And if you want to win, you're going to have to stop the other guy from scoring. That's the way I've been taught to play basketball from day one.

"That's the great thing about going to the Knicks, that I'm playing in a system similar to the one I played in college. They stress defense, don't they? They play a trapping, pressing game, don't they? I like that. If I went to a different club, the adjustment would be bigger."

"You have to have quality big people," said Brown. "And Ewing is probably a better athlete than all of them. He's a genuine intimidator. Last year we blocked 257 shots. Patrick should get over 200 by himself."

"When Patrick was a freshman, he was just a threat to block a shot down low," added Blake. "By the time he was a senior, you could draw a circle 15 feet around the basket, and he'd protect the entire area."

But the standout defender could play offense too.

"His offensive game is going to flourish in the pros," said Brown, "because, unlike college, he is going to be able to catch the ball. There's no doubt that he's going to be double-teamed when he gets it, but then he's a good enough passer to find the open people. Plus, he's going to get a lot of points off the glass, and he's also been an excellent free throw shooter."

The legends were similarly impressed with the young Ewing.

"He's got that Russell look," said Willis Reed in 1985. "Some guys' minds aren't always in the game, but Patrick's out there reading the plays

Left to right, Dave DeBusschere, Knicks GM, Garden boss Sonny Werblin and coach Hubie Brown. On facing page, Ken (The Animal) Bannister throws it down as a future Knick, Charles Oakley, #34, watches.

and seeing the court. He has total concentration. That's the distinction of the great ones."

"I want to be considered one of the best to play the game, but that will only happen if I win," said Ewing. "So I guess winning is my only goal. Being compared to Bill Russell and all that, well, it's an honor, because I think he was the greatest player ever. But I don't model my game after anyone. I can only be Patrick Ewing."

Which, the years would prove, would be more than good enough.

The addition of Ewing to the Knicks was supposed to make a big difference (indeed, he would be named the NBA's Rookie of the Year for 1985-86).

Certainly Brown thought so. In the team's preseason prospectus, he said, "The coming of Patrick Ewing, the seven foot Georgetown star, to New York, the return of seven foot one Bill Cartwright to the Knick lineup after missing the entire schedule last year with a broken left foot are the key ingredients in that quest.

"I always speak from a positive standpoint, and if we have a healthy front-line of Ewing, Cartwright, NBA scoring champ Bernard King and Pat Cummings, we will be able to compete favorably with all the heavyweights in the Eastern Conference."

Hubie's "if" turned out to be pivotal. For as it turned out, the advent of Ewing could not overcome the ongoing injury hex that would strike the team like a blow to the belly. In the absence of King and Cartwright, the Knicks finished in last place again in 1985–86. The loss of Cartwright was particularly galling since he had been expected to return healthy and raring to go. But in his first preseason game, "Mr. Bill," as he was known, reinjured the left foot that had sidelined him the previous year and was finished for 1985–86. Neither he nor King would play a single game while they recovered from their injuries. Ewing, too, was a victim of the injury hex and though he led the team in scoring with a 20 ppg average, he would miss 32 games because of floating soft tissue in his

Patrick Ewing and Dave DeBusschere were all smiles when Ewing became a Knick.

right knee that would require arthroscopic surgery. The team's next-best scorer, 6' 9½", 230-pound Pat Cummings, would also end up on the sidelines after only 31 games with recurring tendinitis.

While manpower shortage would provide playing time for supporting cast members like Gerald Wilkins (brother of superstar Dominique), Rory Sparrow and Ken (The Animal) Bannister, it left the team severely undermanned in 1985–86.

As the season progressed and the Knicks regressed, it prompted some observers to ask aloud whether New York management—DeBusschere really—had done all it could do to fortify the club.

In May 1982, when DeBusschere signed on as a Knicks executive, he had already established himself in the business world through a series of prestigious jobs: vice-president and general manager of the New York Nets; commissioner of

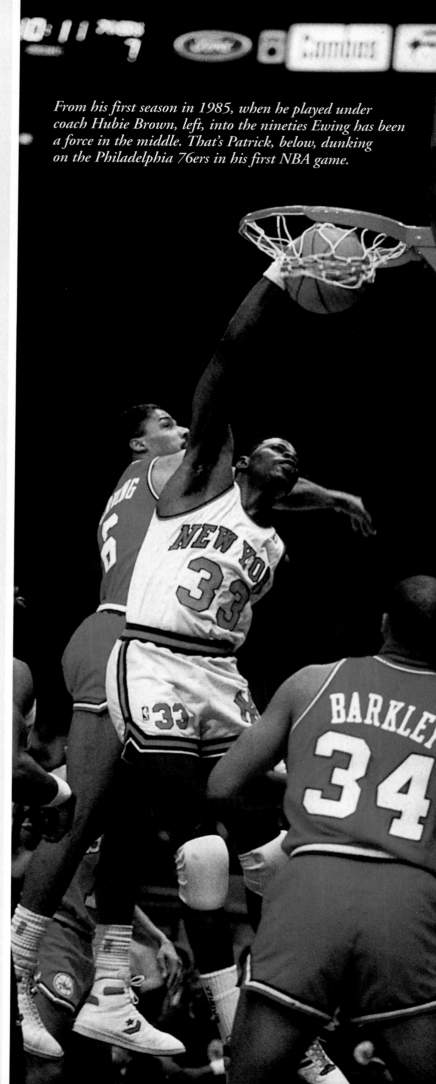

From his first season in 1985, when he played under coach Hubie Brown, left, into the nineties Ewing has been a force in the middle. That's Patrick, below, dunking on the Philadelphia 76ers in his first NBA game.

the American Basketball Association, president of Total Video Inc., a television advertising sales and marketing company, and part owner in restaurants in New York and Boston, and in *The Ring* Magazine.

The public's image of a pro basketball mogul is of a wheeler-dealer with a cigar in the side of his mouth and an unending line of blarney issuing from both sides of it. As this mythical general manager works the phones, action is as easy, and inevitable, as sunset, curbed only by a lack of one man's vigor and acumen.

In real life, though, pro basketball was more complicated.

In real life, there were salary caps that now made trades and free-agent acquisition so difficult that a cottage industry developed for lawyers who were asked to help teams fathom the caps' fine print. In addition, an executive like DeBusschere had to contend with cagey agents, multiyear contracts

21 IN A ROW

and athletes who were deluded as to their worth.

With the Knicks a corporate entity—part of Gulf+Western's Entertainment and Communications Group—DeBusschere

The Knicks shattered a club record in 1989 with their twenty-first straight home victory, celebrated above by head coach Rick Pitino (second from left) and assistants Stu Jackson, Ralph Willard, Jim O'Brien and trainer Mike Saunders.

could not move with the autonomy of, say, Red Auerbach in Boston or Jerry Colangelo in Phoenix.

Player personnel decisions—potential trades, free-agent deals and draft choices—were thrashed over in committee, by DeBusschere, Brown and his assistant coaches and by the team vice-president, Eddie Donovan, and the chief scout, Dick McGuire.

When DeBusschere negotiated with player agents, he was the point man of a corporate process that could include Jack Krumpe, president of Madison Square Garden Corporation, and Arthur Barron, president of the Entertainment and Communications Group at Gulf+Western. "Like the Ewing negotiations," said DeBusschere. "That was a very major contract that was going to have impact on the corporate look, so Gulf+Western kept a close finger on it."

And the press kept a close finger on

Kenny Walker grabs Mike Gminski's last-second miss sealing the Knicks' game two win against the Sixers in 1989. Pitino was gone from such moments the following year, succeeded by Stu Jackson, below.

DeBusschere, who as the GM bore responsibility for the fortunes or misfortunes of his franchise. In this instance, the misfortunes mounted, as did the team's losses. And by January 1986, DeBusschere was fired, replaced by Scotty Stirling.

The Knicks finished last again in the Atlantic Division with a 23–59 record.

In his abbreviated season—55 games—King averaged 32.9 points a game, which made him the NBA's scoring champion. Cummings (15.8), Walker (13.5) and Orr (12.7) were also in double figures. Sparrow, Tucker, Butch Carter, Bannister, Grunfeld and James Bailey also played extensively.

Life on Thirty-third Street did not get any better the next season. Sixteen games into the 1986-87 campaign, the team was 4–12 and looking as though it had had its fill of Hubie Brown. As Marv Albert would say, "Off the court, Hubie was a very personable guy—he went on to make an excellent color analyst—but the players didn't always appreciate his coaching style, his constant rantings and ravings at them, the way he called every play, the way he screamed at them after a mistake. Because of that, Knicks center

173

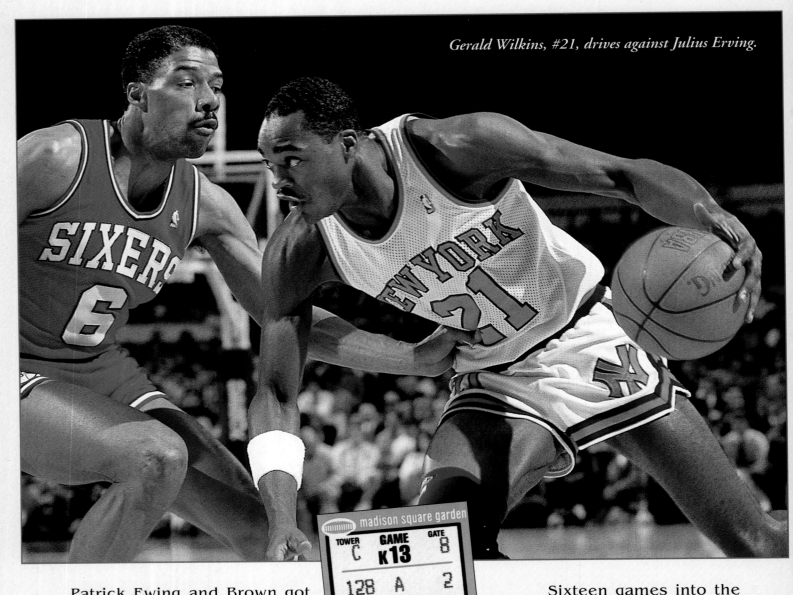

Gerald Wilkins, #21, drives against Julius Erving.

Patrick Ewing and Brown got along like in-laws.

"It's too bad, because Hubie was a genius with X's and O's and he was brilliant when it came to making average players overachieve. I always thought he would have been an outstanding college coach, because players are in school for their two, three or four years, then move on. The shorter exposure to volatile surroundings, the less extensive college schedule and the more impressionable younger players would have been an effective setting.

"Still, I don't blame Hubie. He got killed by injuries. You'd walk into his locker room and you'd have thought you were in the waiting room at an HMO."

madison square garden

TOWER	GAME	GATE
C	K13	8

128	A	2
SEC	ROW	SEAT

1PROM $18.00
EST. PRICE $16.63
SALES TAX $ 1.37

KNICKS

KENNY WALKER
Thurs., Dec. 25, 1986
VS CHICAGO

SEC	ROW	SEAT
128	A	2

Thurs., Dec. 25, 1986

Sixteen games into the season, Brown was let go, replaced by Bob Hill.

A native of Columbus, Ohio, Hill played basketball and baseball at Bowling Green University. Upon graduation he signed a pro contract with the San Diego Padres farm club at Tri-Cities (Kennewick, Pasco and Richland), Washington.

He later returned to Bowling Green, where coach Pat Haley made him an assistant in charge of recruiting. Later he would work as an assistant coach at Pittsburgh and at Kansas.

Even with Ewing leading the team in scoring with a 21.5 average, the Knicks under Hill finished tied for

last in the Atlantic Division with a 24–58 record.

But the tail end of the season seemed to offer a promising glimpse into the future. Bernard King was back, ending a two-year absence and providing an emphatic last word on the rehabilitation program he had undergone. During that time King, the team's recuperating captain, had chosen not to attend Knicks games, a decision that was vigorously defended by King against the criticism of some observers.

"As my family and friends know, it was very difficult for me to make the decision not to attend practices or ball games," King would tell newsmen. "Although my workout schedule did not allow my return, I did not need any distractions. I know no other way but to give it my all."

The proof of King's methods was in

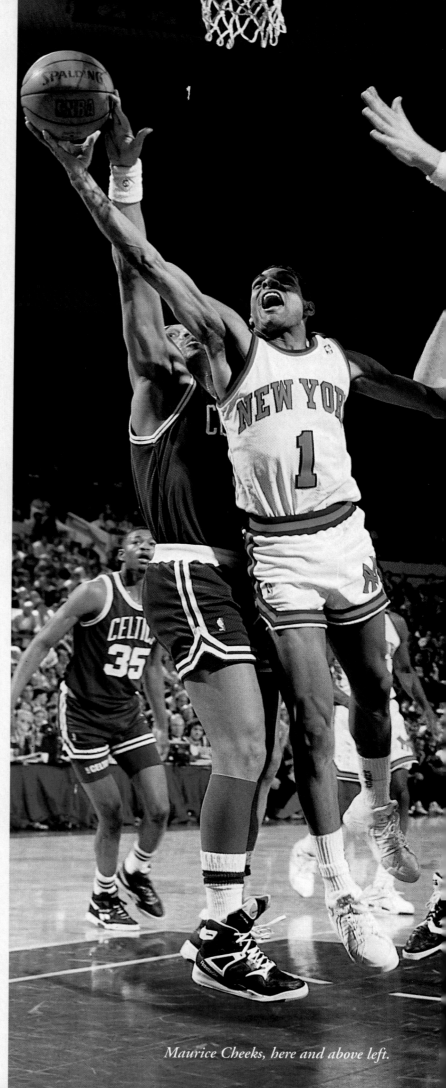

Maurice Cheeks, here and above left.

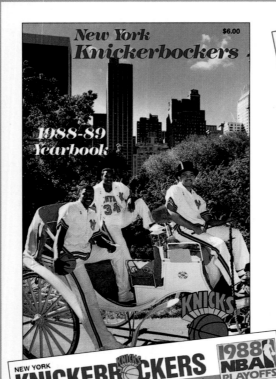

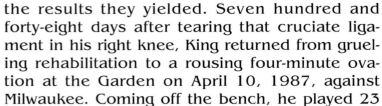

the results they yielded. Seven hundred and forty-eight days after tearing that cruciate ligament in his right knee, King returned from grueling rehabilitation to a rousing four-minute ovation at the Garden on April 10, 1987, against Milwaukee. Coming off the bench, he played 23 minutes that night and scored 7 points. In his next game, against Boston on April 12, he had 20 points. Returning to the starting lineup in the final four games of the season, he averaged 30 ppg while shooting 53 percent from the floor, including a season-high 31 points in the season finale against Cleveland.

While King was obviously back in form, he would not display it in New York during the 1987–88 season. King would end up as a free agent with the Washington Bullets, averaging 17.2 ppg in 60 games. And yet, curiously enough, his leave-taking did not prove the ruination of New York. No sir. Enter Rick Pitino.

Pitino was the boy wonder of the coaching profession. He was the prototypical hoops nut, who could never have enough basketball. As a 12-year-old, he had told his mother, Charlotte, that he wanted to attend three basketball camps over a single summer.

"Ricky, this is expensive, you going to all these camps," said Mrs. Pitino.

"But Mom," replied Pitino,

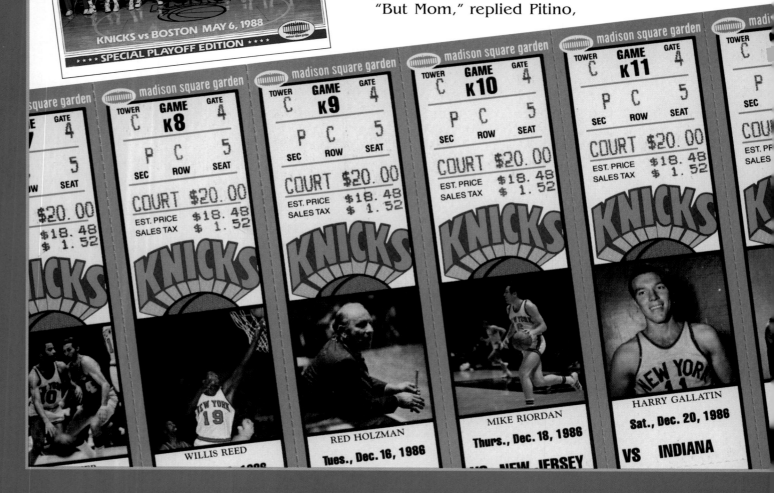

WILLIS REED

RED HOLZMAN
Tues., Dec. 16, 1986

MIKE RIORDAN
Thurs., Dec. 18, 1986

HARRY GALLATIN
Sat., Dec. 20, 1986
VS INDIANA

* *Bob Hill was the Knicks head coach in 1986-87, succeeding Hubie Brown.*

THE CHAMPIONS TWENTY-FIVE YEARS LATER

Here's what became of the Knicks from that championship season of 1969-70:

Dick Barnett earned a Ph. D. in education from Fordham University and for a while headed the Athletic Role Model Educational Institute in New York. In recent years, he worked as a consultant to the Seattle SuperSonics.

Bill Bradley served for seventeen years as a United States senator from New Jersey and delivered the keynote address at the 1992 Democratic Convention at Madison Square Garden.

Dave DeBusschere is a vice-president for the New York–based real estate firm of Williamson, Pickett and Gross.

Walt Frazier is the color commentator for the Knicks on WFAN radio and the Madison Square Garden Network.

Bill Hosket became general manager of Millcraft Paper Company in Columbus, Ohio.

Don May became a purchasing agent for Mosier Industries in Dayton, Ohio.

Willis Reed is a longtime front office executive with the New Jersey Nets.

Mike Riordan owns restaurants in Annapolis, Maryland.

Cazzie Russell coached in the CBA and on the high-school level in Columbus, Ohio. Is presently coaching at a small college in Atlanta.

Dave Stallworth worked in the aircraft industry in Wichita, Kansas.

John Warren is an accountant with Ernst & Young in Manhattan.

Nate Bowman suffered a fatal heart attack in December 1984 following a career as a film and TV actor.

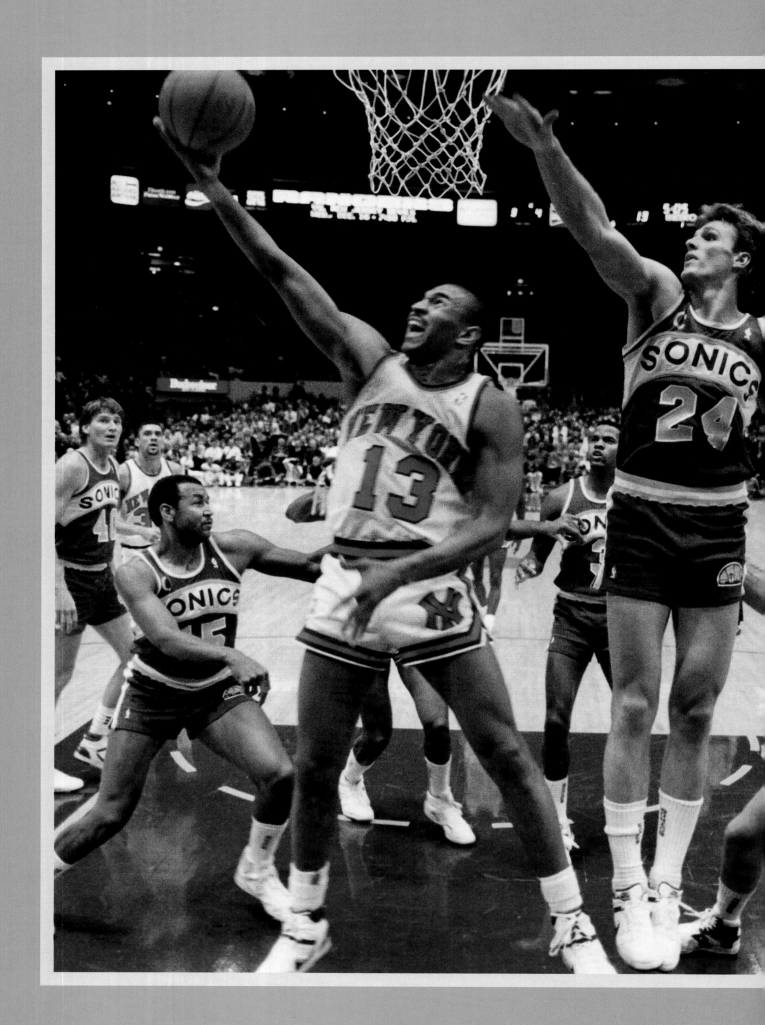

Mark Jackson, #13, drives to hoop against Seattle.

with characteristic self-confidence. "Think of it as an investment in my future."

Later, Pitino was a star guard for St. Dominic's in Oyster Bay, and a youth who gave every indication he had the right stuff to be a coach. As Howard Garfinkel, director of the notable Five-Star basketball camp, recalled: "Ricky really discovered himself. I gave him a stage as a teenager. But if he wasn't insistent and as confident as he is he would have just become another good counselor. Even back then his teams pressed end to end. He had a saying, "Get a fingernail on the ball."

Pitino went on to the University of Massachusetts, where he was captain of the basketball team and a starting guard in his junior and senior years.

He began his coaching career at the University of Hawaii in 1974 as a graduate assistant coach and finished the 1975–76 season as interim head coach, the youngest coach in the nation.

He quickly gained a reputation for being a skilled motivator and knowledgeable basketball man. What's more, he was intense about the game, and obsessive. On his wedding night in 1976, he took a phone call from Jim Boeheim, the coach of Syracuse. Boeheim wanted to speak to him about an assistant's job for Pitino at Syracuse. Pitino went down to the lobby to confer with Boeheim, intending to put off the decision so he could have the pleasure of his bride Joanne's company. Boeheim misunderstood. He interpreted Pitino's reluctance to agree to a deal as a negotiating ploy. Over the next four hours, Boeheim kept upgrading his offer, increasing the money Pitino would make from $12,000 to $16,000.

When Pitino finally got upstairs he told Joanne that not only did he have a job at Syracuse but that the honeymoon would have to be put off so that he could go to Cincinnati and recruit Louis Orr, who did indeed end up at Syracuse.

"That's a sad commentary," Pitino later said, laughing. "My wife's a basketball junkie herself, so she understood. SHe knew I was not well as far as basketball is concerned.

Pitino, top right with 1988 Rookie of the Year Mark Jackson, was not averse to using eight or nine men a game, allowing players like Sidney Green, above, Kenny Walker, below, and Johnny Newman, on opposite page, to tap their potential.

From the age of twenty-five, Pitino was a big-time coach, first at Boston University and then at Providence College, leading the Friars to the Final Four in 1987. At both venues, he showed remarkable organization skills and the ability to motivate his players.

"You must stay positive," was Pitino's motto. "The moment you become negative, you lose the players." And using that theory, Pitino got positive results, turning around both college basketball programs.

"Winning is the common denominator," Pitino said upon his July 13, 1987 appointment to the Knicks top post. "Winning is the only thing that matters in New York. Winning is everything.

"Vince Lombardi was a winner," he continued. "He knew how to get the best out of his people. He knew how to bring his team together. That's what I want to do with the Knicks. People say that having a family atmosphere can only work in college. I don't believe that. I think you should be more like a family in the pros. Your livelihood depends on it.

"I want the Knicks to be together. I want to build team camaraderie. Teamwork is the most important thing, not individual glory. And I'm going to demand it."

His two-year stint as a Knicks assistant under Brown

Charles Oakley, above, tangling with Rick Mahorn under the backboard, and opposite page top, gave the Knicks strength under the boards and on defense. Rod Strickland, below, and Gerald Wilkins, opposite page bottom, were offensive threats.

was brief but eventful.

"Rick was innovative," said Bernard King. "We knew then that he had what it took to be a great coach. We knew he'd be back in the NBA."

"The first thing it (becoming an assistant) did was raise my respect for NBA coaches about ten levels," said Pitino. "Until I got in the league, I probably was your typical college coach who believed all the traditional stereotypes about the pro game. I felt the players were all spoiled athletes who played no defense and the most important part of the game was the last five minutes.

"But as soon as I got in the league, I saw how NBA coaches have to coach under constant fatigue. Constant mental fatigue. You have so little time to prepare for the next game. There are so many moves to make in the course of one game."

And when he returned, he readily accepted the challenge of taking over a team that hadn't won more than twenty-four games in any of the prior three seasons.

"I want to turn it around the first year," Pitino said. "I want to entertain and please the fans. I want this team to hustle, to use every ounce of perspiration.

"The basic premise of my system is to fatigue your opponents with constant pressure defensively and constant movement offensively, using multiple substitutions and ten to eleven players. So when you go into the final five minutes of the game, you're the superior conditioned team.

"I know this is crazy and if anyone heard me say this last year they would have put me in a straitjacket, but before the season I told my Providence team we were going to New Orleans and the Final Four. I'm not naive enough to think that overnight the Knicks are going to win a championship, but we have a solid nucleus of players. We can achieve the level of excellence that New York fans expect and deserve.

"To me, this is my dream job. You don't always get what you dream for, but when you do you have to make the most of your opportunity. And that means winning."

That attitude had an immediate affect on the Knicks: The team hustled their way to a second-place finish in the Atlantic Division in Pitino's first season there, 1987–88, and made the playoffs for the first time in four years. GM Al Bianchi, the career hoop man who replaced Sterling, surrounded his new coach with a revamped roster and it paid off bigtime.

Pitino, who had been an assistant coach with the Knicks under Hubie Brown in 1983–84 and 1984–85, used nine players to implement his uptempo, pressing game. Ewing led the team in scoring with a 20.2 points per game average, with Gerald Wilkins (17.4), Rookie of the Year Mark Jackson (13.6), Bill Cartwright (11.1), Kenny Walker (10.1) and Johnny Newman (10) all in double figures.

The big leap forward came the next year, in 1988–89. New York finished first in the Atlantic Division with a 52–30 record and made it to the Eastern Conference semifinals before losing to the Chicago Bulls four games to two.

Once again, Ewing was the team's offensive leader, averaging 22.7 points per game

Chairman Of The Boards

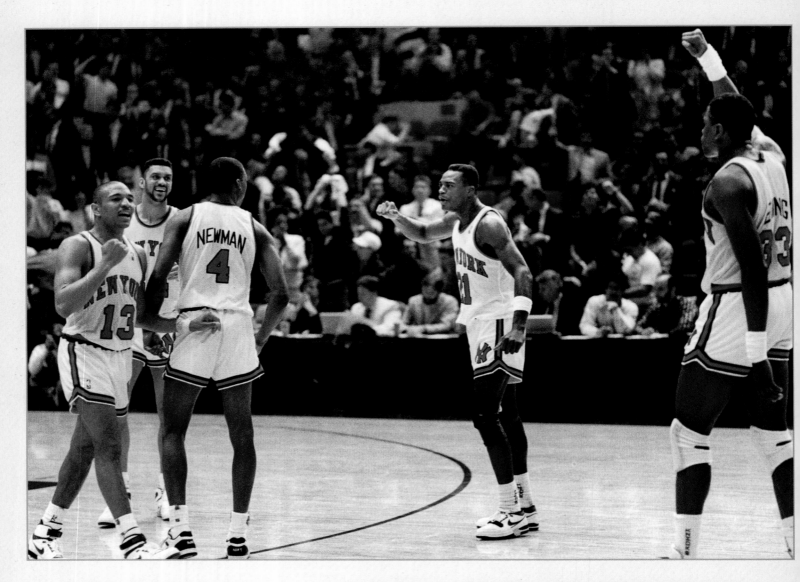

While Ewing, above far right, provided scoring punch near the basket, Pitino, below, encouraged his men to fire up the three-point shot. Trent Tucker, #6 on facing page, was one of several Knicks whose three-point proficiency led them to be called "The Bomb Squad."

while pulling in 740 rebounds. Only the team's new forward, Charles Oakley, had more rebounds, 861 of them. Oakley, who averaged 11.1 points, would prove to be an enduring Knick, giving the team hard-nosed defense and board strength. He was a reliable presence, always very physical and intense.

There were other new Knicks who provided ammo for the team's potent offense: the veteran Kiki Vandeweghe (son of Dr. Ernie, now a pediatrician in Southern California) and a rookie, Rod Strickland. Vandeweghe, traded to New York in February 1989, would average 11.1 ppg in 27 games with the Knicks. Strickland, the Knicks' number one draft choice, who'd played his college ball at DePaul, would average 9.2 ppg while being credited with 319 assists, second-best to Jackson, who had 619.

Jackson had had a big year under Pitino, averaging 16.9 ppg, leading the team in assists, steals and theatrical embellishments after his baskets. But in a season that saw the Knicks accelerate to the top of the Atlantic Division, those hambone touches were merely diverting. The Garden crowd gave Jackson his due. In the seasons to follow, as Strickland matured, a debate

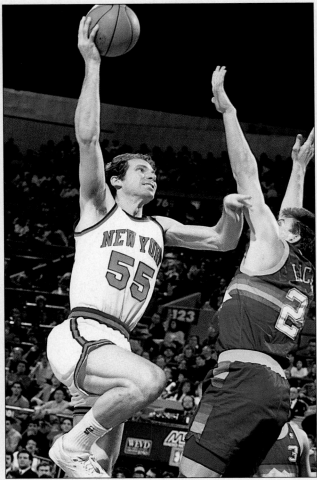

Mark Jackson, above.
Kiki Vandeweghe, #55 top right, is the son of former
Knick Ernie Vandeweghe.
Facing page, from left to right, "The Bomb Squad":
Rod Strickland, Trent Tucker, Gerald Wilkins,
Mark Jackson, Johnny Newman.

would ensue about which guard ought to be starting.

By the 1988–89 season, New York's legitimacy had been re-established. Pitino's club was scrappy and offensive-minded—third in the league in scoring with a 116.7 ppg average, and imbued with a trigger-happy attitude about the three-point shot. Their corps of three-point specialists—Jackson, Wilkins, Newman, Strickland and Tucker—would become known as "The Bomb Squad" for the merry abandon with which they fired the three all season.

With Pitino at the helm, expectations ran high after the 1988–89 season. But while New York fans were excited at what Pitino had wrought, the coach was having second thoughts about remaining in New York.

For one thing, it was an open secret that Bianchi and Pitino were not on the same wavelength about basketball strategies.

For another, Pitino had an offer from the University of Kentucky which he would accept, leaving the Knicks to his assistant, Stu Jackson, who would be named head coach.

BOMB
SQUAD

Celebration: The Knicks oust the Pacers in game seven of the 1994 East finals.

Pitino's departure had an adverse effect on the team.

By 1990–91, when the Knicks lost three straight games to the Bulls and were eliminated from the playoffs, they had lost the zip and panache that they had under Pitino. Up in the boardroom at Paramount, the Garden's corporate parent, it was a Code Red crisis—and time for radically retooling the Knicks organization.

In March of 1991, 35-year-old David W. Checketts was named president of the Knicks. In the eighties, Checketts had revitalized the Utah Jazz franchise during a six-year stint there, and now he was given a mandate to do the same in New York.

With the Knicks, his first order of business would be to find a coach with commanding presence. In an era where multi-year contracts and rocketing salaries often created inflated player egos, coaches no longer had the hire/fire leverage they had possessed years before. It meant that an NBA coach had a trickier time in motivating his teams.

For Checketts, Pat Riley was the antidote to the creeping diminution of authority.

Riley was an intriguing mix of motivator and dictator. On the lecture circuit or in the dressing room, Riley preached the verities of selfless sacrifice for the greater good of the organization. This was not exactly ground-breaking stuff. For decade upon decade coaches had sought to make the team's needs override the individual's. But Riley's approach had the force of his forward-march personality. Riley didn't ask that players fit the team concept, he insisted, communicating in language that was as direct as a left hook to the solar plexus.

For Riley, building the prerequisite togetherness—that one-for-all and all-for-one brio—was the first step in reconstructing the damaged psyche of a team that looked, played and thought like a loser. Riley would reroute a loser's anger and frustration into the purposeful aggression of a winner. Kill the cliques. Work hard, and then harder. And solidify team spirit by creating an us-against-them mentality. Practices would be closed to the media, and the team bus and charter plane would be off-limits to outsiders. In the strongest terms, Riley would insist that whatever quarrels and quibbles players had with him or with one another . . . well, that was family business and not to be aired out in public.

Riley had established his reputation in the eighties during his nine seasons as coach of the Los Angeles Lakers. Those were years in which Magic Johnson, Kareem Abdul-Jabbar, James Worthy and Company wrought wonders in the Fabulous Forum—slick, fast-paced basketball that from 1981 to 1989 produced four NBA championships in seven trips to the playoff finals. They were years in which Riley recreated Riley as the Armani-clad sidelines warrior, hair slicked back, a cool and cagey presence amidst the clamor and glamour that came to be known as "Showtime" at the Forum and ended up drawing a multitude of Hollywood VIPs such as Michael Douglas, Walter Matthau and, of course, Jack Nicholson. Riley had gone from being a reserve player on the Lakers roster, hustling like crazy to keep his job, to being the King Kong of coaches, living in Brentwood and driving his charcoal-gray Mercedes sedan to work.

"They've always written about 'Showtime' and glitter and glitz and clothes and my hair and gel," Riley said. "It's always been that. They've always missed the substance of what the Lakers were, which was a work-ethic team."

With Riley's record for success, Knicks players bought into Riley's work-ethic dogma, and suddenly the defense was swarming, relentless and guard-dog mean. On offense, players collaborated to get the best possible shot. And while the team may have lacked the finesse that Riley's Lakers had, they made up for it with doggedness and a brute physicality that would soon have other teams complaining that the Knicks were turning the game into a rugby scrum.

But the Knicks were no longer losers. By the All-Star break in February 1992, they were atop the Atlantic Division with a 30–16 record, and the Garden once had again become a hive of good-cheer and boisterous support. Yes, a Knicks ticket was a hot item. As in the good old days of Holzman's championship teams, courtside locations were filled with celebrities. A few of them, like Woody Allen, Robert Redford and screenwriter William Goldman, had been there in 1969–70. But this time around there would be plenty of new faces—like Richard Lewis, Spike Lee, Matt Dillon, Danny Aiello, Tony Bennett, Gene Wilder, Michael Douglas, Mike Tyson, Maury Povich and his wife, Connie Chung, and Lou Gossett.

For the players, Rileyball was a new deal, a new chance. Under this coach, no-name players willing to work hard or, in Riley's vernacular, "bust their humps" were upgraded immediately. Playing time was strictly on merit rather than reputation. For two Knicks in particular, John Starks and Anthony Mason, the hardscrabble road to NBA legitimacy would terminate, happily, in New York under coach Riley.

Starks, a former supermarket cashier, had bounced around the game's minor leagues while Mason had been obliged to draw his wages from European teams. In Mason and Starks, the Knicks had uncovered two players who at the outset of the season did not figure, really, in the team's plans. But both men made good on what chances they got, and through perseverance and talent, they had become integral to Riley's blueprint for the Knicks.

That blueprint was steeped in the old *DEE-fense*, *DEE-fense*, a cry that rang once again through the Garden as the Knicks—who had tied with Boston for top spot in the Atlantic Division with a 51–31 record—set a 5-game playoff series record by holding the Pistons to a total of 424 points while eliminating them three games to two in the opening round.

That Riley's Knicks were for real was transparently clear in the seven-game series that followed against defending NBA champion Chicago. Down three games to two, and before a Garden crowd, the Knicks fought back. Ewing would score 27 points, pull down 8 rebounds and block 3 shots even while playing with an ankle sprain suffered in the third quarter. That did not deter him. Eleven of his 27 points would come in the final quarter. Meanwhile, Starks would bolt off the bench and match Ewing's 27 points on 9–14 FGA. New York would even the series with a 100–96 victory.

Though Chicago would win the seventh game and go on to repeat as NBA champions, New York had established that it was no longer a team to take for granted. In Riley's first season, the Knicks had forged an identity as back-alley scrappers—and certainly no fun to have to go up against.

The city's fascination with and its adoration of these Knicks was based on the eternal team/fan equation: winning begets affection and admiration. And these Knicks—driven by Riley, hounded by Riley, worked to exhaustion by Riley—produced. It was not the ripening of that savvy game that Reed, DeBusschere, Bradley, Barnett and Frazier had flashed. This was blood, sweat and tears basketball, rooted in unrelenting defense, with a little bump and bang thrown in for good measure. Theirs was a physical game not photogenic the way, say, Riley's Lakers had been, with Magic's sleight of hand delighting the eye. And Riley and his Knicks made it work. In 1992–93, the defense was the best in the NBA, holding the opposition to 95.4 ppg. The offense ran on two cylinders—with Ewing (24.2 ppg) and Starks (17.5 ppg) providing most of the firepower. But with a little help from their friends—Oakley, Mason, Charles Smith, Tony Campbell, Greg Anthony, the rookie Hubert Davis—they managed to put enough points on the board. The Knicks won 37 and lost only 4 at the Garden, the best home-team record in the league that year, aided no doubt by the fact that every single home game was sold out. The Knicks would finish regular-season play at 60–22, best in the Atlantic Division and best in the Eastern Conference—a record that equalled the all-time club mark set by the 1969–70 champions.

Through the year, Riley kept driving his team. When a magazine writer wondered if the coach was having fun, Riley replied: "Basketball is a business pure and simple. If you want to have fun go to the YMCA."

After winning series from Indiana and Charlotte, once again the Bulls loomed as a formidable obstacle. The fifth game of the Chicago–New York series would be a classic heartbreaker for Knicks fans, as indelible in memory, in its perverse way, as Reed's seventh-game heroics in the championship finale of 1969–70. But here the memory was of the final seconds, Knicks trailing 1995–94, and Charles Smith going up four straight times at arm's length from the basket and falling short with each attempt.

So close to conquering the almighty Bulls they'd been—one shot to climb that rim and fall. But it wasn't to be. And in the next game, Chicago won their fourth straight game of the series, 96–88, to eliminate the Knicks on their way to their third straight NBA title.

It would be a year later when the Knicks would break through to the NBA finals, aided perhaps by Jordan's decision to retire from the NBA and try his luck as a baseball player. New York conquered Chicago and then Indiana to advance to the championship round. Their opposition would be the Houston Rockets, led by Hakeem Olajuwon, a 7', 255-pound center, who could hit the fade-away jumper or turn to the basket with a variety of nimble moves.

But in the end it would not be the shots that Olajuwon hit that people would remember. No, the finals would be marked by three Knicks wins, and the denial of a fourth by the slimmest of margins—Starks' last-second game six miss.

But Riley's instinct was to support his man, for Starks had repeatedly made the big plays during the season. It was the loyalty of a coach for a man who, like the Knicks team, had grown under his command.

The Knicks would come one game shy of seizing the glory, of knowing the exhilaration of a championship, as Houston won game seven 90–84. But in the broad sweep of the team's history, their turnaround under Riley was a success story that one series, one game could not undo.

But Riley appeared to realize the cycle had run its course after the 1994–95 season saw the Knicks slip to second place, behind the Orlando Magic in the Atlantic Division, and then be eliminated by Indiana in the playoffs. When a lucrative offer from the Miami Heat materialized, Riley took it and headed south. He was replaced by Don Nelson, whose methods and manner were relaxed and seemed the perfect antidote to the tightly wound Riley. But in 1995–96, Nelson and his players proved incompatible, and toward the end of the season he was replaced by Jeff Van Gundy, who was in his seventh season as a Knick assistant coach.

The assumption was that Van Gundy would be an interim coach. The assumption was wrong. Under Van Gundy, an Everyman type whom the players liked and trusted, the team began to look like a team again.

Their showing in the playoffs made believers of the world beyond Thirty-third Street. The Knicks swept the Cavaliers in three games and then played a rough-and-tumble series against the Bulls in which their defensive pressure had Chicago looking out of synch—hardly the super team the media had made them out to be. While Chicago would eliminate the Knicks in five games, the games were so competitive that but for a break here, a break there, New York might have beaten the Bulls.

But the Knicks' performance earned Van Gundy an extension of his contract. And it brought 50 years of Knick history full cycle. For a team that had been launched with men who worked routine jobs in the off-season—regular sorts—would face the future with an Everyman coach. And who knew? The magic that Holzman brought, that Pitino imbued, that Riley imparted, maybe Van Gundy will find it in him. And some night, as the sound of DEE-fense, DEE-fense rings out, perhaps another championship banner would be in the offing.

LIFE WITH RILEY

With Pitino headed for the bluegrass country, Bianchi tabbed Rick's first sergeant, Stu Jackson, for the head coaching spot. Jackson, who had played at Oregon as one of the "Kamikaze Kids" before becoming a college assistant, owned a keen sense and was a brilliant student of the game, qualities that would serve him well later as president of the expansion Vancouver Grizzlies.

Still, the 1989–90 Knicks tumbled to third place in the Atlantic with 45 wins. Midway through the season, Bianchi addressed the point guard logjam by sending Rod Strickland to San Antonio for Maurice Cheeks, who had established himself as one of the era's premier backcourt men with Philadelphia and as an unflappable veteran who would provide a stabilizing influence on the young team.

The Knicks were anything but stable in the first round of the playoffs against their old friends from Boston, whose Big Three of Bird-McHale-Parish was heading into what everyone knew would be their last title push. New York lost game one to Boston, then was blown away in game two by the unseemly score of 157–128.

Here's where the schedule came in. Game two in Boston had been on Saturday afternoon. Game three in New York wouldn't be until Wednesday night.

If you're the winning team in this situation, all you want to do is play the very next night, or the very next hour if possible, and close it out. If you're the losing team, you get a whole lot of time to think. And think. And think.

On Sunday, the Knicks were off. On Monday they sleepwalked through practice. On Tuesday, though, a What-do-we-have-to-lose attitude took over, and the Knicks had what coach Jackson termed, "The best practice we have ever had."

Back home on Wednesday for game three, the Knicks eked out a 3-point win, sealed only when Bird unbelievably clanged a wide-open 3-point attempt at the buzzer. On Friday, Ewing poured in 44 points and the Knicks would outscore Boston 70–51 in the second half to win by 27.

And now it was the Celtics who were reeling. In one memorable end-of-the-game sequence, the Knicks' Eddie Lee Wilkins was flattened by a Boston pick. When a few of the Celtics went over to help Wilkins up, Boston's Joe Kleine lumbered over and began pulling his teammates

Facing page, a wide-angle view of John Starks, #3, launching a jump shot.

Below, a close-up view of Starks, in pursuit of a loose ball.

away. Let him lie there. Sportsmen or not, both teams were headed to Boston for a deciding game five.

Of course, the Boston Garden was a place in which the Knicks had lost an amazing 26 straight games, dating all the way back to February of 1984. A parquet chamber of horrors.

But this time, there was a different feeling about it. Oakley would score 26 points and haul in 17 rebounds. Cheeks, the late addition, the old pro, would play the entire 48 minutes, hit 8 of 10 shots and score 21 points. Ewing would add 31 points, including a 3-point bomb from the left corner that he launched while falling over the bench. Knicks, 121; Celtics, 114.

So much more would happen to this team over the next decade, but for anyone who was there, this Sunday afternoon in Boston would retain a special kind of luster (especially for Bianchi, who as a player had experienced so much heartache in Boston and now, finally, had defeated the ghosts). And it really didn't matter that in the next series the Knicks would be run out by Detroit in five.

Fifteen games into the next season, Jackson was let go and John MacLeod, former coach of the Phoenix Suns, took over. The team did not respond to MacLeod either, again finishing third in the Atlantic Division with a 39–43 record.

By 1991, the front office felt an urgency to find a coach who could restore the faith of Knicks fans by putting a competitive team onto the floor. The club's chief executive, David W. Checketts (who replaced Bianchi on March 1, 1991), decided that that coach would have to have the command presence of a Marine first sergeant as well as the ability to communicate his basketball knowhow. Checketts' man was

Pat Riley, the former Laker coach who had been working as a TV commentator after nine seasons in L.A.

Riley took his new team's problems head-on. In the hermetically sealed world Riley created, he worked his players relentlessly, in meticulously organized practices that ran three hours or more. He dissected player performances with an evaluation index of his own creation that went beyond the box score to measure the effort expended by each Knick against his opponent—a kind of "hustle meter."

And as hard as he worked his men, so did Riley drive himself, constantly looking for ways to keep his team on the cutting edge. As Ken Auletta would write in a *Vanity Fair* profile on Riley: "He screens hours upon hours of videotapes of the Knicks and their opponents—two or three times. He hunts through Shakespeare and Sun-Tzu for quotes to inspire the troops . . . He's such a perfectionist that when the team arrives at a hotel at 2:30 a.m. the team trainer immediately plugs in a VCR so that the coach can stay up a few hours watching tapes of the next opponent. He worries about his team so much that he often drops ten to fifteen pounds during the pressure of the playoffs."

It was the portrait of a workaholic, a driven man whose slick image belied the real Riley, some observers insisted. For Riley was the son of a minor-league baseball manager, whose disappointment at not getting his chance in the majors made him turn to alcohol. When the father, Lee Riley, pulled himself together, he ended up as a janitor at a parochial school, where he moonlighted as the varsity baseball coach. He did so only after the school agreed to let him coach in his janitor's clothes.

Starks and Pippen in a frightening tangle under the basket in the 1993 playoffs.

Defense became the Knicks' trademark under coach Pat Riley in the nineties. That's Muggsy Bogues, of Charlotte, opposite with ball.

Wrote David Halberstam in *New York Magazine:* "That was pride, thinks the son, that there be no dissembling. In the eyes of one of Pat Riley's friends, screenwriter Bob Towne, the man in the Armani and the parochial-school coach in his janitor's clothes are the same man; both exist only on their own terms."

Riley made his terms crystal clear to his players. Work hard and the world can be

yours. Fake it and you're gone. For the player who had operated on the fringes of the pro game this amounted to an opportunity, a fair shake. And from the shadows would emerge men after Riley's heart, a pair of unknowns who would will themselves into the Knicks' big picture—John Starks and Anthony Mason.

Starks, a 6' 5" guard, had grown up in Tulsa, Oklahoma, with a schoolboy's love for the game. But a disagreement with the JV coach at Tulsa's Central High would prompt Starks to quit the team and seek his action on playgrounds against the city's better athletes. That led to a basketball transient's journey through three junior colleges and summer wages in a local supermarket, bagging groceries on the late-night shift for $3.35 an hour.

The supermarket wages spurred him to push on with his basketball as a scholarship player at Oklahoma State in 1987–88. There Starks averaged 15.4 ppg on .497 shooting, while making virtually no impression on NBA teams. No NBA organization saw him as prospect who was worth drafting—a bitter blow.

In the years that followed, Starks played in pro summer leagues, had a one-year stint as a benchwarmer for the Golden State Warriors, then a more prominent role in the CBA with the Cedar Rapids (Iowa) Silver Bullets and then with the WBL Memphis Rockers. His play in those minor leagues attracted the notice of the Knicks, and Starks ended up making the

team in 1990–91, playing only occasionally.

Under Riley the next year, 1991–92, Starks' playing time virtually doubled, even though he continued to come off the bench. But now his stretches of court time were comparable to that of starters Jackson and Wilkins. And by season's end, there was Starks averaging 13.9 ppg—only Ewing was better with 24 ppg—and suddenly more than just a guy scrambling for a job. John Starks had become a presence, hoisting up three-pointers, slashing to the basket on drives, taking charges on defense. His emotions were close to the surface, and that made him accessible to the Garden gallery with whom he quickly became a favorite.

Mason's turnabout was every bit as remarkable. After a college career at Tennesse State, Mason was an afterthought to the NBA. He was the fifty-third player selected in the 1988 draft, and the team that chose him, the Portland Trail Blazers, reinforced the general disinterest the league had for him by cutting him quickly.

Mason's life became a hoop itinerant's odyssey. There were seasons spent with European and South American professional teams, there were brief stops in the CBA and with the New Jersey Nets and Denver Nuggets of the NBA.

Finally, he got a chance when Ernie Grunfeld invited him to training camp. Grunfeld thought Mason's physicality would fit nicely with the take-no-prisoners style that Riley was crafting for his new team.

Like Starks, Mason would get serious playing time coming off the bench and he too would deliver: 7 ppg and a total of 573

In one of the defining moments of the Riley Era, John Starks nails down game two against the Bulls in 1993 with "The Dunk."

In the nineties, New York had reason to celebrate, as Doc Rivers, #25 above, is doing.

At left and below, Charles Oakley dives for loose ball and then recuperates from the impact.

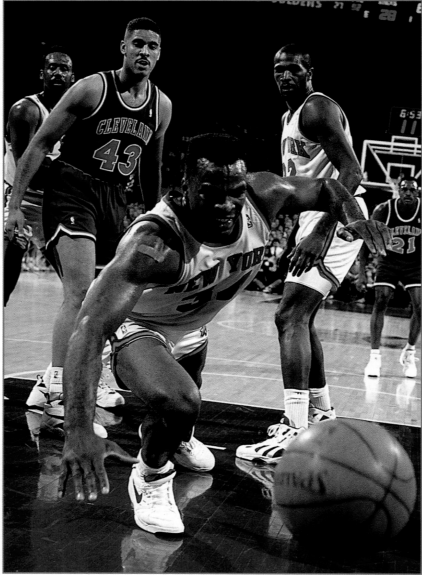

rebounds, third best on the Knicks, behind Ewing and Oakley, and more than starting forward, Xavier McDaniel, would amass.

Together they would be part of the surprising resurgence of basketball in New York, the Knicks' first-place tie with Boston in 1991–92 for the top spot in the Atlantic Division elating the fans and prompting the front office to push even harder to upgrade the team.

With the season ended, Checketts and Grunfeld were busy in the team's new offices at Two Pennsylvania Plaza. When McDaniel defected to Boston as a free agent, New York made a trade for swingman Tony Campbell of Minnesota and then a three-corner deal with the Clippers and the Magic that brought Charles Smith, Doc Rivers and Bo Kimble to New York

and sent Mark Jackson to Los Angeles. Wilkins moved on to Cleveland when the Knicks renounced their contractual rights to him, and Vandeweghe was unconditionally released and ended up as Jackson's teammate on the Clippers. New York traded a future first-round draft pick to Dallas for Rolando Blackman and took Hubert Davis in the college draft.

Riley's Knicks became a unique attraction in 1992–93, setting a team record when 39 regular-season home games were sell-outs, the prior mark of 31 having been established during the championship season of 1972–73. The total paid attendance of 804,840 was also a team record—99.3 percent of seating capacity.

With their first-place finish in the Atlantic Division and their 60–22 record,

Ewing earned high fives from Starks and Oakley and a standing ovation from the Garden faithful upon becoming the Knicks' all-time leading scorer in 1994.

the Knicks justified the renewed interest in the team. That success fed the need to crown the glory in the playoffs.

In the opening round of the 1992–93 playoffs, the Knicks were pitted against the Indiana Pacers, whose leading scorer and spiritual leader was the trash-talking and ever-theatrical Reggie Miller. Miller, who averaged 21.2 ppg during the regular season, had a knack of raising his game against New York, especially at playoff time when the spotlight was most intense.

By game three at the Pacers' Market Square Arena, he and Starks had a grudge match going. The emotional Starks let Miller's needling get to him. As the two players jawed at one another, Starks suddenly cocked his head and slammed it into Miller's face. That headbutt would oblige the officials to call a Phase II flagrant foul and eject Starks from the game. Miller would finish with 36 points (14–22 FGA), the Pacers would nail .603 of their field-goal attempts and win 116–93.

The Knicks would eliminate the Pacers in four games and then dispose of the Charlotte Hornets four games to one to advance to the next round against their old nemeses, Michael Jordan and Bulls. Under Phil Jackson, Jordan and the Bulls had won two straight NBA titles, against the Lakers in 1990–91 and against the Trail Blazers in 1991–92. Now they were intent on a "three-peat."

Their battles in the East against the Knicks were proving to be more than a prelude to the championship round: they had become the playoff match-up, with enough antagonism built in to extend to the coaches, who sniped at one another through the media.

Part of it had to do with the

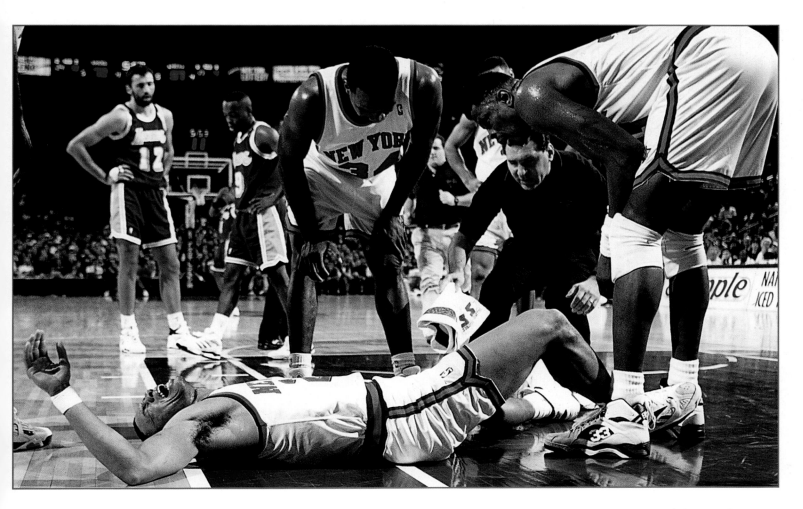

ongoing debate over the physicality with which the Knicks played. Jackson was using the media to make the officials conscious— maybe even sensitive—to what he viewed as "basketbrawling" and to what Riley saw as being competitive to the max. The rest had to do with two prideful coaches acting the part.

Even so, the players took center stage once the series began. The Knicks, owning home court advantage, authored an eight-point win in game one. Then they were able to stave off the Bulls in game two, a contest punctuated by a final-minute play that symbolized all that was outrageously wonderful about the Riley Era: a driving, lefthanded tomahawk slam by Starks, splitting Jordan and Horace Grant along the baseline for what would be forever known as "The Dunk." But the Knicks found the going rougher in Chicago, losing the next two games. Still the Knicks were determined to upend the Bulls. But in pivotal game five, with the series tied at two games apiece, the Knicks experienced the agony of defeat when Charles Smith missed four times in the final seconds, shooting the ball from underneath the basket. The heart seemed to go out of the Knicks, who lost the next game to Chicago and were eliminated.

River's all-out style, exhibited against Bogues, below, resulted in a serious knee injury against the Lakers, in 1994.

A SEASON TO REMEMBER

The master roster change for 1993–94 would be the midseason trade that sent Tony Campbell and a conditional draft pick to Dallas for 6' 4" veteran guard Derek Harper. The move was made in response to the torn anterior cruciate ligament and torn medial meniscus of the left knee that Rivers suffered on December 16, finishing his season.

Harper was an eleven-year veteran, who still had quickness and a decent outside shot and was a strong defender. For the past six years at Dallas he had been clockwork regular as a scorer, notching 17 or 18 points a game. He was a capable driver, able to take it all the way to the basket or dish off to the open man.

The other big change came when Michael Jordan shocked the sports world with his decision to retire from the NBA and try his luck as a baseball player. By now Jordan and his Bulls had become the most celebrated team in the game, and Jordan was a pop icon who transcended his sport. Like Muhammad Ali, he was known all over the globe, his fame spread nearly as much by the commercials he did as by the high-wire game he played.

But basketball aficionados saw beyond the glitz to the heart of the player. For beyond the photogenic smile that graced the billboards and made advertisers think "crossover" attraction was the drive and fierce resolve of a winner. Jordan had the ability, not to mention the need, to conquer. The Bulls would miss him, and his departure would create an opportunity for the Knicks.

The Knicks took advantage of the opportunity. During the regular season,

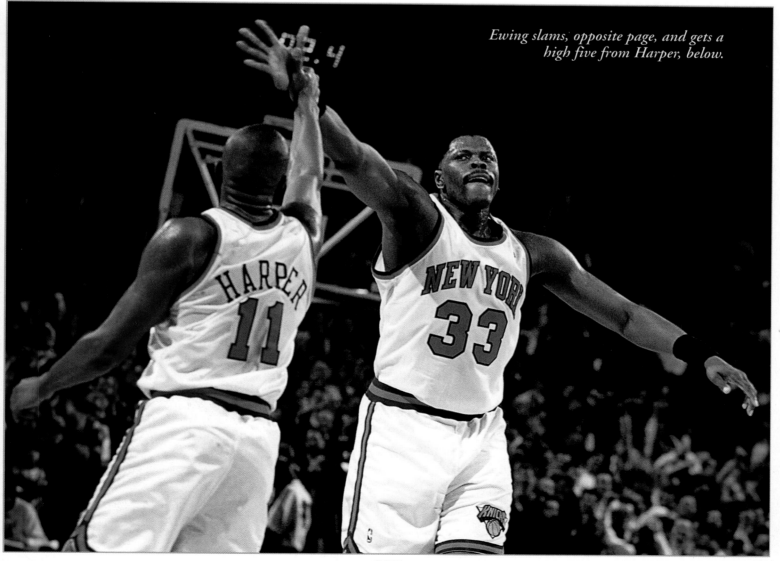

Ewing slams, opposite page, and gets a high five from Harper, below.

Riley's first Knicks team, 1991–92. Sitting on ground: Xavier McDaniel, Charles Oakley; first row (seated): Greg Anthony, Gerald Wilkins, Patrick Ewing, John Starks, Mark Jackson, asst. trainer Tim Walsh; second row (seated): Anthony Mason, Patrick Eddie, James Donaldson, Tim McCormick, Kennard Winchester, Kiki Vandeweghe, asstistant coach Bob Salmi; standing: head coach Pat Riley, trainer Mike Saunders, asstistant coaches Jeff Van Gundy, Paul Silas, Dick Harter, strength and conditioning coach Greg Brittenham.

Rolando Blackman

the team had a record of 57 wins and 25 losses—its third straight 50-plus-win season—good for first place in the Atlantic Division.

Ewing would once again provide the firepower on offense. Playing in 79 games, he would average 24.5 ppg while hauling in a total of 885 rebounds, second only to Oakley, who led the team with 965. On December 16, Ewing scored 27 points against the Lakers to become the Knicks' all-time leading scorer, passing Walt Frazier's 14,617 points when he nailed a 12-foot baseline jumper with 9:39 left in the third quarter.

By the end of the regular season, Ewing had a total of 16,191 career points. That put him fifty-fifth on the all-time NBA list, just behind Randy Smith (fifty-forth at 16,262) and Paul Arizin (fifty-third at 16,266). Ewing also was the all-time leading Knick in blocks (1,984) and games in which a Knick had scored 40 or more points (27).

New Knicks coach Pat Riley.

But Ewing had a fine supporting cast in 1993–94. Starks had had another big season, averaging 19 ppg and totalling 348 assists in 59 regular-season games. Other Knicks in double figures were Oakley (11.8), Hubert Davis (11) and Charles Smith (10.4).

The Knicks had become a team the city could not resist. All 41 home games were sell-outs, a team record. Indeed, the Riley era had virtually assured a full house every night out. And now those fans had expectations that only another NBA title would satisfy.

On to the playoffs.

In the opening round of the playoffs, New York went up against their metropolitan rival, the New Jersey Nets, in a best of five series. New York led two games to one when they traveled to the Meadowlands in New Jersey for game number four. That night Ewing came up big, scoring 36 points and grabbing 14 rebounds while blocking 4 shots, in leading New York to a 102–92 victory. Charles Smith came off the bench to score 18 points and get 8 rebounds in 35 minutes while Oakley had 16 points and 9 rebounds.

Next came the Eastern Conference semifinals against the Jordan-less Bulls.

With Jordan a minor-leaguer in the Chicago White Sox farm system, it made things easier for the Knicks. Easier but not easy. The Knicks needed seven games, finally, to vanquish the Bulls. New York did it with its ever-reliable defense and with balanced scoring.

The series would provide one of the NBA's strangest moments in game three when the Bulls' star, Scottie

MASE

For five years with the Knicks, Anthony Mason was a crowd favorite, as much for his physical play as for the ever-changing hair carvings that adorned his head.

Mason's tenure in New York ended after the 1995–96 season when he was traded to Charlotte for Larry Johnson. But by the time he left New York, he had gone from basketball no-name to high-priced star.

Like teammate John Starks, Mason had to work his way up from the basketball boondocks. But that was no surprise, Mason was no natural at the game. On the asphalt playgrounds of Baisley Park in Queens, where future pros like Mark Jackson, Pearl Washington and Kenny Smith would strut their stuff, grade-schooler Mason would be maligned for having no game.

But like Starks, Anthony George Douglas Mason had faith that with time he would measure up. At Springfield Gardens High, varsity coach Kenny Fiedler was a believer in Mason's potential and imbued the player with his conviction. At Springfield and later at Tennessee State, Mason worked hard and saw his game improve.

In New York, under Riley, he would come into his own.

ON TO THE FINALS

Pippen, would refuse to come off the bench for the final sequence because coach Phil Jackson had decided the crucial shot would be taken by Pippen's teammate, Toni Kukoc. Kukoc hit the shot from the top of the key to break a 102–102 tie and give the Bulls the victory.

That narrowed the Knicks series lead to two games to one. Even without Jordan, Chicago was no pushover. After six games, the Bulls had tied the series at three games apiece.

At Madison Square Garden, the Knicks finally bumped Chicago out of the playoffs, quashing the Bulls' three-year reign as NBA champions in a 87–77 victory. Ewing shook off a scoreless first half (oh-for-three field-goal attempts in 15 minutes) to lead the Knicks with 18 points and 17 rebounds. Oakley had 17 points and 20 rebounds.

In the final quarter, with textbook defense, the Knicks held the Bulls to 14 points on 6–20 FGA.

With the Bulls finally beaten, New York moved into the Eastern Conference finals against the Pacers. The series was tied two

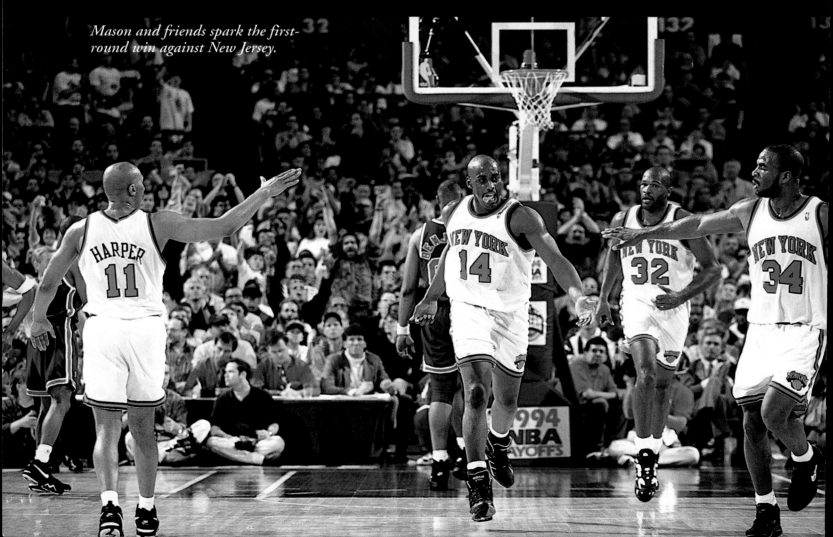

Mason and friends spark the first-round win against New Jersey.

games apiece—each team winning their games at home—when the Pacers came to the Garden for game five. Suddenly the home-court advantage was subverted by skinny Reggie Miller, who fired off a barrage of three-point shots and harangued and gestured at courtside spectator Spike Lee as the shots went in.

It was the game of his life for Miller, who scored 27 of his game-high 30 points in the fourth quarter, wiping out a double-digit Knicks lead and giving the Pacers a 3–2 series edge before a stunned MSG crowd. The final was 93–86. Miller set an NBA record for the most 3-point goals in a quarter with the five with which he sank the Knicks and derided filmmaker Lee.

Afterward, the cocksure Miller would tell newsmen that the Knicks were quitters and chokers. No surprise, those words figured prominently in the headlines in the next day's newspapers and even persuaded some fair-weather Knick fans.

As Riley would later note, exaggerating for effect: "There was a massive thud of everybody jumping off the bandwagon. There will be the same resounding thud of people jumping back on. What I can't understand is the questioning of their heart. Heart is what this team is all about."

Bye-bye Bulls: The end of years of playoff frustration.

The heart of the Knicks offense in the nineties was Patrick Ewing, #33.

Two days later, in Indiana, Miller's nemesis, the tempestuous Starks, gave Reggie and the Pacers their comeuppance in game six. As *New York Post* columnist Wallace Matthews would write:

"On this night, Starks fought through screens and picks and fought with the temptation to give in to his favorite indulgence, his boyish temper. Mostly it is born of enthusiasm, but often it turns self-destructive. Starks can unravel faster than a $40 suit in a rainstorm. His excitability can light his team up or burn it down. Last night, Starks glowed."

Starks scored a game-high 26 points, making 8 of 11 field goals and 5 of 6 of his 3-point attempts. While Miller would end up with 27

points, his shot was not the guided missile it had been in the previous game. Miller would make only 8 of 21 from the floor and even miss 3 of his 12 free-throw attempts.

The crucial seventh game would come down to the final 34.5 seconds, with the Pacers leading 90–89. That's when Starks missed a driving lay-up that was salvaged by Ewing, who snatched the ball in midair and slammed it through the hoop to give the Knicks a 91–90 lead with 26.9 seconds left.

When Oakley forced Miller's final-second shot off course, and a frustrated Miller then committed a flagrant foul on Starks, the Knicks had the game, the series and a ticket to the NBA finals against the Olajuwon-led Houston Rockets.

It was not exactly late-breaking news that in facing the Rockets the Knicks would be up against one of the game's best pivotmen, Hakeem Olajuwon. Olajuwon, a U.S. citizen born in Nigeria, had outside shots and slick moves to the basket. He could shoot, he could rebound, he could block shots. At 7', 250 pounds, Olajuwon was a formidable presence.

But he was not the only threat to the Knicks. Coach Rudy Tomjanovich's team had capable forwards in Robert Horry, Carlos Herrera, Otis Thorpe and Mario Elie. Horry and Thorpe were quick off their feet, routinely snatching rebounds above the rim, with Thorpe among the NBA leaders with an average of 10.6 rebounds per game. Elie was a tough defender, and could take the ball to the basket. Herrera was a rugged athlete, too.

Against a physical team like the Knicks, the Rockets were not lacking the big bodies, the powerful leapers to rumble with New York.

What's more, in Horry the Rockets had a big man who could fire the three-point shot. Another big man, Matt Bullard, also specialized in nailing the long-range three.

The backcourt featured Vernon Maxwell, Kenny Smith and Sam Cassell. As steady as Smith was, Maxwell was a streak shooter and emotional. But the surprise of the series would be Cassell. In a series where Smith would struggle to penetrate against Harper, Cassell would repeatedly drive the middle and improvise either a shot for himself or a pass to an open teammate. Though he was new to the pro game, the pressure hardly affected him.

During the regular season, Olajuwon had finished third in scoring in the NBA with a 27.3 points per game average, topped only by David Robinson of San Antonio and Shaquille O'Neal of Orlando.

He was also among the league leaders in field goal percentage (.528), rebounds (11.9 a game) and

When Doc Rivers injured his knee in 1993-94, the Knicks front office traded Tony Campbell for Derek Harper, #11, above.

blocked shots (3.71).

Houston had made it to the finals by beating Portland three games to one in the opening round, by eliminating Phoenix in the Western Conference semi-finals four games to three and by dumping Utah four games to one in the conference finals.

The Knicks–Rockets series would prove to be a bruising, very physical seven games, with the accent on defense. Neither team was able to score 100 points in any game.

Here is a recap, game by game, of the first six games of this thrilling series:

Game One (June 8 at Houston): Rockets, 85; Knicks, 78.

Poor shooting (31–91 FGA, .341) turned out to be the Knicks' undoing as they dropped the opening game of the finals. Ewing led the Knicks with 23 points and Olajuwon paced the Rockets with 28. Otis Thorpe had 14 points and a game-best 16 rebounds for Houston.

Trailing by 9 points (72–63) after three quarters, the Knicks put their defensive stamp on the fourth quarter yet again, holding the Rockets to 13 points on 2–13 FGA. New York, however, scored just 13 points on 6–24

Starks and Mason celebrate Eastern Conference finals victory over the Pacers.

in the quarter. They got as close as 3 points in the final minutes, but no closer. The two teams combined for 63 points in the second half and 28 points in the fourth quarter, both all-time NBA finals half/quarter lows.

Game Two (June 19 at Houston): Knicks, 91; Rockets, 83.

The Knicks rode clutch performances by Ewing, Starks and Harper to stifle a fourth-quarter Rockets surge and even the series in front of a Summit sell-out crowd. The victory snapped an overall six-game losing streak at Houston and was the Knicks' first win at the Summit since November 15, 1988. Starks bounced back from his 3-for-18 outing in game one to score a team-high 19 points. Harper scored 18 points with 7 assists and Ewing scored 16 points and had a game-high 13 rebounds, along with 6 blocked shots.

Olajuwon led the Rockets with 25 points.

The Knicks shook off their first-game shooting slump by going 10–19 FGA in the first quarter to take a 24–20 lead, but the Rockets forged a 42–42 tie at half-time. Starks scored 11 points in the third quarter as the Knicks took a 72–65 lead.

Houston responded with a 14-4 run to open the

fourth quarter, capping the rally on Maxwell's lay-up and free throw that gave the Rockets a 79–76 lead with 6:32 left.

But the Rockets would go 0 for 12 the rest of the way as the Knicks ran off a game-deciding 15–4 surge. Harper gave the Knicks the lead for good (81–79) by burying a 3-pointer with 4:30 left. After a block from behind by Ewing on Olajuwon at 2:14, Harper hit another 3-point shot with two minutes left to give the Knicks an 87–81 edge.

After two defensive stops, the Knicks sealed the verdict as Starks stole the ball from Maxwell and fed a trailing pass to Mason for a slam dunk and an 89–81 lead with just :43.9 seconds left.

Game Three (June 12 at MSG): Rockets, 93; Knicks, 89.

Cassell's 3-point bomb with 32.6 seconds left was the difference as the Rockets prevailed at the Garden. Harper led the Knicks with 21 points, Starks added 20 points and a game-high 9 assists and Ewing recorded 18 points, a game-high 13 rebounds and 7 blocked shots. Olajuwon paced the Rockets with 21 points and 11 rebounds.

Houston led by as many as 16 points in the second

New York City mayor Rudy Guiliani, above, kibitzes with Doc Rivers, left, and Patrick Ewing, right.

Riley, below, with Indiana Pacer coach Larry Brown.

The play that sent the Knicks to the finals, opposite at bottom: Ewing's follow-up slam that gave New York the lead for good in game seven against the Pacers.

John Starks in a quiet moment of prayer before game six.

quarter (42–26) and by 14 points in the third quarter (59–45) on Olajuwon's slam with 7:49 left. Then the Knicks rallied to close the gap to 69–63 after three quarters.

The Knicks outscored Houston 14–8 to open the fourth quarter, climaxing the uphill climb with Starks' lay-up that tied the score at 77–77 with 5:14 left. Inside the final minute, Harper's jumper with :52.7 seconds remaining gave the Knicks an 88–86 lead.

With the Knicks' defense smothering Olajuwon, Hakeem passed the ball out to Cassell, who nailed what proved to be the decisive 3-pointer for an 89–88 edge.

On the Knicks' next possession, Ewing was called for an offensive foul with :23.7 left. Starks' subsequent 3-point miss and 4 free throws by Cassell put the game away for Houston.

Game Four (June 15 at MSG): Knicks, 91; Rockets, 82.

Monstrous efforts by Oakley, Harper and Starks staved off a 32-point, 8-rebound, 5-block game by Olajuwon as the Knicks evened up the series.

The Knicks won at a raucous MSG, which only 24 hours earlier had hosted the Rangers' first Stanley Cup celebration in 54 years.

Harper scored a team-high 21 points for the second straight game, going 5 for 10 on 3-point shots. Starks added 20 points, 11 in the fourth quarter. Oakley had 16 points and a game-high 20 rebounds.

The Knicks took the lead for good on Ewing's short jumper, which gave them a 74–72 lead with 5:31 to go.

The key play down the stretch was Oakley's out-of-bounds save off the second of Ewing's two missed 3 throws. Starks converted the save into a 3-pointer that gave the Knicks an 80–74 lead with 3:39 left.

Game Five (June 17 at MSG): Knicks, 91; Rockets, 84.

The Knicks came up big again down the stretch, holding the Rockets to only one field goal over the game's final 4:25 to negate a storming Houston comeback and take a 3–2 series lead.

Ewing led the Knicks with 25 points and 12 rebounds, adding a club playoff record 8 blocks (tying a finals mark). Starks scored 19 points and Mason came off the bench for 17 points and 9 rebounds in 30 minutes.

Olajuwon paced the Rockets with 27 points.

The Knicks took a 13-point lead (56–43) midway through the third quarter, but then the Rockets took off to outscore the Knicks 18–5 for the rest of the quarter, forging a 61–61 tie after three quarters.

The Rockets led by as many as 4 points in the fourth quarter (67–63) before the Knicks came back for their final push.

After Kenny Smith lost the ball out of bounds with 2:34 left and Houston up by 2, the Knicks took the lead for good when Starks hit a 3-pointer with 2:22 left for an 81–80 lead.

Harper's two free throws with 1:50 left made it 83–80. Robert Horry missed a 3-point shot, with Oakley hauling in the rebound and Harper converting to a driving Mason for a slam dunk and an 85–80 lead with 1:25 left.

Game Six (June 19 at Houston): Rockets, 86, Knicks, 84.

The Rockets survived a 16-point fourth-quarter assault by Starks and held off a furious Knicks charge down the stretch to send the finals into game seven before a delirious sell-out crowd in Houston.

Starks led the Knicks with 27 points, including 5 for 9 from 3-point range. Starks hit 5 of 7 field-goal attempts and 3 of 4 from downtown in the fourth quarter.

Olajuwon led the Rockets with a game-high 30 points.

Houston took a 9-point lead (72–63) with 9:18 left in the game. But the Knicks would close out the game with a 21–14 run to fall an eyelash short.

The run began on Starks' 3-point bomb with 9:11 left, starting a stretch in which he would score 15 of his 16 fourth-quarter points in the final 9:11.

Starks' lay-up (1:33) and 3-pointer (1:17) brought the Knicks within 2 points (84–82). Hakeem's two free throws made it 86–82 with :39.3 seconds left. Mason hit a short jumper to bring the Knicks to within 2 (86–84) with :32.0 left, then grabbed the rebound off a Smith miss to give the Knicks a shot to tie. But Starks' potential title-winning 3-pointer with 2 seconds on the clock was deflected by Olajuwon.

In the end, there would be a climactic game seven and a sudden-chill in Starks' outside shooting. Rockets, 90; Knicks, 84.

Twenty-five playoff games. No team had ever played more. And in the end: One win short.

The long season ended in bitter disappointment. But what a ride it had been.

Just inches away: Starks lets fly in the final seconds of game six.

New York's heartbreaking loss to Houston was, it turned out, a psychological breaking point. Thereafter Riley's authority would diminish in New York. Not exactly shocking. Riley was a hard, driven man, who kept the pressure cranked up on his teams. That sort of unrelenting push tends to wear thin when a championship does not become part of the equation soon enough.

Riley had made his mark—his Knicks teams had character and drive. They only lacked the title.

The team fell to second place in the Atlantic Division in 1994-95 and was then eliminated by Indiana in the playoffs. They fought the Pacers back from a 1–3 deficit to force game seven, only to see Ewing miss a last-second one-hander that would have forced overtime. The season was over and Riley seemed to sense his time in New York had passed.

Riley would move on to the Miami Heat as coach and team president. The new Knicks coach was Donald Arvid Nelson.

Don Nelson was an NBA veteran. He had played fourteen seasons, the majority of them with the Boston Celtics during their glory years. He had been an integral part of five World Champion Celtics teams—1966, 1968, 1969, 1974 and 1976. He had forged a reputation as a cagey operative, who used his wits to maximize his talent.

Nelson retired as a player in 1975–76. In the very next season he would begin 18 years of coaching, 11 years with the Milwaukee Bucks and 7 years with the Golden State Warriors. His Milwaukee teams would finish first seven times in the Midwest and then the Central Division. During his Milwaukee tenure, he also served as director of player personnel and later as vice-president of basketball operations.

He joined the Warriors as executive vice-president in 1987–88. The following season he became the club's head coach and general manager, serving in that capacity until February 13, 1995, when a highly public dispute with Warrior star Chris Webber prompted Nelson to retire. As Warriors coach, Nelson posted a 277–260 record, including two 50-win seasons (55–27 in 1991–92 and 50–32 in 1993–94). He came to New York with 817 career wins.

"To be in New York is a dream come true," Nelson said after being named the 17th head coach in Knickerbockers history on July 6, 1995. "There's no place like New York, and if I can make it here, I can make it anywhere."

GM Grunfeld, who played for Nelson at Milwaukee, called the new coach "an innovator, a motivator, a teacher and a man who has a real passion for the game of basketball. His resume has 'Hall of Fame' written all over it."

For all his years as a coach, Nelson had never won an NBA title.

"It's something I would like to do before I hang up my coaching sneakers," he said. "And I think I have that opportunity here."

The opportunity was short-lived. Nelson, thought to be the antidote to the control-oriented Riley, certainly offered the Knicks a difference. His practices were more brief and not so kamikaze intense. His offense offered opportunities for a variety of Knicks.

But things did not work out quite the way Nelson and the Knicks anticipated. It was a sticky situation. The inevitable happened. Nelson would not last the 1995–96 season—an incompatibility problem, it seemed—and that would lead to long-time assistant coach Jeff Van Gundy being named coach.

Van Gundy, 34 years old when he took over the Knicks, had started the 1995–96 season in his seventh year as an assistant coach.

Van Gundy was from a basketball family. His father, Bill Van Gundy, had been coaching for more than three decades and was in his thirteenth season as head coach at Genessee Community College in Batavia. Jeff's brother Stan was in his first year as an assistant coach with the Miami Heat, after a distinguished college coaching career at Fordham, Lowell (Mass.) and the University of Wisconsin.

"The foundation for all my love of the game came from being around my dad and my brother, who are 'lifers' in coaching," said Van Gundy.

A 1985 magna cum laude graduate of Nazareth College in Rochester, New York, Van Gundy played point guard for two seasons and helped the 1983-84 squad to the NCAA Division III Eastern Regional title.

Van Gundy's coaching career began in 1985–86, when he was head coach at McQuaid Jesuit High School in Rochester. Then came two years on the coaching staff of Providence College, as a graduate assistant to Rick Pitino in 1986–87 and as assistant coach under Gordon Chiesa the following year. In 1988–89, he served as an assistant under Bob Wenzel at Rutgers.

He joined the Knicks on July 28, 1989.

Van Gundy had an unassuming style, both as a coach and a civilian. This was a man who drove a Honda Civic and for dinner ate Big Macs regularly at a McDonald's on Tenth Avenue. He told writers that his annual wedding anniversary celebration with his wife Kim was a Broadway show preceded by dinner at Howard Johnson's in Times Square. "Best apple crisp in New York," he would say.

It was certainly not the portrait of a big-time image-conscious coach. No, Van Gundy hadn't either the slick image of a Riley or the deep NBA background of a Don Nelson. Yet he had been around these Knicks for a while, and they found him easy to co-exist with. They liked him, and they felt he had a special feeling for them.

Van Gundy was named coach on March 8, 1996, via an early-morning visit from Grunfeld to his Philadelphia hotel room. That night, the Knicks went into the Spectrum, where they had won 8 of their prior 9 games, and were promptly drubbed, by eight, by a Sixer team that would win all of 18 games. A memorable debut, it was not.

And it wasn't going to get any better. Two days later, the Chicago Bulls, who had won 54 of their first 60 games, would visit the Garden before a national TV audience. Van Gundy's debut in front of the home folks figured to be a rough one.

It was a memorable, surreal afternoon. The Knicks, who had lost to the hapless Sixers just two nights before, scored 31 points in the first quarter against a 54–6

Charlie Ward

team and never looked back. They outscored the Bulls 54–30 in the second half. They got 26 points from Ewing and 23 from Harper. They allowed 32 points to Jordan, but just 19 to the rest of the starters. They hit 10 3-pointers. They won by 32 points, 104–72. And a stoic Van Gundy allowed himself, yes, just the tiniest of smiles as the final seconds ticked away.

During the stretch run of the regular season, the slumping Knicks would come together and, in the 23 games that Van Gundy coached, win 13 and lose 10.

Van Gundy's late-season tenure as head coach was marked by a renewed commitment to rebounding and defense.

"I haven't done anything to change

Perennial springtime nemesis Reggie Miller.

For the Knicks and the rest of the league, Michael Jordan, #45, was virtually unstoppable. While Jordan was around, he was a formidable obstacle for the likes of Patrick Ewing, right.

this team," Van Gundy would say soon after his appointment. "The veterans have changed the attitude of this team and they deserve credit for that.

"We've got to get our attitude strong and our game will follow. It can't be the other way around. We've got to be resilient in the tough times. If we're all pulling the same way, on the same page, with the same goals, we have a chance to do a lot of damage the rest of the way."

Van Gundy proved right. In the playoffs, the Knicks blitzed the Cavaliers, sweeping the series with a steady barrage of three-point shots. Starks was deadly from behind the 3-point line, as was Harper. Ewing hit the fade-away jumper with clockwork regularity, and Oakley and Mason were The Bruise Brothers under the backboards. The Cavaliers were no match for the Knicks.

Chicago was tougher. But the Bulls, who would stampede through the rest of the playoffs, didn't have their way with New York. Although the Bulls won four games to clinch, the final result was no indication of how Chicago struggled.

Game one would haunt the Knicks

When Riley was with the Knicks, Don Nelson, shaking hands with Riley, right, was coaching Golden State. It was Nelson, in subway photo below, who moved in when Riley moved on to the Miami Heat as coach and team president. Both Riley and Nelson depended on Charles Oakley, #34, above.

throughout the series. They held Chicago to just 38 percent shooting and 91 points, but could not capitalize. The Knicks ran off 13 straight points in the third quarter and were within 1 point in the final minutes, but could only score 15 points in the fourth quarter and lost by 7. Jordan, who had 44 points in game one, added 28 in game two as the Bulls won again.

But the Knicks were coming home now, to a Garden audience that had grown accustomed to Knicks-vs.-Bulls as a Big Apple springtime tradition. And game three would only serve to add to the tradition. Jordan scored 46, including 8 straight points in the final 2 minutes to wipe out a Knick lead. But Ewing would take over in overtime, with two vital field goals in the final 90 seconds. Up by 3, the Knicks emerged

Sweet-shooting Hubert Davis.

victorious—102–99—as Pippen's 3-point attempt from the left wing hit the front rim as the buzzer sounded.

That was Saturday. On Sunday, they were right back at it again.

The Knicks fought from behind all game, down by 10 with less than eight minutes left. Then they ran off 13 straight points, the last 4 by Ewing, to move ahead. Rodman found Bill Wennington twice under the basket, negating another last-minute Ewing basket. Down by 3, the Knicks had one last shot. But Starks was called for traveling, just before draining a last-second 3-pointer that could have tied it. That the Knicks were even in a position to win was amazing, having been outrebounded 46–28. The final point margin was just 3—94–91—but enough.

Following that, the Knicks didn't have a whole lot left heading back to Chicago for game five. Still, the issue was in doubt most of the way. Jordan scored 35, but the game was really decided early in the fourth quarter when the Knicks held the Bulls to just 4 points over a 5:20 span but could score only 6 points themselves. That and a late 12–5 run did it. 94–81 was the final.

The Knicks' hard-nosed defense made the Bulls look tentative and nothing like the team that had swept through the regular-season schedule with a 72–10 record and the accompanying hoopla that made them out as possibly the greatest team in NBA history. Time and again in the series, the Knicks were in position to win ball games that they simply failed to seize. A turnover here, an error of omission there, and it could have been a life-and-death series for Chicago.

But the Bulls recognized that they had a struggle on their hands. Michael Jordan acknowledged how tricky a series it had been when he told newsmen after the first four games with Chicago leading three games to one: "They can look back and say they could have won all four games."

Could-have, should-have: those are the catchwords of a losing team. But for New York the series revealed what their tenacious defense might beget if the team could become mistake-proof at crunch time.

As for Van Gundy, assumed to be a mere interim coach when he replaced Nelson—well, he had restored cohesion and mellowness to

Mase exhibits his trademark ferocity.

the ball club.

"He is a very good communicator, very honest, and created a head coach's presence because of his knowledge," Grunfeld would say after the season.

"He created an environment in which the players wanted to come to work," said Grunfeld. "When a lot of (top) coaches are under contract, why go around looking when we are comfortable with what we have right here?"

As *The New York Post's* Jay Greenberg would write: "The key word, indeed, is comfort. Without that level of trust between player and coach, an NBA team is doomed to the level of failure we saw from the Knicks in February."

Van Gundy would say: "One of the benefits of being an assistant in this league is that you can analyze why teams are successful. And it really comes down to players. That's why I know my role, but it's a small one. I'm not going to be the reason why we win."

Wrote Greenberg: "This essential understanding of a professional coach's limitations

Assistant coach Jeff Van Gundy, opposite, replaced Don Nelson late in the 1995-96 season. Although New York lost four games to one to a Bulls team featuring Dennis Rodman, #91, and Michael Jordan, #23, their strong defense gave the Bulls problems.

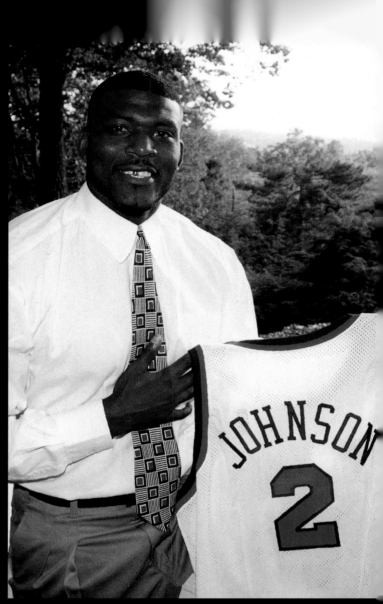

can save one from his own stubbornness. It gives Van Gundy, who until March was perfectly happy to be a career assistant, a chance to be the best possible head coach for the talent he is given. Which, in the NBA, means a fine coach indeed."

And when the dust settled in mid-July, Van Gundy was looking at a new-and-improved Knicks team, with the additions of Allan Houston, Chris Childs, and Larry Johnson, and rookies John Wallace, Walter McCarty and Dontae' Jones. The new-look roster followed a change in ownership, with ITT/Cablevision having assumed control of the Garden and its organization the following year.

Larry Johnson, acquired from the Charlotte Hornets in exchange for forwards Anthony Mason and Brad Lohaus, is a two-time NBA All-Star and the 1992 Rookie of the Year. In five NBA seasons

the 6' 7", 253-pounder averaged 19.6 ppg with the Hornets, where he recorded nine 30+ point games. Johnson was the first overall selection in the 1991 draft; he attended UNLV, where he helped lead the team to the 1990 NCAA championship.

Chris Childs, a point guard, will begin his third NBA season with the Knicks, following two years with the New Jersey Nets. A former Boise State star, Childs also played for five seasons in the Continental Basketball Association.

Twenty-five-year-old Allan Houston comes to the Knicks following his best NBA season, with the Detroit Pistons. An outstanding shooter, the 6' 6" Houston averaged 19.7 ppg last season. Houston was the eleventh player selected in the 1993 draft, from the Tennessee Volunteers, where he is the school's all-time leading scorer.

Forward Buck Williams was also secured for the Knicks 1996–97 roster. Heading into his sixteenth NBA season, Williams is a three-time NBA All-Star and a four-time NBA All-Defensive team selection. At 6'8", Williams "will fill a void in our frontcourt and provide veteran leadership," said head coach Van Gundy. "He's a terrific low-post defender, a rebounding force, and he's been a consistent winner." Williams has played with the New Jersey Nets (from 1981–82 to 1988–89) and the Portland Trail Blazers (from 1989–90 to 1995–96). He holds a career average of 13.5 ppg and heads into the new season as the fifty-seventh leading all-time scorer in NBA history with 16,117 points.

With the influx of fresh rookie talent, combined with the energy from the new trades, a new coach and the solid talent already on the Knicks team, the 1996–97 season should prove to be an exciting one to watch—once again.

Above, left to right, Dave Checketts, Jeff Van Gundy and Ernie Grunfeld (at right) welcome new Knicks players Chris Childs (center) and Allan Houston (second from right).

Opposite page: left, NBA veteran Buck Williams, #52, is acquired by the Knicks for the 1996–97 season; right, Larry Johnson, #2, a two-time NBA All-Star, joins ranks for the first full season under head coach Jeff Van Gundy.

THE GARDEN EXPERIENCE

In the beginning, there was the BAA...and not much public interest. That league's first season grossed little more than $1 million in ticket receipts—the equivalent of one NBA bench-warmer's salary these days.

But even then, back in 1946–47, New Yorkers turned out for their Knickerbockers—scoring the second-best paid attendance in the league. Basketball is and always has been The City Game, with enough hard-core fans to satisfy the franchise's box office.

However it wasn't until 1969–70 that it became chic to be courtside at the Garden. That's when the first conspicuous wave of celebrities began flocking to the Garden, and they have kept coming ever since. If, as F. Scott Fitzgerald said, the rich are different from you and me, so are the celebs. They get the best seats *and* their pictures in the next day's tabloids. So it goes...

But the excitement of the game wouldn't be the same without the yells, cheers and hollers of the Knicks fans who occupy over 19,000 seats behind the players' benches. Not often an easy crowd to please, Knicks fans are certainly among the league's most supportive and appreciative as late April rolls around each year. And for the last 50 years, through victories and defeats, the fans always returned for another season of renewed hope and passion for their team, The New York Knickerbockers.

✴ *Clockwise from top left, Bill Bradley shares a moment with entertainer Barbra Streisand; for the average fan or for a celebrity like Bill Cosby, Bradley was a Knicks favorite; Mary Stuart Masterson and Gene Wilder, two Hollywood stars who turn out for Knicks games; and "Dancing Harry," a Garden fixture who would gyrate and lead the crowd in cheers.*

* The 1969–70 Knicks drew the likes of Peter Falk, above left, Robert Redford, middle right, and NY Mets legend Tom Seaver and his wife, Nancy, below right. Woody Allen has been supporting the Knicks over many decades. Above right, Allen's pictured on Willis Reed's show in the 1970s along with Pete Maravich; and, below left, he's catching a game with girlfriend Soon Yi in the 1990s.

✳ Comic Knick-watchers, at left top to bottom, Jerry Seinfeld, Billy Crystal and Jay Leno. Above, Patrick Ewing has a moment with TV's Emmanuel Lewis. Stars of the silver screen Sharon Stone, below left, and Ma Dillon, below right, catch a court side glimpse of the Knicks.

✱ *Celebs on left, from top to bottom: singer Tony Bennett, actor Danny Aiello and comedian Richard Lewis. Notable spectators on right, from top to bottom, former heavyweight champion George Foreman, actor Lou Gossett Jr., actor Arnold Schwarzenegger and Dr. Ruth Westheimer chatting with Dr. Joyce Brothers.*

✳ In the nineties, basketball at the Garden could be something of a spectacle—from sign-waving fans, left top and bottom, to the attractive and talented Knicks City Dancers, above, and entertainment luminaries like Tom Cruise, left center, Madonna, near left, and John F. Kennedy Jr., near right.

✳ *And then there are those Hollywood types who can't seem to get enough of this East Coast game: far right, top to bottom: actors Michael Douglas, Jack Nicholson and Dustin Hoffman.*

✳ *In the 1950s, Marv Albert had been president of the Knicks fan club and a ball boy for the team; but his ambition was to be a sportscaster. In that role, Albert, above, is seen interviewing a smiling Walt Frazier.*

✳ *Bob Wolff, below at right, with Cal Ramsey, began announcing pro basketball in 1946-47. In those days, Wolff did the telecasts of the Washington Capitols of the Basketball Association of America, a team coached by a young Red Auerbach.*

In the beginning, there was the voice of Marty Glickman, whose sweet humming line of on-the-court action made friends and influenced basketball people.

There are folks who, these 50 years later, will insist that talented as those announcers were who followed him— Bob Wolff, Les Keiter, Jim Karvellas, Marv Albert—Glickman is and was *the* forever voice of Knicks basketball.

Well, the pleasure of the broadcast sound is in the ear of the beholder. But suffice it to say that when Glickman's voice filled the airwaves, folks paid attention.

"Basketball broadcasting didn't exist before 1945–46," Glickman said. "As an aspiring young broadcaster, I recognized that through certain sports, guys became prominent. Bill Stern and Ted Husing were known for football. Mel Allen and Red Barber for baseball. Don Dunphy for boxing. Clem McCarthy for horse racing. There was no basketball announcer. I wanted to be *the* basketball announcer. I'd played in high school—one year varsity for James Madison High in Brooklyn. I was a New York City kid. What the hell, it was our game. Basketball was like a religion: I'd go to Hebrew school, and then play basketball. Saturdays, I'd go to synagogue, and then play basketball the rest of the day. And all day Sunday. But basketball simply was not broadcast.

"During the war, I'd write from overseas to Bert Lee, the general manager of WHN radio, telling him I wanted to broadcast basketball when I was mustered out of the military. Nineteen forty-five, forty-six, I began announcing college basketball doubleheaders.

"In the early days of the game, the NBA needed help to draw crowds. The Harlem Globetrotters were important to the BAA and NBA. They'd often play the first game of a doubleheader. Marques Haynes and Goose Tatum were very, very popular. At the end of their game, maybe half the people would go home."

Glickman's voice helped change all that.

Like Glickman, Bob Wolff's roots are deep in the pro game. As the telecaster for the Washington Caps in 1946–47, he got to know the team's coach, Red Auerbach.

"We lived four, five blocks from one another," said Wolff. "Every once in a while we'd go over to a playground, and shoot baskets. Red was a good two-handed shooter. One day we played against a bunch of kids. One of them asked Red his name. 'Red Auerbach,' he told them. The kid didn't believe him. He figured what would a big-time coach be doing shooting hoops in a playground. But Red just wanted to play."

It's the chance to sit courtside and maybe shoot a few baskets with one of the greatest coaches in the game that keeps kids dreaming of becoming basketball broadcasters.

Left to right-Bob Wolff, Marty Glickman, Marv Albert, John Andariese, Jim Karvellas celebrate Marv Albert's twenty-fifth year as a Knicks broadcaster.

Walt Frazier, pictured above with broadcast partner Mike Breen, has been a color commentator on Knicks games since the late 1980s. Frazier's narrative is given to polysyllabic words, the use of which has become as much his trademark as the name "Clyde" was when he was a ballplayer. Breen has been the radio voice of the Knicks in the nineties over the WFAN/MSG Radio Network.

Jim Karvellas and Butch Beard, below with TV's Emmanuel Lewis, were a broadcast team in the eighties over the Madison Square Garden Network.

THE GUY WITH MARV

For more than a decade, John Andariese, second from right, above, has sat alongside Marv Albert as color commentator on MSG Network's coverage of Knick games. Besides offering insights on the developing game action, Andariese often is the object of Albert's tongue-in-cheek barbs. Their repartee has become part of their popular broadcasting format.

Andariese is a 25 year veteran of basketball broadcasting, serving 8 years as color commentator on MSG Network radio, including the Knicks' second championship season in 1972-73.

A former hoop star at Fordham under Johnny Bach, Andariese is co-founder of the New York Pro and College Summer Basketball League, a member of the national sports committee of the Leukemia Society of America, celebrity chairman of the YMCA's "1 in 10 Club" and president of Petry Networks, a division of Petry Inc.

✳ *Through the thrill of victory, and the agony of defeat, there have always been Knicks fans. Young and old, they have filled the Garden for fifty years. On occasion the generations gather, as occurred on the night tennis star John McEnroe and son, left middle, were spectators. Compared to Stanley Asofsky, at bottom in sports jacket and glasses, and his friend, Fred Klein, standing next to him with upraised arms, the McEnroes were relative newcomers at watching Knicks games. Asofsky in particular went way back, having first seen the team play using a friend's student discount card in 1946-47 to get into the old Garden on Eighth Avenue, between Forty-ninth and Fiftieth Streets.*

✳ *In the VIP seats at courtside or in the upper reaches of the Garden (see opposite page), Knicks fans share the same passion for their team. Whether urging defense with a novelty sign or helping cushion Patrick Ewing's fall, they put their hearts, heads and voices into the game.*

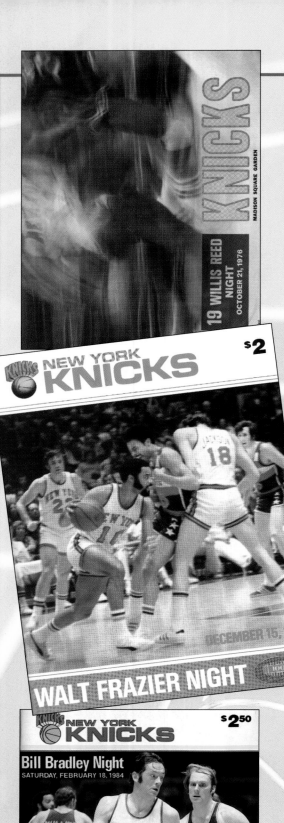

NEW YORK KNICKS

$2

DECEMBER 15, 1979

WALT FRAZIER NIGHT

NEW YORK KNICKS

$2.50

Bill Bradley Night
SATURDAY, FEBRUARY 18, 1984

SPECIAL COLLECTORS ISSUE

If you look up to the rafters of the Garden, you'll find hanging there the jersey numbers of memorable Knicks.

Only a few players have been honored in this way. In numeral order they are: Walt Frazier (10), Dick Barnett (12), Earl Monroe and Dick McGuire (both wore 15), Willis Reed (19), Dave DeBusschere (22) and Bill Bradley (24). But the numbers are merely triggers, evoking vivid memories of these unique players, the best in the franchise's history.

Reed's was the first retired, Barnett's the most recent. Reed always drew the deepest affection from the fans and the front office. His gimpy heroics in the seventh game of the 1969–70 NBA finals are the stuff of myth and lasting memories. The Cap'n had plenty of gumption and we sure as heck remember it.

Willis Reed, above, holds up his number "19" jersey on the night the team retired his number.

Below, Earl Monroe being congratulated by Bill Bradley when his jersey numeral was retired.

Barnett? Well, he was a man who hadn't much use for public relations, and pretty much kept his own counsel. Where Reed was more public, more user-friendly, Barnett was a private character who saved his sly humor for teammates. That insularity probably cost him brownie points with the media and the public, who unfortunately never really got to know him.

But for those in the know, Barnett, like Reed, was a gamer. From 1959 through 1974, he averaged 15.5 points a game while shooting .456. But beyond the numbers lived a player who could hit the clutch shot, a player who defended against the opposition's top gun so teammate Frazier could more readily doubleteam, a player who rarely made a mistake. Barnett was rock solid, and his numbers prove he was good.

As Barnett's movements were unorthodox, Monroe's were too. But there was a difference. The Pearl's had the improvisational twist, the unexpected spinning, dipping, zippety-do flourish that made you gasp aloud.

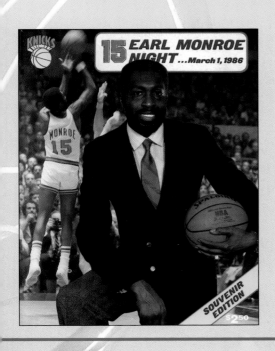

The greatest honor the Knicks can bestow on a player is to retire his jersey. Those players honored this way have been Walt Frazier, Dick Barnett, Dick McGuire, Earl Monroe, Dave DeBusschere, Bill Bradley and Willis Reed. The game programs from those special nights (shown on opposite page and on this page) have become collectors' items, and they feature photographs of some of the most spectacular moments of the athletes' careers. Such memorabilia becomes cherished souvenirs for those who watched each Knicks' legend play.

THE GARDEN MARQUEE

The marquee is the image many fans conjure up when they think of Madison Square Garden.

Some people see the old Garden's black letters on a glimmering white background; others envision today's electronic version with digital graphics. In either case, the marquee has heralded the events of the world's most famous arena.

From the *Fight of the Century*, between Muhammad Ali and Smokin' Joe Frazier, in 1971 to the 1994 Stanley Cup Champion Rangers, tennis, track and field, volleyball, dog shows, the circus and all the concerts in between.

Today's arena opened on February 11, 1968, and is the fourth structure to bear the honor and distinction of being Madison Square Garden.

The first was P.T. Barnum's *Great Roman Hippodrome*; it was renamed *Madison Square Garden* on May 31, 1879. The next was thirty-two stories of Moorish architecture designed by Stanford White which soared above Madison Square Park on the same location.

The third Garden eventually became the home of the Knicks. It opened on November 24, 1925, and on December 6 hosted the first professional basketball game with the original Celtics defeating the Washington Palace Five, 35–31.

It's a place of glamour and excitement, and over the years it has been the stage of some of the biggest sporting events in history—with the marquee lighting the way.

✴ *In his playing days, Dick McGuire wore #15. Above right, he and Earl Monroe appear together in 1992, when McGuire's number was retired. Monroe, who also wore #15 for the Knicks, already had his jersey retired in 1986. Below, in a rare honor, the Knicks held "Dr. J Day," an appreciation for an opposing player, Julius Erving.*

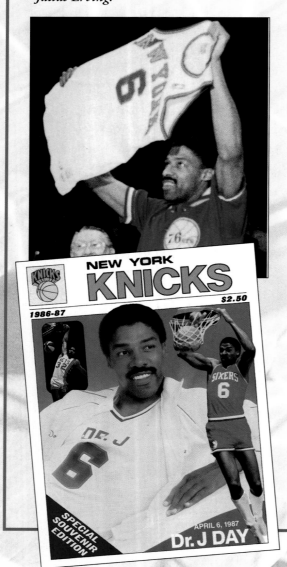

Barnett's shots were one like the other, only the wiring was not standard-brand. You saw that clinking, clanging jump shot again and again—some ungainly stroke—and you shook your head that that junkyard shot of his went in.

Reed? He was a no-frills kind of player. It was written of him: "The Cap'n...worked the boards with the kind of cruel insistence that Marciano put on a man. There was often inelegance to his art—a weary Reed ran like a girdled damsel—but his body was like that of an overweight tapdancer, capable of surprises. Reed striding across the lane, his chest inflating, limbs stretching, had a kind of striking majesty."

Dave DeBusschere was like Reed in his absence of flair. Whatever poetry there was in his game was not calculated: he was a thoroughgoing pragmatist. In the words of another heavyweight, Joe Frazier, DeBusschere's objective was simply to "get the job done."

Bradley and McGuire, of different basketball generations, shared an appreciation and talent for team ball: selfless, savvy team basketball. The right pass was as sweet to them as the shot that dropped through the hoop.

They were different players with various styles, but they were all good enough to end up with their jerseys in the rafters.

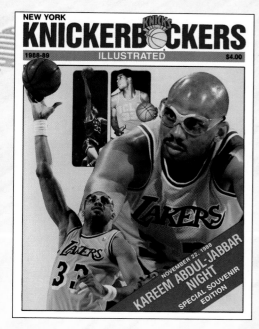

* Kareem Abdul-Jabbar, above, was a New Yorker—he had played his high school ball at Power Memorial in Manhattan—whom the Knicks organization thought enough of to honor with a special night.

* The last of the 1969-70 Knicks to have his number retired was Dick Barnett. On the night he was honored, March 10, 1990, so was Red Holzman. Holzman not only coached Barnett, but hired him as an assistant coach following Barnett's playing days.

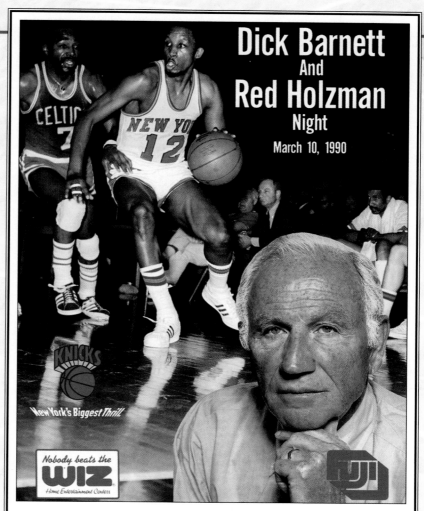

Dick Barnett
And
Red Holzman
Night

March 10, 1990

MARCH 10, 1990

On March 10, 1990, the Knicks retired the number "613." What was the significance of that number? Well, it was the number of regular-season victories that Red Holzman had won as a Knicks coach. And on that night, Holzman became the first—and, so far, the only—Knicks coach to have his number retired.

Holzman earned Hall of Fame honors in 1985, and he continues to work with the Knicks organization as the club's basketball consultant.

Dick Barnett, #12, from the championship 1969–70 team, also saw his number retired that evening.

acknowledgments

This book is for all the players who helped make my career a joy and who will always be a very important part of my life.

A project of this magnitude owes a great deal to the talent and efforts of many individuals—especially the players, coaches and my colleagues who make up the New York Knicks organization. My sincere gratitude to all of my loyal friends who have given me support, encouragement, and who have shared their love when I needed it most.

David W. Checketts, President and CEO, Madison Square Garden
Ernie Grunfeld, President and General Manager, New York Knicks
Frank Murphy, John Cirillo, Pam Harris, Ed Tapscott

Editorial and Production Staff: Traci Cothran, Vincent Gatti, Phil Berger, Dennis D'Agostino, Maria Massey, Chris Dreyer, Ken Samelson, Betsy Becker, Len Lewin, Red Holzman.

Memorabilia and Photographs: Marty Appel, The Topps Company; Sonny Hertzberg, Ralph Kaplowitz, Ray Lumpp, Fuzzy Levane, Fred Podesta, John Goldner, Bob Rosen, Gwynne Bloomfield, Al Marchfeld.

Additional Photography: Bob Olen, pages 197, 216 (bottom); NBA Photos; New York Knicks files; *New York Daily News* pages 22, 23, 26, 28, 29, 37, 39, 40, 41, 46; Betsy Becker; Ray Amati.

A special thanks to my friends and family who have always been in my corner from the beginning: Joe Cohen, Dr. Norm Scott, Dr. Irv Glick, Herb Schwartzman, Lee, Rachelle, Ellen Sue, Larry, Sadye, Fay and June.

George Kalinsky

I wish to extend my thanks to the following men who took time to reminisce about their association with the Knicks: Sonny Hertzberg, Ralph Kaplowitz, Ray Lumpp, Marty Glickman, Bob Wolff, Marv Albert, Richie Guerin, Fuzzy Levane, Bill Bradley, Ernie Vandeweghe, Stanley Asofsky and Ossie Schectman.

As a journalist, I have written about the Knicks from time to time. Some of the material in this book is excerpted from articles of mine on Red Holzman, Sonny Werblin, Patrick Ewing, Phil Jackson, on the 1969–70 team, and on Knicks fan Stanley Asofsky. Excerpts were also taken from my book on the 1969–70 team, *Miracle on 33rd Street: The N.Y. Knickerbockers Championship Season* (reprint Four Walls Eight Windows) and from taped interviews done back in 1969–70 with Carl Braun and Dolph Schayes. My thanks to those two great players, and to Bud Palmer, whom I interviewed in the early eighties for a series on the NBA's first season, 1946–47.

My thanks to Marv Albert for allowing me to quote from his informative and entertaining book, *I'd Love To but I Have a Game: 27 Years without a Life* (Doubleday).

Thanks to Bill Bradley for permission to quote from his observant book on NBA life, *Life on the Run* (Bantam Books).

Thanks to Willis Reed and George Kalinsky for permission to excerpt from *A Will to Win: The Comeback Year*, a detailed and lively account of the 1972–73 season (Prentice Hall Inc.).

For those interested in early NBA history, I recommend *Vintage NBA: The Pioneer Era (1946–1956)* by Neil D. Isaacs (Master Press).

My gratitude to Isaacs for allowing me to excerpt from his book.

Finally, I'm appreciative of the help given by Dennis D'Agostino, Director, Publications and Information for the Knicks; by Leonard Lewin, executive director of the Knicks Alumni Association; and by Traci Cothran, who edited this book.

I've dedicated this book to my mother, Fanny Berger, and to my daughter, Julia.